Prime Minister Portillo ...

... and other things that never happened

PRIME MINISTER PORTILLO ...

... AND OTHER THINGS THAT NEVER HAPPENED

edited by

DUNCAN BRACK

and

IAIN DALE

POLITICO'S

First published in Great Britain in 2003.

This paperback edition published in 2004 by Politico's Publishing,
an imprint of Methuen Publishing Limited
215 Vauxhall Bridge Road
London SW1V 1EJ
www.methuen.co.uk/politicos

10 9 8 7 6 5 4 3 2 1

A CIP catalogue record for this book is available from the British
Library.

ISBN 1 84275 111 5

Printed and bound in Great Britain by Bookmarque Ltd.
Designed and typeset in Bembo by Duncan Brack.

Contents

Introduction

I have come across men of letters who have written history without taking
part in public affairs, and politicians who have concerned themselves with
producing events without thinking about them. I have observed that the
first are always inclined to find general causes whereas the second, living
in the midst of disconnected daily facts, are prone to imagine that everything is attributable to particular incidents, and that the wires they pull are
the same as those that move the world. It is to be presumed that both are
equally deceived.

Alexis de Tocqueville

Here in this book you will find twenty-one examinations of
things that never happened, from Michael Portillo becoming Prime Minister, to J. F. Kennedy dodging the assassin's bullet, to
Margaret Thatcher being unceremoniously removed as Conservative
leader after losing the 1978 election, to Lenin's sealed train never
reaching Petrograd in 1917.

As one or two of our contributors observe, historians have tended
to look down on the study of counterfactuals, the 'what ifs' of history. To a certain extent this is fair enough. Even if a particular inci-
dent turned out differently – an election lost rather than won, a man
lived who might have died – who can really tell what would have
happened afterwards? And furthermore, as de Tocqueville observed,
history is more than simply a series of incidents; underlying general
causes may sweep events on to much the same conclusion regardless
of whoever thinks they are in charge. Two of this book's chapters
make much the same point: even if Ted Heath had won the February
1974 election, or even if Willie Whitelaw had become Tory leader in

place of Margaret Thatcher, it is not clear that the ultimate outcomes would have been very different.

And yet ... in some cases, clearly a single decision or person or event obviously did make a real difference, as de Tocqueville, clearly trying to have it both ways, also held. There was nothing inevitable, for example, about Jim Callaghan's decision not to call an election in 1978, when, as it turned out, he was much better placed to win a contest than he would be the following spring. After all, the choice of election date is solely the Prime Minister's. Arthur Scargill could have held a nation-wide strike ballot of the NUM in 1984, and probably would have won. Lee Harvey Oswald could have missed. Lord Halifax could have become Prime Minister in 1940 instead of Churchill – at the time it seemed more probable. John Smith could have lived, as could Nye Bevan. Roy Jenkins could have joined the Liberal Party, rather than founding the SDP, in 1981. Mrs Thatcher could have resigned over Westland in 1986; at one point it looked likely. Tony Blair could have stuck to his half-promise to Paddy Ashdown, and invited the Liberal Democrats into government in 1997. In the chaos of eastern Europe in 1917, Lenin's train could have been turned back, or derailed, or blown up.

A stronger heart, a trembling trigger-finger, a decision, on finely balanced arguments, to tip one way rather than the other – all of this reminds us that chance and circumstance do play a major role. History without the study of counterfactuals runs the risk of making everything seem predestined, of removing any element of choice. Individuals, as our contributors demonstrate through their studies of what might have happened if people had chosen differently, or been absent or present at key moments, can make a difference.

Other chapters look at the combined effect of groups, rather than particular individuals, choosing slightly differently. This is at its most obvious in election results. Labour almost won in 1970; almost everyone expected them to. The Liberal-SDP Alliance could have come second in 1983; they almost did. The Tories could have won in 1964.

And, of course, Michael Portillo could have held his seat in 1997. Again, these were finely balanced outcomes; not much of a shift in voters' behaviour was needed. Most strikingly, in 1981 Tony Benn could have beaten Denis Healey for the deputy leadership of the Labour Party; in fact, as our contributor argues here, maybe he did.

Other what ifs arise from collective decisions over strategy or policy. The Liberal Party could have disappeared entirely in 1951; if the Tories had contested sitting Liberal MPs' seats, instead of giving most of them a free run, it probably would have done. Over the following decade or two, the Liberals could have pre-empted Thatcher by staying true to their Gladstonian heritage of free markets and small government rather than New Liberal interventionism; many of them wanted to. In 1969 the government and the unions could have decided to agree *In Place of Strife*. In 1916 the Liberal leadership could have decided to stick together rather than tear their party apart. All these possible outcomes are, at the least, plausible.

Other volumes of 'what ifs' have tended to concentrate, not surprisingly, on military history, the outcome of battles and wars often resting on chance, accident and fine decisions. It is our belief that politics is just as prone to analysis through counterfactuals, and here we present twenty-one cases; we hope you find them enjoyable, thought-provoking and – sometimes – amusing.

We hope in due course to publish a second volume of political 'what ifs'. Ideas for contents and volunteer authors are very welcome; please email us on iain@iaindale.com and/or dbrack@dircon.co.uk.

Maybe one of the next book's chapters will deal with our favourite 'what if', sadly not included here, but attributed to Chairman Mao. He was asked what he thought would have happened if, in 1963, Khrushchev had been assassinated instead of Kennedy. 'Well, I'll tell you one thing', he replied. 'Aristotle Onassis wouldn't have married Mrs Khrushchev.'

Duncan Brack and Iain Dale   *August 2003*

Chapter 1

What if the Liberal Party had emerged united from the First World War?

Richard S. Grayson[1]

The history of twentieth-century British politics is marked by the rise and fall of political traditions and political movements. At different times, all three main parties have dominated. The Liberal Party seemed unbeatable in 1906, with over 400 seats at Westminster. Labour seemed to be similarly dominant in 1945, and again in 1997. Yet in the 1950s and the 1980s, people have wondered if Labour could ever win again, and the same question has been asked of the Conservatives post-1997. This seems to be the natural order: parties rise, fall, reinvent themselves, and (not always) rise again.

In tackling these issues, some historians are a little sniffy about counterfactuals. Asking 'what if?' is, in theory, not the business of historians. Yet there are areas where, in assessing the relative importance of different causes, historians look at what might have happened if one factor had been missing or reduced in scale. If there is one area of twentieth-century British political history where such a counterfactual approach has been almost unavoidable, it is the decline of the Liberal Party.

Although historians never go so far as to ask directly 'what if?', decades of historical work has been focused on the importance of the Great War in Liberal decline. Did the Great War deal a hammer-blow to the Liberals without which the party would have survived and prospered? Or was the Liberal Party likely to decline in any case, due to the growth in popularity of the Labour Party, on the basis of a growing class-consciousness? At the risk of not doing justice to a vast field of sometimes complex theories, it is possible to divide the historiography of Liberal decline into two broad camps: 'Great War' versus 'class war'.

The 'Great War' approach argues that the Liberal Party entered the war relatively united, but the conduct of the war led to serious rows and divisions over issues such as the adequacy of munitions supply to the army or whether to introduce conscription. The personal rivalry between Lloyd George and Asquith plays an important role in this argument. In December 1916, Lloyd George ousted Asquith as Prime Minister to become head of a coalition with the Conservatives and some Labour figures. Then in the May 1918 Maurice debate in Parliament, Asquith led the charge against the government, criticising its record on sending reinforcements to France. The government was backed by seventy-one Liberal MPs, Asquith gained the support of ninety-eight, and eighty-five abstained. Over the course of 1918–19, things did not improve for the Liberal Party. The 'coupon' general election of 1918 saw those Coalition Liberals who supported Lloyd George slump to only 133 seats, while Asquith's followers fared even worse, securing just 28. Asquith himself lost his seat and, as he did not return to the House of Commons until the 1921 Paisley by-election, the party was temporarily led in Parliament by Donald Maclean.

The 'class war' camp starts from the different view that Liberalism itself had run out of steam by 1914, and, more fundamentally, that it was ill-suited to dealing with the emerging class basis of politics. By 1918, with the adoption of a programme based clearly on social-ist principles, Labour was better placed than the Liberals to appeal to working-class voters, who had become more class-conscious, and radicalised, through trades union membership. The massive expan-sion of working-class voters through the 1918 Representation of the

People Act thus led to significant progress for Labour, which continued through the 1920s to the detriment of the Liberal Party.

Proponents of the Great War approach have responded that the Liberals were making good progress among working-class voters prior to the war, but the debate is not resolved, and it is increasingly clear that the situation was highly varied across the country. It simply is not possible to reconcile these arguments, especially in a short piece such as this, and there are plenty of studies that rehearse the arguments in more detail.[2] However, to aid the 'what if?' exercise, there are some themes that do emerge from the debate on Liberal decline.

First, there is no doubt that the Labour Party was having *some* success in developing a form of politics that was more appealing to *some* working-class voters. In the absence of the Great War, that appeal might have remained limited to a minority of the working class, with the majority staying with the Liberal Party. But it was a factor, and it is unlikely that there would have been no significant Labour Party. After all, there was a significant socialist working-class movement in every other European country.

Second, we do know that the Liberal Party had enormous problems getting a clear message across to the voters about what it stood for in 1918, due to the fact that Liberals were fighting Liberals. One Liberal leader was a Prime Minister who had essentially ousted another Liberal leader so that he could lead a Tory-dominated coalition. That disunity must have had an impact on Liberal fortunes.

The alternative

In answering the question: 'what if the Liberals had emerged united from the Great War?', a number of assumptions have to be made about what united meant, and what happened during the war. The assumptions here are that Britain won the war, and instead of a coalition, there remained a united Liberal government (though dependent on the support of Irish Nationalists from 1910 onwards). Asquith remained as Prime Minister throughout, with Lloyd George as Chancellor of the Exchequer. One must also assume that the Liberals took better decisions on issues such as munitions, meaning that the serious questions about the ability of a Liberal government to fight a war did not arise. In such circumstances, it might actually be of little importance whether or not there was a wartime coalition with the Conservatives, as the Liberals could have been united in 1918 in either circumstance. However, it is assumed here that if the Liberals were already fighting the war effectively, they would not seek Conservative support, and thus the Conservatives would have ended the war as a clear and distinct party of opposition, with Labour growing but still clearly in third place. Implicitly, this all means that issues such as conscription were resolved without difficulty for the Liberal Party. That may not mean stretching credibility all that far, for we know that recruitment slowed after conscription was introduced, and it is possible that had it not been, the feared absence of volunteers may never have occurred.

So where do these assumptions leave the Liberal Party in 1918? First, there is a united leadership, so the party is more united on the ground. Second, Asquith has the aura of a Prime Minister who has led his country to victory. Third, the Liberals are well positioned as the party most able to deliver the reforms needed at home – to build a 'fit country for heroes to live in'.

And this is what happened: a Liberal election victory in 1918, which delays Lloyd George's ascent to the premiership. Austen Chamberlain does not lose his place as Conservative leader in 1922, and goes on to be Prime Minister. But he only leads a minority government, and there are two Lib–Lab coalitions, one led by Lloyd George, another by Churchill. Labour never governs alone, and although it splits, it does so over different issues, at different times, and with different leaders. Yet the fundamentals of the economy remain the same, though it is a Baldwin government that takes the blame for the economic collapse of 1931. There are still storm clouds in Europe and the Far East. All of this has a major impact on the careers of two men: Winston Churchill and Oswald Mosley …

Liberals win the khaki election of 1918

Like the election of 1900, the December 1918 contest was a 'khaki election', which Asquith fought on the slogan: 'punish the Kaiser'. Many people at the time saw the hand of the Chancellor, David Lloyd George, in this; he made no secret of wishing to extract reparations from Germany to pay for the heavy costs of the war borne by the allies. On a wave of patriotic fervour, the Liberals gained over 80 seats from the Conservatives, ending the campaign with 344 seats to the Conservatives' 200. It was not all progress for Asquith, however: the Liberals lost nearly 20 seats to Labour, who won over 60 seats, under the leadership of Arthur Henderson.

With the Irish Nationalists performing exactly as in the last election before the war, winning 84 seats, Asquith's majority of eighteen was slim; but an alliance of the Conservatives with Labour and the Irish Nationalists was very unlikely, and made his majority more secure than it looked. The Conservatives took solace in the fact that although they had lost many seats, they were still a clear second. Much attention among the chattering classes focused on the steady progress of the Labour Party, most attributing this to the new franchise which had given all men over twenty-one the vote, and women over thirty. Many speculated that had the Liberals not emerged from the war as a viable progressive force, Labour might have done even better.

The Liberals now had to pick up the pieces of war. During the election, they had pledged to build a 'country fit for heroes', but the economic problems they faced meant in practice they were able to deliver little. Asquith began his peacetime government in a difficult economic situation. The shipbuilding and cotton industries were poorly structured. The British Government was owed massive debts from foreign countries who could not or, like Russia, would not, pay. The National Debt was fourteen times its pre-war level. As the 1920s approached, coal miners went on strike for higher wages. At the same time, exports fell as European markets struggled to recover from the war. Industrial owners used the only economic weapon they believed they had – cutting wages. As unemployment steadily rose, the Liberals counted the cost of the increases in unemployment insurance benefits that they had introduced immediately after the war in a time of higher employment.

They also had to face problems in Ireland. The minister tasked with implementing the provisions of the 1914 Home Rule Act was Winston Churchill – not a wise choice in practice, given his supposed promise to leave Belfast 'in ruins in twenty-four hours' if home rule was resisted in 1914. Growing public support for the Protestants, based partly on memories of the sacrifices made by regiments such as the 36th (Ulster) Division on the Somme, allowed the Conservatives to play the orange card. By-elections in both Liverpool and Glasgow saw Conservative gains, but even more worrying were shock losses in Wales and Cornwall, where Nonconformists turned out in support of their Protestant brethren in Ulster. There had already, in 1914, been much talk of partition, with various options on the table, but the Act as placed on the statute book at the outbreak of the war did not include any such provisions. The Conservatives' deployment of the orange card, together with public opinion, meant that Churchill had no choice but to introduce home rule on the basis of partition, with six northern counties becoming part of Northern Ireland and remaining in the United Kingdom. One outcome was a civil war in the Irish Free State over whether or not to accept this settlement.

At the same time, Labour made gains in by-elections in working-class areas, as former soldiers grew increasingly frustrated at rising unemployment and the terrible state of housing. Labour was given a harder edge in 1920 when Ramsay MacDonald replaced Henderson as leader. By-election gains by Labour and the Conservatives meant that the Liberal majority had been whittled down to just four by 1923.

Austen Chamberlain's minority government

After seventeen years of government, the Liberals faced the 1923 election without optimism. The Conservatives, now led by Austen Chamberlain, had developed an alternative programme of using tariffs to protect British industry and raise money for social reform. The tariff reform programme was essentially that put forward by Austen Chamberlain's father, Joseph, in the early part of the century. It offered the British people a clear choice: Conservative rhetoric combining patriotism and a promise of better living standards against a Liberal agenda widely viewed to have delivered little in the post-war years.

There is no doubt that the Conservative agenda possessed some appeal, but overall voters seemed simply to want a change rather than enthusiastically embracing tariff reform. The result was that in the February 1923 election, the Conservatives became the largest party, although with 278 seats they were 30 short of a majority. The Liberals suffered major losses to Labour, but were still clearly the second party, retaining 230 seats compared to Labour's 107. The Conservatives formed a government but, lacking a majority, were able to achieve very little. A handful of Labour MPs backed tariffs, but the party was still held in thrall by the Liberal belief in free trade, and the Conservatives were unable to force their plans through Parliament.

Major developments took place in the opposition parties over the following year. Lloyd George, who replaced Asquith as Liberal leader immediately after the 1923 election, developed a series of ideas for saving British industry through a partnership between workers and capital. He drew together a range of leading thinkers to produce *Britain's Industrial Future,* better known as the 'Yellow Book', a series of proposals for modernising the economy. It called for investment in public works programmes, but stopped short of endorsing forms of public ownership and the creation of an Economic General Staff which was advocated by the more radical Liberals.

Labour had adopted a socialist constitution in 1918, committing itself to the common ownership of major industries. This, it was argued by people like Ramsay MacDonald, would help the party secure significant working-class support. Labour's failure to make major gains in both 1918 and 1923, however, led some to ask whether the future for Labour still lay in cooperation with the Liberal Party. This was the case argued by Oswald Mosley, who had been elected as a Labour MP in 1923 after unsuccessfully running as a Unionist in 1918. He challenged Ramsay MacDonald for the leadership in early 1924. As a newcomer, Mosley failed to win on the first ballot, but did enough to force MacDonald to resign. Mosley then did creditably in the next ballot, but Arthur Henderson, the compromise candidate, returned as leader with a combination of trade union and socialist backing.

While Labour debated its future, some leading Liberals privately wondered whether the Liberal Party had any future. In particular, Winston Churchill was becoming increasingly concerned over whether Liberalism could resist the spread of what he termed 'Bolshevism'. Austen Chamberlain approached him immediately after the 1923 election, offering him the post of Chancellor of the Exchequer if he could bring enough Liberals with him to secure a majority for the Government. Churchill eventually refused, however, deciding in the end that with the Liberals still a viable force, it was not the right time to throw in his lot with the Conservatives. As he had judged prior to the Great War, the best way to stave off radicalism was through progressive social reforms aimed as satisfying working people's concerns. With Lloyd George developing a new reform agenda, and a strong Lib–Lab element emerging within Labour, Churchill soon realised that he had made the right decision. In any case, it was doubtful whether the 'scourge of Ulster' would have been welcome in Tory ranks, given his recent record in forcing through home rule.

Lloyd George's Lib–Lab Coalition

All these developments meant that when Austen Chamberlain called an election in November 1924, hoping to secure a majority, the Liberals were in better shape than they had been the year before. But the result was almost exactly the same as in 1923, the Conservatives gaining only two seats overall – though around thirty seats changed hands, mainly due to local factors. The parties therefore emerged from the election as follows: Conservative 280, Liberal 228, Labour 107. Sensing failure, Chamberlain announced that he would not seek to form another government, and the King invited Lloyd George to try to assemble an administration. Persuasive as ever, he convinced the Labour leader, Arthur Henderson, to join him in government as Foreign Secretary. This was not an easy decision for Labour to make; the party was divided between those who were prepared to accept coalition as a means of achieving practical reforms and those more ardent socialists who anticipated the collapse of capitalism. Stanley Baldwin, the new Conservative leader, looked forward to his party reaping the benefits of a chaotic Lib–Lab government.

Yet the coalition began well. Winston Churchill, the new Chancellor of the Exchequer, took a lead, along with Lloyd George, in implementing the main proposals of the 'Yellow Book'. They focused in particular on housing, funded by modest income tax rises, which in turn created new jobs in construction, and began finally to provide homes fit for heroes.

The Conservatives soon drew strength, however, from the controversial decision to grant diplomatic recognition to the Soviet Union, one of the prices extracted by Labour for entering the coalition. This deeply alarmed many Liberal voters, who were horrified by the stories of the brutalities emerging from the Russian Civil War. From a different perspective, concern was also generated over Lloyd George's continued intransigence towards Germany. Gustav Stresemann, the liberal German foreign minister, was seeking revision of the Treaty of Versailles, in a bid to prove to German public opinion that moderate parties could achieve more than extremists like Adolf Hitler, and in 1925, Stresemann proposed that Germany should meet Britain and France at a venue such as Locarno in Switzerland. Lloyd George would have none of it, and overruled Henderson, who thought it was worth pursuing. Instead, he reached a new security pact with France, guaranteeing to come to its aid if it was attacked by Germany. This made the French far less fearful of Germany, and removed any incentive for them to negotiate over issues such as reparations. Stresemann's position was thus rendered untenable, and he retired from politics in 1926. He went on to write the standard study on the work of Goethe, politics' loss becoming literary studies' gain.

Domestically, having proved that tax rises could fund better housing, Labour MPs argued for further increases to fund better pensions and benefits. Churchill obliged. But he did not do enough to satisfy many Labour MPs, while middle-class voters began to be alarmed. They saw few benefits from the tax hikes, partly because a significant part of the increases simply filled the holes in the budget as the economy slowed down and tax revenues fell. This caused problems for the coalition, with a core of the more left-wing Labour MPs regularly voting against the government. In time, this took its toll on the party leadership, and Henderson resigned in October 1928. Oswald Mosley once again contested the Labour leadership, this time against the fiery Clydeside orator James Maxton, who pledged to lead Labour out of the coalition towards a more radical socialist platform.

Maxton spoke to Labour's heart. But many Labour MPs liked exercising an influence over government and delivering tangible, if less than revolutionary, results for the people who had sent them to Westminster. Mosley won with a narrow majority. There was an immediate split, and Maxton led fifty-two Labour colleagues out of the coalition, adopting the old label 'Independent Labour'. The trades unions tried to support Maxton by organising a General Strike but its impact was patchy across the country. Mosley remained in the Government, taking over from Henderson as Foreign Secretary – but as he led only fifty-five Labour MPs, the government lost its majority.

Baldwin and the Great Depression

Meanwhile, the Conservative leader Baldwin had made progress in developing his party machine. Biding his time for the right moment, he communicated a sense of quiet patriotism embodying the values and virtues of the English countryside. Against a backdrop of a frankly too exciting government, led by brilliant but erratic politicians, Baldwin's offer of 'safety first', including only modest measures of tariff reform, gave the Conservative Party, with 338 seats, a 30-seat majority in the November 1928 general election; the other parties fell to Liberal 180, Independent Labour 51, Labour 46. A heavier defeat for Labour was avoided by there being very few instances of Labour and Independent Labour candidates fighting each other.

The country was ready for calm, and one of Baldwin's first acts reflected this: the withdrawal of British troops from the Rhineland. He also persuaded the French to do likewise. Many in Britain had hoped for this under the previous Liberal Government, arguing that it was both indefensible and costly, and it was hoped that it would help prevent the rise of extremism in Germany.

Baldwin could not have banked, however, on what was to come. Although it is difficult to blame them for the Great Depression, the Conservatives were in power when the economy finally crashed in the summer of 1931. Higher tariffs were introduced in an attempt to protect business, and they did begin to have some effect. After the Liberals refused to join a coalition 'National' Government, Baldwin went to the country, hoping to increase his slender majority by persuading the voters that the Liberals had acted in a partisan spirit at a time of national crisis. But his tactic backfired hideously, and it was Baldwin's party that was punished by the voters, falling from 338 MPs to only 187.

Winston Churchill was the main beneficiary. After Lloyd George had stood down as Liberal leader in 1929, believing that the persistent rumours about his alleged involvement in the sale of honours would fatally damage the Liberals' chances of returning to office, Churchill had taken over. The Liberals were returned with 318 seats – a majority of only 10, but a real recovery from their previous position, even if it was based overwhelmingly on a negative vote against the Conservatives.

Churchill was faced immediately with the decision on whether to keep or abandon tariffs. On simple practical grounds – they were starting to work – he had already decided before the election to keep them in place. Fearing that some of the more ardent free trade Liberal MPs would not back him, however, he invited Oswald Mosley, leader of the declining Labour Party of twenty MPs, to join his Cabinet, again as Foreign Secretary. Meanwhile, Maxton's Socialist Party (as Independent Labour now called itself), had steadily been replacing Labour as the voice of the working class, winning ninety seats in the election and securing the backing of all the major trades unions.

Churchill as Prime Minister

As Prime Minister, Churchill played a major role in foreign policy. In 1931, he became increasingly anxious about Japanese intentions in the East after Japan's invasion of Manchuria. Always the ardent imperialist, Churchill feared for the security of India, and on taking office, introduced a rearmament programme, largely funded by the revenue from tariffs. Many orthodox Liberals had gave doubts about this, but Churchill's Chancellor, the brilliant economist John Maynard Keynes (ennobled by Churchill in order to bring him in to the government), seemed to be able to persuade the Liberal Party that anything was justifiable if it got people back to work.

Other clouds were gathering nearer than the Far East. Churchill recognised the threat posed by Adolf Hitler, who had come to power in Germany in 1933. He believed it might be worth trying to negoti-ate with the National Socialist regime, and despatched the Foreign Secretary, Mosley, to meet with the German leader. Mosley came back a partial convert, having been impressed by Hitler's public works schemes – but his reports, together with Churchill's own instincts, persuaded the government that there was no deal on the table.

The downfall of Churchill can largely be attributed to his late Vic-torian mindset, and the poor judgement that many people believed had afflicted his earlier career. The first problem he faced was India. There was considerable pressure, both from Liberals and Labour, for reform in the sub-continent. Many Liberals had always believed that there would come a time when Britain's work in its Empire would be over, allowing a graceful withdrawal and the steady growth of self-government by the 'native peoples' that the colonial governors had 'trained' to manage themselves. Gandhi's campaign of civil disobedi-ence had focused attention on Indian affairs, and Liberal opinion was broadly persuaded that reforms were needed. Yet Churchill was stead-fastly opposed; even after pressure for reform by the Conservative former Viceroy of India, Lord Irwin, he would not move. The issue deeply divided the Liberal Party, with a minority of mainly older MPs backing the Prime Minister, but a majority of younger ones sens-ing betrayal of the Liberal view of Empire. Several pressure groups formed within the party, and the internal dissension greatly sapped Liberal strength; instead of focusing on bread-and-butter issues of concern to the electorate, the party spent much of its time debating a problem for which it seemed to have no solution.

Churchill's judgement was also called into question in 1936 when the new King, Edward VIII, told his Prime Minister that he wished to marry the American divorcée Wallis Simpson. Churchill fully supported the as yet uncrowned King, and there was a strong body of Liberal opinion which saw nothing wrong with the idea. But when the issue was discussed in Parliament, it became clear that the Conservative leader, Baldwin, better represented the fundamentally traditional view holding sway in the country at large. Sensing the political mood, the King abdicated before Parliament was forced to a decision.

Time was up for Churchill. There had to be a general election by the end of 1936, and he pushed his period in office to the limits, sensing his support ebbing away and waiting for something to turn up. But nothing did, and the government went into the election with a general air of incompetence. The Conservatives, the party which had always presented itself as the defenders of Empire, ironically had developed a moderate package of reforms deemed enough by many voters to meet India's short-term aspirations, and Baldwin led a more united party than did Churchill. The Conservatives also hinted that they might seek an accommodation with Hitler – a popular move among the many voters who feared the prospect of another terrible European war.

The Liberal collapse of 1936

The Conservatives won the 1936 election narrowly with 319 seats, while the Liberals plummeted to 161. The official Labour Party fared even worse, winning just 4 constituencies, with even Mosley losing his seat, as the Socialist Party made significant gains, winning 131 after offering working people a vision of a dramatically better society. Sadly for Maxton, his own ill health forced him to resign the leadership in 1937, and he was replaced by Clement Attlee, a more moderate figure, who immediately applied himself to developing a programme that would make socialism work.

Churchill resigned the Liberal leadership immediately after the election, and was replaced by Archibald Sinclair. Though a former comrade of Churchill's from the Great War trenches, he had been one of the leading imperial reformers in the party, and his ascendancy to the leadership marked a resolution of the India debate. The Liberals soon found themselves arguing for bolder proposals than those put forward by the new Conservative Government.

Churchill, however, was not yet finished. Fundamentally opposed to the Sinclair's position on India, he resigned the Liberal whip and started describing himself as an Independent. In making strident speeches against Indian reform, he found himself regularly allied in Parliament with right-wing Conservatives, and there was even talk of him standing as a Conservative at the next election. He also found common cause with Conservatives on a different wing of the party over the Government's policy towards Germany, delivering powerful warnings about Hitler, with whom Baldwin had hinted that he would be prepared to negotiate. Some called Churchill a warmonger; others observed that if he was right, at least the country knew who to ask to be its war leader – particularly as, despite his position on India, he steadily emerged as the only figure able to link Conservatives with the bulk of the Liberal MPs, similarly concerned about the Government's policy of appeasement of Hitler.

As for Oswald Mosley, he realised that the official Labour Party was finished, but recoiled from the class war preached by Maxton and even Attlee. After spending time travelling throughout Europe in 1936–37, fulfilling a lucrative contract to write a book on European politics from the perspective of a recent Foreign Secretary, he returned home to form his own National Socialist Party.

With so much change at the top of the Labour and Liberal parties, and even in the monarchy, the country expected Baldwin to provide stability. This he did – but only for a year, when he handed over the Conservative leadership to Neville Chamberlain. And the rest is history …

Conclusions

Alternative general elections

	1918	1923	1928	1931	1936
Liberal	334	230	180	318	161
Conservative	200	278	338	187	318
Labour	60	107	46	20	4
Independent Labour / Socialist	–	–	51	90	131

Of course, things wouldn't have been *exactly* the same after 1937. It is assumed that the Second World War would have happened for similar reasons at a similar time and, with Churchill becoming an Independent post-1936, it is possible that he could have been acceptable to the Conservatives as leader of a wartime government. But party politics would have looked very different in 1945 had the Liberals entered the war with 161 seats instead of 20. It is possible that Labour could have grown from its 131 (only 20 or so fewer than it actually won in 1935) to gain a majority under Attlee in 1945, if it had been the beneficiary of the growth of public belief in central planning, one of the side-effects of the war. However, it is equally possible that the Liberals could have benefited from the same mood, had they been associated with a social democratic agenda before the war, as indeed they are in this alternative history. It would take another essay to go beyond this point, but it almost goes without saying that had the Liberals entered the Second World War with healthy parliamentary numbers, any number of outcomes post-1945 would have been possible.

However, this article is about the inter-war years rather than what followed. What are the differences in this alternative history stemming from the Liberal Party emerging united from the Great War? How far-reaching would these differences have been?

Perhaps one of the most obvious features of the alternative has been how much remains the same. Lloyd George eventually takes over from Asquith. There are splits in the Labour Party. The Conservative Party campaigns on tariff reform. Broadly the same people lead the same political parties. These similarities are based on the assumption that talented people would still have risen to the top, and many of the factors that brought those people to the top, such as their background and general political views and talents, would have stood them well in the alternative. Certainly in the Conservative Party, there is no reason to believe that the likes of William Joynson-Hicks, Birkenhead, Leo Amery or Samuel Hoare would have been chosen over Stanley Baldwin or the two Chamberlains. 'Safety first' still tapped a vein in Conservative thought, although in the alternative it is used more successfully, and a year earlier than in reality. The Liberals still publish a 'Yellow Book', though several years earlier, and with fewer radical proposals. It is also assumed that the Liberal Party's good health has relatively little impact on broad trends in international affairs, even if the nuances of British policy might have had a greater impact on the careers of individual overseas politicians, such as Gustav Stresemann.

Other similarities are more to do with broad economic trends. There is no reason to believe that the long-term effects of the Great War, and the fundamental weaknesses of the British economy, would have had a different impact on Asquith as Prime Minister than on Lloyd George as Leader of a coalition government. There is no reason to believe that the Conservatives in government could have averted the crash in 1931, or that the policies a Liberal government might have introduced afterwards would have had a major impact, other than through the jobs created by earlier rearmament.

Some parts of the alternative occur only slightly differently. It is assumed that at some point in the 1920s, the Liberal Party would have felt the need to review its policy, much as it did in 1928. However, in the alternative, it happens earlier and is consequently less radical than the real 'Yellow Book', which was produced when the Liberal Party had both the luxury of opposition and more time to think boldly.

This alternative history becomes more interesting when one looks at the more marked differences. In this alternative, they are embodied in the careers of two men.

Take first the career of Oswald Mosley. No doubt many will find it implausible, perhaps even shocking, that in this alternative, the man who was actually the Leader of the British Union of Fascists, instead becomes Leader of the Labour Party – though eventually he forms his own National Socialist Party. It is less implausible, however, when one remembers that he was a rising star of the Labour Party in the late 1920s, following his 1926 by-election victory. He was considered so brilliant by so many that he was easily able to overcame suspicions about his earlier career as a Unionist and then an Independent. Mosley was one of those political figures who seized on new ideas and ran with them, and his proposals for tackling unemployment bore a marked similarity to the sorts of schemes advocated by, for example, Franklin D. Roosevelt and Lloyd George.

Meanwhile, the kind of argument that splits Labour in this alternative – saving capitalism through support for a Lib–Lab coalition, versus awaiting its collapse and adopting a true socialist path – could easily have become a live debate in the Labour Party in the 1920s, focused on Mosley, just as it became an issue in 1931 focused on MacDonald. Had the party been offered a different chance of power than the one it actually gained in 1923 (the chance to govern alone), this is not so far-fetched. The split that actually occurred over the National Government in 1931–32 could well have occurred in the late 1920s, with Mosley as MacDonald and Maxton as Lansbury. The only difference here is that the Socialists break away from the formal Labour Party, rather than taking it with them.

The second career to change is that of Winston Churchill. His actual career in the 1920s was shaped by one key decision. Following the collapse of the Lloyd George Coalition in 1922, Churchill came to believe that British politicians faced a choice between order and chaos. He saw the Liberal Party as finished, and decided that the Conservatives were the only practical opposition to socialism. The result? In 1924, he became Chancellor of the Exchequer in Baldwin's second Conservative Government.

But what if the Liberal Party had not collapsed in 1918? What if it had remained a viable alternative to socialism, with people like Churchill believing that it had enough life left in it to stave off revolution through reform, just as they had prior to the Great War? We would then see Churchill, along with the hundreds of thousands of Liberal voters who took a similar view, able to stick with the Liberal Party. Given this situation, he could certainly have emerged as Liberal leader, as one of the great talents in the party. But none of that would necessarily have altered his attitudes to the Empire and the monarchy, both of which are advanced here as factors in the end of the Liberal government in 1936. And more importantly, the survival of the Liberal Party as a party of government into the 1930s would have made little impact on the pressure for Indian reforms in India itself, or King Edward VIII's preferences for companions, which would still have caused major problems for Churchill in the mid-1930s. Ironically, this split with the Liberals by Churchill also puts him in a position to become Britain's war leader in 1940. Had he remained a Liberal in 1936, it is unlikely that the Conservatives would have turned to him to become Prime Minister, looking instead to one of their own; but in working with Conservatives against Indian reforms, and voicing both Liberal and Conservative concerns over appeasement, it is suggested here that he does just enough to remain an option in 1940 as a unifying force.

All of this suggests that the main impact of the Liberal Party emerging united from the Great War would have been to prevent the Conservatives' inter-war hegemony. That is not because the Liberals would have been a better opposition to the Conservatives than Labour managed to be, but because they would have had a greater appeal to more centre-minded Conservatives than socialism ever could have. It is sometimes assumed by political commentators that the story of inter-war politics is one of Liberal replacement by Labour. Yet it is arguable that the real story was how the Conservative Party took over from the Liberals as the party of more moderate reform. In a world in which the Liberals were united, the Conservatives therefore had even more to lose than Labour.

Notes

1   Author's note: I am very grateful to Lucy Grayson, Andrew Thompson and Claire Chandler for their comments on drafts of this chapter, although inaccuracies and implausible plots are my own responsibility.
2   For a useful summary, see, Keith Laybourn, 'The Rise of Labour and the Decline of Liberalism: The State of the Debate', *History* 80, 259 (June 1995), pp. 207–26.

Chapter 2

What if Lenin's 'sealed' train had not reached Petrograd in 1917?

Helen Szamuely

The real twentieth century was shorter than others. It began in Sarajevo in July 1914 and ended, with a breathtaking circularity also in Sarajevo, during the bloody Balkan war in the 1990s. The shots fired by the Bosnian Serb Gavrilo Princip that killed the Archduke Franz Ferdinand and his wife ushered in what turned out to be a nightmarish period of unparalleled violence and viciousness. It is all the more fitting, therefore, that the last burst of that was back in the Balkans in a war that mixed nationalism, Communism and a plethora of newer ideologies. One of the prolonged battles of that war was the siege of Sarajevo by the Serbs in an attempt to destroy the newly created state of Bosnia–Herzegovina.

A yet more crucial event, historians have argued, was the Bolshevik coup of 1917. By taking power the Bolsheviks unleashed a civil war on Russia, wrenched that country definitively from the course of gradual democratisation and liberalisation it had taken before 1914, instituted a political system that survived on extreme terror and spread their ideology far beyond their country's borders. Even after the collapse of the Soviet Union and the ostensible discrediting of Communism the traces remain, not least in the reluctance to judge the system and its participants displayed by so many in Russia and the West. Not the least of the problems the Bolshevik coup introduced into political and intellectual life, particularly for those on the left of the spectrum, has been a moral slovenliness that has allowed an easy dismissal of mass murder and slave labour provided it was all done 'with the best intentions' and in the name of some nebulous general good.

In October 1917, political discourse changed for ever. Would any of this have happened without the presence of Vladimir Ilyich Lenin? The leader of the Bolshevik party was an apparently insignificant little man, with Tatar eyes and cheekbones, a reddish beard and bald pate; a man who had been dismissed by the great leaders of the European socialist movement as a dishonest schemer, even a thief, as his elder colleague Plekhanov put it, as an authoritarian intriguer and a complete fantasist – but also a man who was clearly seen by the German government and high command as a useful ally, and even tool, in the war against Russia.

The February Revolution swept away the Tsarist system and established the Provisional Government with remarkable ease. This government grew out of the semi-democratic Fourth Duma and consisted largely of left-leaning liberal and various socialist leaders of the radical intelligentsia. Contrary to subsequent accounts, the Provisional Government had a reasonable amount of support, bearing in mind that Russia was in the throes of a crisis induced largely by the war and the hardships it imposed on the population. It had, after all, been a bread riot that had triggered off the relatively peaceful revolution of February 1917.

Abdicating, Tsar Nicholas II instructed the army to obey the Provisional Government; the existing administrative structure, including the vital provincial governors, was ready to accept the new ministers. Partly this can be put down to the traditional Russian acceptance of central authority, but it can also be attributed to the widespread feeling that the Tsarist Government was corrupt and incompetent and a new political system was needed to bring some kind of order as well as a democratic structure to Russia, and to prosecute the war efficiently – an important consideration at the time. There was, however, a problem with the new Government: though skilled in politics, its members were novices in administration. Intent on an immediate dismantling of the old system, they thus deprived themselves of a potentially useful and probably loyal administrative structure without which they could produce edicts but could not enforce them. The dismantling of the structure was partly ideological, as the renowned historian of Russia, Professor Richard Pipes, points out, but also partly careerist. Many a dreaming intellectual now found himself (despite revolutionary and egalitarian fervour it was mostly men who took the leading positions) in an office, surrounded with all its paraphernalia. The only two things lacking were administrative ability and inclination.[1]

The other problem was the immediately reconstituted Soviet of Workers and Peasants and, in particular, its Executive Committee (*ispolkom*) that gathered in Petrograd (as St Petersburg was renamed in the early weeks of the war), intent on undermining the power of the Provisional Government and gathering it into its own hands. Within the Soviet were all the socialist parties, including the Bolsheviks, who at this stage were prepared to work with their brethren, even the Mensheviks, the other branch of the Social-Democrats.

Where was Lenin? He was, as Trotsky was later to describe, pacing up and down as if in a cage, in exile in Zurich.[2] He had spent most of his adult life in foreign exile, writing vehement articles and pamphlets, organising clandestine Bolshevik activity inside Russia and, above all, conducting vigorous fights and intrigues within the international socialist movement. A born politician, he knew that one's worst enemies are always on one's own side. His colleagues in the movement, particularly in the Russian branch of it, were all too well aware of his ruthless, authoritarian behaviour and complete amorality when it came to furthering the cause of his own group, but had never managed to deal with the problem. He was, after all, one of them – or so it seemed. They allowed him to splinter, first the Russian, then the international, socialist movement.

In his determination to acquire and preserve control over a social-ist group, Lenin did not scruple to use or allow himself to be used by agents of the enemy. The Bolshevik party, in common with other socialist organisations, was riddled with police agents in the years before the First World War. The most outstanding of these was Roman Malinowski, who had infiltrated the group after the 1905 Revolution, becoming one of Lenin's closest associates and, eventually, the leader of the Bolshevik group in the Fourth Duma. Malinowski helped Lenin to set up two clandestine Bolshevik publications inside Russia: the newspaper *Pravda* and the periodical *Nash Put'* (Our Path). Both of these were protected and possibly financed by the Okhrana, the secret police, whose aim coincided with Lenin's: they both wanted to split the socialist movement. Malinowski's cover was blown in 1914 by the new Deputy Minister of the Interior, Dzhunkovskii, who thought the use of *agents provocateurs* was wrong and undignified. It is not clear whether Lenin was fully aware of Malinowski's role but when the latter was put on trial as an agent of the Okhrana in 1918, mysterious hints indicated that he did know but felt that one way or another the Bolsheviks were getting more out of the deal than the police. Malinowski, no longer useful to his leader, was shot.

By 1914 Lenin had other worries and other dubious allies to deal with. He had spent the previous two years in Cracow, where he came to an understanding with the Union for the Liberation of the Ukraine. In return for lending his support to Ukrainian national aspi-rations he received funds from the organisation. These had originated in Vienna and Berlin, the Union operating under the Austro-Hun-garian Ministry of Foreign Affairs. In August 1914 Lenin, his family and entourage were arrested as enemy aliens but released on instruc-tions from the Austro-Hungarian government and allowed to leave for Zurich. In an early rehearsal of subsequent events, they left in an Austrian military train.

The First World War split the international socialist movement. There had been an assumption that the working class and the social-ist parties were above nationalist feelings and, therefore, would not participate in wars between nations. This was taken more seriously by the Russian socialists than the Western ones, partly because they, having spent so much time abroad, had shallower roots in their own country and did not feel the patriotism their German or British counterparts recognised; partly, they knew that the only chance they had of ever coming anywhere near power – again, in contrast to their Western colleagues – was by exploiting 'the economic and political crisis caused by the war'.

The start of the war saw most of the socialist parties abandoning international brotherhood in favour of patriotism. A sizeable minority, including almost all the Russian delegates to the various congresses, attacked capitalist warmongering and called for the speedy cessation of hostilities. Lenin, together with his immediate acolytes, distanced himself from both stances, demanding that the Socialist International should call for the transformation of the nationalist war into a class war. He despised pacifism and had no time for international or any other brotherhood, but fixed his sights firmly on the fact that an all-embracing war would provide him with a completely unexpected opportunity to edge his group somehow nearer to the seat of power, though, if truth be told, he had no real idea of how to do this in 1914. Still, in Zurich he wrote *The Tasks of Revolutionary Social Democracy in the European War,* in which he posited that the least worst outcome would be a defeat for Tsarism. This blatant attack on his own country at a time of war shocked even the Russian socialists. Those that might have followed his lead knew that inside Russia they ran the risk of being arrested, imprisoned and, possibly, executed as traitors while Lenin was safe in his Swiss exile. His ideas may not have percolated to Russia but the first accusations of his being a German agent were beginning to be heard.

Throughout his Zurich stay Lenin was in touch with the German authorities through other socialists like Parvus, who had decided that the overthrow of the Russian government was essential and that it would be accomplished most efficiently by German arms. The German Foreign Ministry, on the other hand, had taken the view that they needed agents inside all their enemy states to stir up trouble and weaken the war effort. As the war was fought by empires that consisted of many different nationalities on both sides, each side viewed the oppression that existed inside enemy states with self-righteous indignation.

In March 1917 Lenin was approached by several German and Swiss socialists and it was suggested to him that he might like to go back to Russia to fight the good fight. He accepted the offer of a train – not sealed, but treated as extraterritorial – and money to return to the motherland and proceed to deepen the anarchy there. The Germans were gleeful and their pleasure increased markedly as Lenin's activity in Russia became more visible. Lenin, on the other hand, considered that once again, he gained more than he lost. He was careful in his dealings, leaving no immediate trace of negotiations, insisting that the train passing through Germany be treated as an extraterritorial entity and not be boarded by German officials, never openly acknowledging his dealings with the socialist emissaries of the German authorities. He knew that accusations of being a German agent would be fatally compromising; he did not see his own activity in that light. To him patriotism or love of country were of no importance. He did not even think in terms of a Russian revolution. The aim at all times was a world revolution – which seemed, by some historical freak, to be beginning in Russia – conducted according to ideas expounded by him. To that end all means were acceptable.

If Lenin was worried that his method of travel through enemy territory would be used against him once he arrived in Petrograd in April, he need not have done so. The leaders of the Soviet and the Bolshevik party, which had been functioning reasonably well without his presence, welcomed him with great pomp, only to find themselves lambasted for taking a tactically incorrect road. Lenin dismissed the notion that the Provisional Government was legitimate or could ever be popular; he did not consider an efficient prosecution of the war desirable and ideas of democracy left him cold.

Even the devout Marxists did not accept Lenin's ideas that the bourgeois and socialist revolutions could somehow be telescoped into several months in Russia. While the Soviet contented itself with undermining the Government and gathering as much power as it could in the circumstances, Lenin proclaimed the need to overthrow the new rulers just as the old ones had been. Furthermore, he ruled, to his subordinates' discontent, that the Bolsheviks had no business working together with the other socialist parties. These were traitors to the cause and, most likely, agents of the Provisional Government, if not of the old Tsarist clique. (The Tsarist clique, as a matter of fact, had long ago disappeared, but it remained a useful bogeyman with which to frighten the socialists.)

In response, there were accusations of treason. The method of Lenin's return was brought up and he was described as a German agent, a traitor to Russia, and, most awfully of all, a traitor to the revolution. He managed to dismiss all these accusations. The details of his dealings with the German Foreign Ministry were not known and the various stories were disbelieved by the socialists he was busy attacking and threatening.

There were problems with the Bolsheviks themselves. They had already suffered because of his pronouncements in Switzerland in 1914 and, having returned from Siberian exile in February/March 1917 they managed to set up a party organisation and restart the publication of *Pravda*. The immediate reaction of the local Bolsheviks like Molotov, Stalin and Shlyapnikov, to Lenin's denunciation of the colleagues with whom they had developed a good working relationship was an embarrassed silence. His *April Theses* and first speeches were not published immediately in *Pravda;* they were eventually put in only under pressure and accompanied by a disowning editorial. (All this 'faintheartedness' would later be recalled by both Lenin, in his famous *Last Testament,* and Stalin, as he purged the party in the 1930s.)

But the Bolsheviks did not stand a chance against the force of Lenin's personality. Gradually, and often reluctantly, they fell in behind him, allowing him to organise three abortive Bolshevik uprisings in April, June and July. After the last one, even Kerensky's Provisional Government decided that enough was enough; leading Bolsheviks were either arrested or fled into exile. Lenin himself went to Finland – which had, by this stage become virtually independent – and continued haranguing his followers from there. The October coup was organised by Trotsky, who had decided that Lenin's ideas could not be put into effect by supposedly popular uprisings and street violence. A definite political putsch was indicated, in which the centre of power would be seized and control in the country taken later. Both Trotsky and Lenin, who returned to Petrograd secretly, without his beard – a fact rarely acknowledged in subsequent pictures and films – found that many of the leading Bolsheviks in their leader's absence had once again backslided, preferring to work with the other socialist groups in the Soviet to take power eventually, perhaps through the forthcoming elections for the Constituent Assembly.

The October coup was carried out in the name of the Soviet, as both Lenin and Trotsky realised that 'all power to the Bolsheviks' would not be a popular slogan. The Soviet, on the other hand, had managed to convince many that it was the true representative of the 'masses' and keeper of the revolutionary flame, while the Provisional

Government was the representative of the bourgeoisie. Having taken power in the name of the Soviet, Lenin invaded the Second Congress and informed the assembled delegates that the Bolsheviks were the true representatives of the Soviet who would now have to fall in with them.

This was not the end of the story, or even the end of the beginning. The elections for the Constituent Assembly went ahead, though in an atmosphere of increasing authoritarianism. Liberal politicians were arrested and even murdered; at the very least, they were prevented from conducting anything resembling an election campaign. The Menshevik-controlled trade unions went on an all-out strike which was subsequently put down. Lenin discarded any ideas he may have had of sharing power with other socialist groups with the exception of the Left SRs (Socialist Revolutionaries), and even these were variously dispensed with after an attempted uprising in July 1918.

By December 1917 the new Bolshevik Government had set up the first of its series of secret police organisations, the Cheka (the initials stood for *Chrezvychal'naya Kommissiya*, or Special Commission). This was headed by the ruthless and formidable Pole, Felix Dzerzhinsky, who was not, as it happens, a Bolshevik but a Left SR. The Constituent Assembly, in which the SRs won an overwhelming majority and the Bolsheviks were left with a small percentage of the seats, opened in January 1918 and was closed after a day's deliberations by the sailors who had been assigned to guard it under Zheleznyakov, who announced that they were all bored with endless speeches and discussions. Russia's brief experiment in liberalism and freedom came to an end for over seventy years as the country plunged into a ferocious civil war complicated by half-hearted Western attempts to intervene.

~

Clearly the German Government had been right: Lenin's presence in Russia was crucial for the complete destruction of the Russian order. They were wrong, however, in supposing that his influence could be contained within Russia. Churchill's description of Lenin being transported like a tuberculosis bacillus in a 'sealed train, a sealed envelope being too small', was nearer the mark. Though Lenin's own dream of a world revolution did not come true, the influence of the Communist system he established in those bloody years after his arrival at the Finland Station in April 1917 has spread wider than anyone could have predicted at the time and is still noticeable in international politics as well as intellectual developments. Could it have gone differently?

The train might never have got there. Though orders were given to let it travel through Germany undisturbed, and guards were provided for the periods when it was stationary, the chaos of war may well have prevented those orders from reaching everyone. Some official could have stopped it, some stray military detachment could have derailed it completely. The Russian Provisional Government and the Soviet need not have welcomed Lenin but could have arrested him for clear dealings with the enemy in wartime.

What if Lenin had never reached the Finland Station? Undoubtedly, there would have been no Bolshevik coup, as without him they would not have been bold enough, or organised enough, to take power. Probably it would not have occurred to them. There was every indication that in Lenin's absence the Bolsheviks were happy to work with other socialist groups within the Soviet and would probably have been happy to do the same in the Constituent Assembly. On the other hand, Lenin did not create the chaos that was Russia in 1917, or the impossible structure of the weak government undermined by the ever-more demanding Soviet. That being so, and the war going the way it was, the Germans would still have tried to meddle in Russian affairs. Given the lack of success their other agents had in Britain and France, however, it is probable that anyone apart from Lenin would not have been so useful to them.

After the failure of the July offensive Russia was effectively out of the war and the Western allies' main concern was to prevent her from signing a separate peace. The likelihood is that sooner or later any Russian government would have realised that a peace would have to be signed but the likelihood is that, in the absence of the October Revolution it would have taken longer to arrive at that conclusion. Had the separate peace been signed in the summer of 1918, the German offensive in the West in March would not have happened and the arrival of the American troops would have put the Western allies in an overwhelmingly favourable position. How many months of fighting would that have saved? A couple, maybe, and many thousands of lives.

The collapse of the German and the Austro-Hungarian empires would still have followed, together with the republican revolutions, but these would not have developed into the more vicious Soviet republics either in Hungary or in Bavaria, which, in turn, would have prevented much of the 'White terror' that followed across Central Europe. In fact, the newly formed countries would have stood a reasonable chance of developing into stronger liberal democracies, or, at least, relatively free authoritarian states, despite the problems induced by the settlements at Versailles. After all, Hitler's rise was greatly eased by the widespread fear of Bolshevism and, in more practical terms, by the usual Communist intrigues that prevented the formation of a united front against the Nazis in Germany in 1930–32.

What of Russia? Where would the chaos of 1917 have led that unfortunate country without the overwhelming presence of the determined Bolshevik leader? No other Bolshevik could have taken his place, the only one even remotely close to him in talent being the not-very-popular Trotsky who had joined the party very recently. So we can discard the idea of a Bolshevik dictatorship and the consequent civil war as well as, probably, the reluctant Allied intervention. It is, however, difficult to imagine that Russia would have made an easy transition to a democracy. Kornilov's failed military coup of September 1917 would not have been the last such and, just possibly, one would have succeeded; after all, Lenin's coup did. However, Russia does not have a tradition of military rule. The Guards Regiments may have got rid of rulers in the eighteenth century but only at the behest of supposedly rightful other rulers.

Hope would have lain in the Constituent Assembly, led by the SR Chernyayev and the Menshevik Tsereteli, both able men and capable of adjusting to new developments. Left to itself to deliberate, the Assembly, undoubtedly, would have taken far too long to make any decisions but, once they were made, they would have had a legitimacy that most of the country would have acknowledged. Putting the decisions into effect would have been difficult as the administrative system was non-existent. The Government under Kerensky was of little use and some form of administration would have had to grow out of the Assembly, prepared to take unpalatable actions if necessary.

Almost certainly the Assembly would have carried on with the redistribution of land and would not have turned that process into collectivisation, a peculiarly Bolshevik idea. Equally, it would have found itself forced to sign an agreement with Germany, which would probably have lost Russia as much land as was lost in any case through the Brest-Litovsk Treaty. Many of the other republics would have split off and become independent. But the chaos of the country would have necessitated some force to impose law and order – not an immediate liberal democracy but an authoritarian government with some democratic overtones which, as it became stronger, would have wanted to impose Russian influence on the surrounding newly independent states.

It is possible that Russia would have ended up with something like President Putin's rule eighty years earlier and without the terror and bloodshed that came between the present leader and Lenin. Crucially, without Bolshevik rule, Russia would have acquired a clearer understanding of private property and economic freedom. Once order was established, as it had been after the revolution of 1905, she would have learnt to live without fear and would have reverted to the hopeful developments of period between 1907 and 1914. Not that the scars of the First World War and of the 1917 Revolution would have disappeared – but, at least, Russia and the rest of the world might have been spared the full horrors of the short twentieth century.

Notes

1   Richard Pipes, *The Russian Revolution 1899–1919* (Collins Harvill, 1990), p. 322.
2   Quoted in Pipes, p. 386.

Chapter 3

What if Halifax had become Prime Minister in 1940?

John Charmley

Revisionist historians have made something of a splash recently with the claim that Winston Churchill might have become Prime Minister in May 1940. The notion that a few moments of silence from the great orator might have secured him the supreme office is one that has been around for a long time. Its origins can be traced to that great fabricator of myths, Brendan Bracken, who in his ghost-written memoirs claimed that he had advised Churchill not to speak first because he thought that Halifax would not want the premiership. It is a pretty conceit, but it falls at the first hurdle of counterfactual history: it ignores the context of British politics in May 1940. Prime Ministers do not exist in a vacuum, they need a power base and they need supporters. Halifax had both – Churchill had neither.

In the first place, the Conservatives, who were the majority party in the coalition, wanted Halifax. He was their ideal: aristocratic, intelligent (without making a fetish of it) and, above all, 'sound'; Churchill was a half-American adventurer with bad judgement. Nor was it just the Conservative 'men in grey suits' who favoured Halifax; he was the choice of the Labour leader, Clement Attlee, who admitted in his memoirs that the thought of Churchill becoming Prime Minister gave him 'a stomach ache'. Even the Liberals favoured Halifax, not that anyone really cared about their opinion. King George VI was, as so often, entirely in tune with what his people wanted. He knew Churchill as the man who had tried to lead a 'King's party' in 1936 to make political capital out of the abdication crisis; the people remembered him as the man of Tonypandy, Gallipoli and, most recently, Narvik. Seen in this context, it is absurd to suppose that a few moments of silence from Churchill could have made him Prime Minister; the only silence that could have done that was Halifax's.

The so-called 'constitutional' argument against Halifax becoming Prime Minister proved to be purely academic. The Commons passed emergency legislation allowing Halifax to speak in the Commons for the duration of the war, and his conversational style, reminiscent in so many ways of Baldwin's, proved to be just what the House needed. Halifax's political instincts proved to be first-rate, as his choice of Anthony Eden to lead the Commons showed. Eden's legendary charm and diplomacy, combined with his left-of-centre views, made him the ideal man for the job; if the famous family temper occasionally erupted, that did no harm either. Eden's loyalty to Halifax during the war cemented his position as heir-apparent, ensuring his succession to the leadership of the Conservative Party in 1945. It is surprising that in none of the many 'Churchillian' counterfactuals has any comment been made about the fact that had Churchill actually become Prime Minister, Eden might have had to wait until the mid-1950s before succeeding him; given his highly-strung temperament, the effect on his health hardly bears thinking about.

The immediate inclusion of Eden (despite advice from the Whips' Office) was symptomatic of Halifax's desire to create a truly National Government. He had often advised Chamberlain to be less combative with the opposition; in office he practised what he had preached. He could easily have done what Asquith had in 1915 and formed a government that was 'national' in name only, but Halifax realised the need to rally all parts of the political spectrum. His decision to offer

Churchill his old job at the Admiralty was politically acute, but there was a price to be paid for it, and by December 1940 the old boy's interference in every aspect of the war was becoming more than a bore. Fortunately (although not for him) Lord Lothian died at this point, and Halifax's choice of Churchill as the new ambassador to Washington showed his genius for putting octagonal pegs in the same shaped holes. Churchill's bumptiousness, which often grated on English sensibilities, made him ideal for America; no one ever forgot that he was half-American by birth, and his obvious love for the country and its people gained American hearts and won him a reputation as the best ambassador Britain ever sent to America. Churchill swiftly established a good relationship with Roosevelt, and it is said that one of the bonds between Halifax and the President was their aristocratic tolerance of Churchill's eccentricities.

There were other inspired choices which demonstrated the new Prime Minister's desire to achieve national unity in the face of the enemy: David Lloyd George as Minister of Information provided a mellifluous voice from a golden past to ease the pains of a sombre present; making Attlee his Deputy secured the Labour Party; but the stroke of genius was to appoint the trades union leader Ernie Bevin as Minister of Labour. This not only secured the loyalty of organised labour, it brought into the heart of the government the man who would run the Home Front during the period that has become known as 'the armed peace'. Some historians have commented how strange it was that during its greatest crisis in modern times, the country should have turned to an aristocratic leader; but as A. L. Rowse remarked: 'the English have always loved a Lord'. There was something immensely reassuring, solid and English about Halifax; people trusted him. His appeal for national unity went down well.

The need for that unity was very swiftly demonstrated. The Anglo-French armies reeled under the German onslaught, and after the German breakthrough at Sedan, the British army retreated to the coast, ending up at Dunkirk. The new Foreign Secretary, Sam Hoare, let it be known through the good offices of Mussolini that the extermination of the British Expeditionary Force would make any talks with Berlin about an armistice impossible. Historians will always argue about the influence of this initiative, but the fact was that Hitler allowed the BEF to retire from Dunkirk in good order, with their weapons. The Führer had never wanted to invade Britain, simply to remove it from his advance eastwards; Dunkirk gave him ample space to demonstrate this. His actions certainly helped matters when Halifax announced, as the last of the BEF disembarked, the opening of talks: 'We shall negotiate on the beaches', he said, 'and on the landing grounds, we shall talk in the streets and in the houses, we shall never cease from our search for peace'. The Cabinet minutes, in their usual anodyne way, note dissent from Churchill, but even he could not suggest an alternative.

The crunch came at the Cabinet meetings of 27–28 May. Halifax outlined the case for negotiation: Hitler had defeated the Anglo-French armies; we had been lucky to escape from France with our army intact; Hitler was willing to talk: above all, how did anyone propose that we should carry on the war? Our credit was all but exhausted, our ally defeated and our peril greater than ever before. At least according to Hoare's diaries, there was a silence at this point. Churchill broke it, arguing that Britain had not been successfully invaded for a thousand years and that instead of negotiating on the beaches we should be fighting on them. More in the same vein followed unstoppably until the Prime Minister suggested that the Cabinet break for refreshment. In the garden of 10 Downing Street Halifax walked with Churchill, trying to persuade him that his preferred policy was impracticable: 'And how shall we win in the end, Winston?', was one comment overheard by Sir Alexander Cadogan. An animated Churchill did most of the talking. When the Cabinet resumed, Halifax announced that there would be a meeting of the full Cabinet in the morning.

Halifax wrote to Chamberlain that evening, urging him to ensure that the Conservative Party atoned for its vote over Narvik by pressing its ministers to stand behind him. Before the Cabinet met, Chamberlain, Hoare and Kingsley Wood assembled at Rab Butler's Belgravia home to hear what the Chief Whip, David Margesson, had to say. There was, he said, universal desire to see whether a negotiated peace was possible, but anything smacking of surrender would bring the government down. At about the same time, Halifax was meeting Attlee, Sinclair, and most significantly, Lloyd George. It was the last who rallied them all, reminding them that 'Winston's judgement has always been bad: quite apart from the Dardanelles, the Gold Standard, India, the Abdication and Narvik, the fellow joined the Tory Party twice. Don't forget', he added, 'I saw how he dragged Asquith into the Dardanelles, I am not going to see that happen again!' Churchill, too, had spent the morning with his supporters, but Amery, Lloyd, Duff Cooper and Bracken had no place in the Cabinet, and little contact with Labour and the Liberals; a bunch of Tory die-hards along with a few Baldwin rejects was not going to swing many votes.

After the intrigues of the previous twelve hours, the Cabinet itself was an anti-climax. Halifax, after outlining the deteriorating situation, suggested that they use the British Minister at the Vatican to sound out Mussolini about a repeat of the Munich conference. Churchill slammed his papers on the table, declaring that 'he would not be a party to any shameful surrender, and that he would rather die in the last redoubt than surrender to That Man.' There is some dispute about Halifax's exact words, but all versions agree on their sense. As Hoare recorded them, they were: 'Winston, don't talk such frightful rot! It is better to seek terms now than after London has been razed to the ground by bombing.' When Churchill tried to counter, Halifax, for the first time anyone could remember, raised his voice and seemed close to losing his temper: 'Winston, enough! How many more British lives must be sacrificed on the altar of your ambition before your ego will be satisfied – enough, I say!' Churchill glared at Halifax before gathering up his papers; he looked at him and declared: 'I shall have no part in this shameful surrender, and I shall stand on every platform in the country against you!'

It was at this point that Lloyd George made his crucial intervention: 'You do just that, Winston – but as the man who won the last war, I'll respond that the only way to win this one is an armistice now, and let's see who the country believes.' It was Halifax who saved the day. With his shrewd reading of Churchill's nature, he changed tack, saying: 'Gentlemen, with the country on the brink of disaster we cannot and must not argue among ourselves. Winston, only you can stiffen the nation's sinews in the way required – and how shall we replace your experience at the Admiralty? Surely you would not desert your post at this time?' According to Lloyd George's account, tears came into Churchill's eyes as he turned to the Prime Minister and said: 'Edward, you are right. We must all of us brace ourselves to do our duty. I shall not quit my post when the fighting is thickest.' The unity of the government was maintained.

Darcy Osborne in the Vatican delivered the British request to Mussolini. Within hours a message came back that the Führer would, indeed, be interested in opening talks with the British Empire. In a broadcast from Berlin the following day, Hitler paid tribute to the fighting spirit shown by the British, and declaring himself no enemy of the British people, made an appeal for talks to begin about a peace settlement. This was the cue for Halifax. The following evening Lloyd George made his now famous broadcast, with its memorable peroration: 'There is no shame in fighting the mighty German war machine to a standstill; as we look across the ravaged continent of Europe, we can help bring an end to this senseless war; it is for us, here in this island, as the leader of the greatest Empire the world has ever seen, to light the way to peace. That would, indeed, be an act worthy of the British people, and if the Empire lasts a thousand years, men would still say: this was their finest hour.' For the next two days the diplomats on either side worked hard drafting clauses that would make Lloyd George's dream a reality.

Halifax's dramatic flight to Vichy on 5 June produced the first public sign of what was going on. The British Prime Minister came away with an agreement that France would be allowed to negotiate her own peace with Germany; in return, the French fleets in Mers-el-Kebir and Alexandria would be handed over to the British and, to secure the French Empire from German control, Pétain announced that France, the home of liberty, was bestowing that gift upon her former colonies – under French viceroys. The one unfortunate appointment was that of General de Gaulle as Viceroy of Syria; elsewhere British and French proconsuls cooperated cordially, but in Syria de Gaulle's Anglophobia had free reign, and there was plenty of evidence to suggest that the 1941 Jerusalem riots against the British mandate were inspired by Gaullist agents. It was not until he overstepped the mark in 1943 by removing the elected Lebanese government that de Gaulle was removed. His subsequent employment in Algeria in the late 1950s was proof, should any be needed, that French governments do not learn from experience.

France's withdrawal from the war left the road open for Anglo-German negotiations. During this period, Halifax held frequent talks with the American ambassador, Joe Kennedy. One of Churchill's lines, paraded in the *Daily Mirror*, was that America would help Britain stay in the war, and was about to enter it herself. Kennedy told Halifax plainly that this was the result of Churchill's 'two-fisted drinking'. America, he explained, was not going to enter this war, not ever, but particularly not in an election year; she would, of course, be happy to sell Britain all the aid she needed, and even extend credit when the cash ran out – but in return Britain would be required to disinvest her overseas assets and dismantle the sterling area. It was reported that Roosevelt was irritated at Kennedy's candour: 'old Churchill', he told his son Elliot, 'wouldn't have been so miserly'. This was exactly what Neville Chamberlain had been telling the Prime Minister from the start, so there could be no complaining from Washington when, on 18 June 1940, Halifax announced that preliminary negotiations for an armistice had opened in the French city of Amiens. 'We have', Halifax announced, 'lost a battle, but not the war'.

During the next few weeks the most difficult task facing the government was dealing with the susurration of rumours about the settlement: the Empire would be dismantled; Britain would be disarmed; British Jews would be deported; British women would be required to 'service' German soldiers who would be stationed in England; Hitler would demand Buckingham Palace; the Duke of Windsor would be put on the throne; Churchill would be shot – all these, and more, circulated from sources close to Churchill or to the Soviet Embassy. Halifax, it is said, had to tell Churchill to mind his tongue when in public, but most historians now believe that the Prime Minister was happy to let him spout such arrant nonsense because it would so soon contrast with the truth.

The terms were laid before the Commons on 14 July and quite justified Hitler's reported comment: 'I stand amazed at my own moderation'. Britain was required to 'withdraw her forces from the European continent'; this had already happened at Dunkirk. She was also required to accept the terms of the German–Polish peace settlement, another foregone conclusion. The British guarantees to Rumania and Greece were to be given up, a loss of face that had, as Halifax said, become inescapable. At Halifax's own suggestion (it was said) there was a twenty-year non-aggression pact between the two countries, and Britain promised Germany 'most-favoured nation' status when it came to trade. Diplomatic relations between the two powers were resumed, but not even Ribbentrop supposed that he should be the man to renew them.

The Commons heard the terms with amazement; as Chips Channon put it, 'Not a single British virgin was to be sacrificed to the German dragon'. What no one told the House was that there was a confidential annex to the Treaty of Amiens. In it, Britain agreed that in the event of a German invasion of the Soviet Union she would remain neutral and should, in no circumstances, supply the Soviets with military or financial aid. Ribbentrop, always unable to restrain his tongue, had told the chief British negotiator, Rab Butler, that the Germans were so anxious to get on with their planned war against the Bolsheviks that they would have accepted peace on even milder terms; Rab's mordant comment that 'I can't imagine what those might be', caught the spirit of the British reaction.

Churchill's doom-mongering was now firmly discredited. He tried to make what he could of the proposal that Britain should share the sovereignty of Gibraltar with Spain, but neither that, nor the cause of the British settlers in Tanganyika, which was to be handed back to Germany over a ten-year period, aroused mass support against Halifax, whose popularity soared to the heights Chamberlain had enjoyed after Munich. He resisted, however, the temptation to stand on the balcony at No. 10 and proclaim that it was 'peace in our time'.

He did so for one simple reason; Halifax knew that it was nothing of the sort. For all the nonsense spouted by Churchill about it being folly to trust Hitler, Halifax knew that the truce of Amiens was based on nothing more than mutual convenience. Britain could not have stayed in the war without sustaining damage (fatal damage in Halifax's view) to her ability to remain a great power. We know, from his diary, that Halifax had considered the Churchill option carefully. All he could see, he told Butler, was mass German bombing of British cities as a prelude to invasion. Even had we survived the invasion, how, he repeatedly asked, were we to win the war? As far as he could see, America would strip Britain to the bone financially as her price for aid, and even then, there was no guarantee that the US would ever enter the war herself. Indeed, there were indications that the other price America would exact would be British cooperation in an economic boycott of Japan, which, as Halifax said, would put the whole of the vulnerable British Empire in the Far East at risk. No, Churchill was wrong but romantic, and however repugnant to his senses as an Englishman, what Halifax did was right. It also suited Germany, where the Führer's impatience to attack Russia was growing. The most disappointed man in Europe after Churchill was Mussolini, who had to scrap his plans to attack British Somaliland and Egypt.

It is clear that Halifax always regarded the armistice as a temporary affair. *Pace* Churchill, no one imagined that Hitler could be trusted, but an essential breathing space had been gained. The main dispute among historians is whether the Halifax government took full advantage of it.

There was one area where this was certainly the case: the general election. The last election had been in 1935, so when Halifax announced in September that the King had agreed to dissolve Parliament, no one could accuse him of having whatever the peaceful equivalent of a 'khaki election' was. The Prime Minister himself played curiously little part in the campaign, confining himself to election broadcasts and one big speech at the Caxton Hall. One of his problems was the sudden illness of that vital figure, Neville Chamberlain. Despite the attempts of the Beaverbrook Bolsheviks to smear him as a 'guilty man', Chamberlain's earlier failures had been rehabilitated by the success of Halifax's peace overtures; Hitler, it seemed, could be negotiated with. As leader of the Conservative Party, and chairman of the Cabinet committees on domestic matters, Chamberlain played a key role, so his illness and retirement in October placed Halifax in a dilemma. Should he, as many advised, become leader of the Conservatives? Instinctively he was against the idea. He wanted to go into the election as a 'national' leader, not a party one; on the other hand, Sam Hoare was unpopular, while neither Rab Butler nor

Eden had quite the weight required. So, in the end, he agreed to lead the party, but only until the next election, by which time he expected another leader to have emerged.

Many people prophesied a result of 1931 proportions for the National Government, but Halifax always doubted that. Channon's diary quotes him as saying that: 'A government responsible for our greatest defeat since Yorktown cannot expect universal approbation'. Still, bearing that in mind, the election went well enough. The Conservatives lost sixty seats, but since some of them were occupied by the likes of Brendan Bracken and Leo Amery, the Chief Whip was hardly too upset. Churchill's deal with his local Liberals ensured that he held on to his seat, but those Liberals and Labour candidates who took the Tory seats were, on the whole, supporters of the National Government; it was significant that Lloyd George was elected unopposed at the Caernarvon Boroughs. Chamberlain's old seat at Ladywood was held by a young army officer fresh back from the front, whose local credentials were impeccable – Enoch Powell, of whom much would be heard in the future.

With a secure majority in the House, the Halifax Government had to face the problem of preparing for an uncertain future.

Halifax always claimed that there was no real risk in negotiating with Hitler. There was one area where the Führer's word could be trusted – his anti-Bolshevism. With Britain out of the war, Hitler was free to go ahead with his great crusade against Communism, and in May 1941 he launched Operation Barbarossa. At first it seemed as though the USSR would collapse like a house of cards, as the Red Army was driven back with the loss of hundreds of thousands of prisoners. But despite the terms of the Treaty of Amiens, the British, like the Americans, kept the Soviets supplied with armaments and equipment. Hitler's protests against this were dismissed, with Eden reflecting to Halifax that if the Germans wished to disengage any of their forces from the eastern front to open up a war in the west, he for one would welcome it. Nor was the reason hard to seek. In the nine months after Amiens, with American help, the British had rearmed and re-equipped their forces. The RAF and the chain of radar stations stood ready to fend off any German air attack, whilst the British Expeditionary Force was more than ready to defend the home islands. For all his huffing and puffing, Hitler knew that he could not afford to remove troops from the east.

By the end of 1941, faced with 'General Winter', the German armies had come to a halt, and although further major advances were made in the summer of 1942, the Red Army slowly began to hold the German attack; by mid-1943 the Germans had effectively been fought to a standstill. The limitations of the German war machine became increasingly apparent: Hitler was ready to win a *blitzkrieg*, but the Germans were not armed in the depth required to win a war of attrition against a Soviet Union that refused to collapse. The heavy losses incurred at Stalingrad could not be replaced, and the fresh armaments supplies to the Russians from Britain and America helped give Stalin the edge over his rival dictator – though only at a terrible cost in Soviet lives. Furthermore, the increasingly erratic orders from the Führer put the German army in impossible positions. The key moments in the war came in 1943, with the German surrender at Stalingrad and the Soviet victory at Kursk; from August the Nazis were in retreat.

Soviet successes, combined with the improvements the Halifax Government was able to make in the Far East, dissuaded the bellicose Japanese from adventurism, whilst American sanctions brought the regime into a more amenable frame of mind. This was as well for, as Halifax later admitted, the British Empire in the Far East would have collapsed very quickly. Here he did less than justice to himself. As the author of the idea of Dominion status for India, Halifax was ideally placed to guide the sub-continent towards that goal; his choice of Butler as Viceroy after Linlithgow gave the process just the momentum needed. It was said that Nehru and Gandhi rather resented the failure of the Japanese threat to materialise, but they were both realists and worked with Butler to secure Indian independence in 1946.

The turning point for British foreign policy came in the summer of 1944. By then the Soviets had advanced to the outskirts of Warsaw, where they once again showed their true character by leaving the Polish uprising to be suppressed by the Nazis; even the British Communist Party took time to find an excuse for that one. The Nazi satraps were all busy trying to persuade the British and the Americans to enter the war in order to save them from the Russians; rhetorically this became 'we must preserve the balance of power in Europe'. Halifax and Roosevelt met in Washington in June and launched the famous 'peace initiative' in which the two sides were given an ultimatum: if they did not come to terms within six months, Britain and America would have no alternative but to intervene militarily. This forced the Soviets to press on, which, in turn, revealed how overstretched the Soviet military effort had become. By the turn of the year the Nazis and the Soviets had fought themselves to a standstill. It was only Stalin's determination to take Berlin regardless of cost, and Hitler's to stay there on the same basis, that led to the suicide of the latter and the end of the war in Europe.

The war-ravaged continent and the bloodied victors needed nothing so much as injections of cash and supplies of food. Stalin, worried by the Bomb and by Soviet weakness, proved more cooperative than old-style anti-Communists like Ambassador Churchill had predicted. It is perhaps worth the revisionists reflecting that had Churchill become Prime Minister and had Britain stayed in the war, the most likely outcome following the defeat of Hitler would have been an increase in Anglo–Soviet antagonism, instead of the period of détente that actually followed the war.

The final area in which the Halifax premiership proved itself a useful transition period between the problems of the thirties and the opportunities of the fifties was on the Home Front. The human and social consequences of a continuation of the war after 1940 can only be surmised. At the very least there would have been great loss of life and property, large areas of our industrial cities would have been devastated, and economic activity would have come to a standstill. When the cost of carrying on the war is added to this list, it is hard not to conclude that Britain would have been bankrupt by the autumn of 1940. The choice then could have been between becoming an American pensioner (always supposing the Americans would have been willing to pay the pension) or concluding peace on whatever terms the Germans wanted; either way, British 'independence' would have become a qualified term. Withdrawal from the fighting war in 1940 allowed the government to turn to problems on the domestic front.

Those who had followed Halifax's career from its early days when, as Edward Wood, he was firmly identified with the social-imperialist wing of the Conservative Party, were not surprised when he allowed a fairly free rein to Ernest Bevin and Rab Butler. The Butler–Bevin (or 'Butlin') consensus that emerged in the mid-1940s has, in itself, become the focus of revisionist debates, arguing that there was, in fact, a substantial difference between the liberal conservatism of Butler and the labourism of Bevin, but most historians still accept that the reforms narrowed the ground between the two major parties. One notable achievement was the consolidation of the railways and the power-generating industries into a smaller number of companies with mixed public–private ownership and funding, thus cutting through the sterile arguments both of the socialists, claiming they wanted 'public' ownership but never defining how it would have worked, and of the Tory Right, who seemed to want a return to the 1840s. For those with a taste for the morbid, it is worth thinking what might have happened had Herbert Morrison's idea of public ownership through nominated boards of control been put into effect; even his grandson, Prime Minister Mandelson, has agreed that the effect would have been to channel vast amounts of public money into unaccountable bodies which would have been impossible to reform.

Once Halifax stood down in the summer of 1945, the continuing National Government under Eden's leadership made an excellent instrument for the introduction of a long period of liberal Toryism, during which Britain was able to take the lead in building a European Community of nation-states. It was all less glorious than a Churchillian twilight of the gods, but ultimately more fruitful for Britain and the United States of Europe.

Chapter 4

What if the Liberal Party had broken through from the right?

James Parry

Neither the Government nor the local authorities make any wealth or have any money of their own. If we want them to spend more and more we have to pay. The remedy is in our own hands. Stop running to them asking them to do this, that and everything under the sun – and demand instead that they stop doing and spending so much.

Jo Grimond, February 1957[1]

Our long-term objective is clear: to replace the Labour Party as the progressive wing of politics in this country.

Jo Grimond, November 1958[2]

There has developed a tragic chasm between the two sides of the liberal tradition. Those who care most about civil liberties, open government, limitation of police powers and similar matters have drifted to the left, while those who have been most concerned with economic liberalism have drifted to the right. Both sets of ideas have become impoverished as a result.

Samuel Brittan, 1990[3]

There are three major national parties in British politics. At various times since the 1920s, one of them, the Liberal Party, has teetered on the brink of destruction. Yet over the past half-century it has clawed its way back to the front rank of politics. In its modern incarnation of the Liberal Democrats,[4] the party now regularly wins around a fifth of the votes in general elections, holds more than fifty seats in the House of Commons and substantial representation in the European and Scottish Parliaments and the Welsh Assembly, and has thousands of local councillors throughout the country. These gains have been built up in a succession of waves of revival – in the early 1960s, the early 1970s, the early 1980s and the general elections of 1997 and 2001, each tide leaving the party in a stronger position as it ebbed.

There have been high points – briefly after the Orpington by-election victory in 1962, or in 1981–82 as the Liberal–SDP Alliance carried all before it – when it seemed that the third party might break through to remould British politics and regain the position it had lost after the First World War as one of the two major parties of government. These moments have passed, and the domination of the Labour and Conservative Parties has been reasserted, but few would deny the achievement of the Liberals in re-establishing a strong position in British politics.

There are, however, two paradoxes about this development.

The recovery in Liberal electoral fortunes in recent decades has coincided with the renaissance of economic liberalism, including many of the ideas the Liberals were closely identified with when their revival began. Yet there is very little connection between these two trends, except perhaps in the negative sense that the Liberals have benefited electorally from the backlash against the neo-liberal policies pursued by the Thatcher and Major Governments. The Liberals who defended economic liberalism through thick and thin in the years of their decline seemingly abandoned the cause to the Conservatives in the latter part of the twentieth century, just as its resurgence was beginning. The result has been what one commentator has described as the 'dismemberment of liberalism into political and economic segments'.[5] The Liberals' commitment to social and political liberty is not in doubt, but the party has ceased to be the natural home of economic liberals.

Secondly, for more than four decades the Liberal strategy has been to reshape British politics from the left as a radical alternative to the Labour Party, replacing it as the opposition to the Conservatives. In many ways this seemed the natural order of things, a reversion to the pre-1920s' pattern of Liberal–Conservative rivalry that Labour had disrupted. The Liberals have prospered, but their objective of realigning the left by replacing Labour has evidently failed to occur. The rise of New Labour, accompanied by the first large-scale gains in seats by the Liberal Democrats, has seemingly buried this prospect. Recently the Liberals' hopes of remoulding politics have been pinned rather on the disintegration of the Conservatives, a scenario that looks increasingly plausible as Tory support drops below that of the Liberals in many regions and amongst key groups of voters.

This prompts some fundamental questions about the Liberal strategy. Not only has the party failed in its objective of replacing Labour but, positioned on the centre-left, it is awkwardly placed to take advantage of the recent decline of the Conservatives. Perhaps its relative electoral advance in recent decades hides missed opportunities for greater success.

What might have happened if the Liberals had adopted a different strategy? Was the goal of a 'realignment of the left' a dead-end? Would they have achieved more by aiming from the start to reshape British politics from the centre-right? How might this have impacted on the Liberal revival, and how might it have affected British politics more widely?

Liberals and economic liberals

Is it plausible to suggest that the Liberals *could* have adopted a centre-right stance? Parties are shaped by their history, their values, their

53

leaders and their supporters. They are not free agents to pick and chose which ideas to follow. Were the Liberals destined by their tradition and outlook to follow a centre-left course?

Nowadays it requires a feat of imagination to visualise the Liberals as a centre-right party. For a long time now they have been associated with the social liberal, not to say social democratic, cause. Today the great majority of Liberal leaders and activists are of the centre-left, if not the left, in their outlook. At the 2001 general election a number of commentators placed the Liberals somewhat to the left of the Labour Party in many of its policies.

However, looking across Europe, left-leaning British Liberalism is an exception. In Germany, Belgium, Denmark, Italy and elsewhere liberal parties after the Second World War found a niche for themselves and sometimes prospered as market-oriented parties of the centre-right. The archetype is perhaps the Free Democratic Party in Germany which, despite periods of coalition with the Social Democrats, essentially chose to be an economic rather than a social liberal party in the 1960s, and remains so to this day. Indeed, in the rest of Europe the term 'liberal' is associated more with the right of politics than the left; just think of the connotations that 'liberalism' has in France, for instance.

Historically also, British Liberalism for much of its existence was not identified with the centre-left. Such a term had little meaning until the advent of the Labour Party and class-based politics after the First World War. True, the Liberals were the alternative to the Conservatives, but as we shall see, in some respects the Liberals took positions that we would today see as being on the 'right', while the Conservatives were more on the 'left' – most obviously over the issue of protectionist intervention in the economy.

During the years of their decline, from the 1920s to the 1950s, it would be most accurate to say that the Liberals were unable to find a home on the left–right spectrum. They were generally seen as a centre party. At certain elections such as 1929, when Lloyd George was leader, and 1945, when Beveridge was their most prominent campaigner, their appeal inclined to the centre-left. At other times, such as 1931 or 1950, they were oriented more to the centre-right. Throughout the period in some areas they provided a radical challenge to the Tories and in others a moderate alternative to Labour. However despite this ambiguity and uncertainty, there is no doubt that until the early 1960s the Liberals were, far more than their opponents, the party of economic liberalism, the open economy and free markets.

The Liberal Party had been founded as a champion of the open economy. It was created, following the mid-nineteenth-century realignment provoked by Peel's repeal of the Corn Laws, as a coalition of Whigs, Radicals and Peelites around the cause of reform, retrenchment and free trade. Retrenchment meant limited public expenditure and balanced budgets, and free trade referred not just to international trade but to free exchange and competition throughout the economy. Cobdenite political economy formed a ideology for the mid-Victorian party which, if by no means unchallenged as the century wore on, remained hugely influential. Liberal governments vigorously sought lower public expenditure, balanced budgets, and free trade against the background of a sound currency based on the gold standard.

Despite the rise of the New Liberalism and the social reforms of Asquith and Lloyd George before 1914, the legacy of Cobden and Gladstone continued to exert a powerful influence on Liberal ideas. In the 1920s and early 1930s the Liberals continued to fight for free trade and retrenchment. Even a confirmed New Liberal such as Herbert Samuel, who led the party in the early 1930s, retained an unshakeable belief in these fundamentals.[6] In 1932 he led the Liberals out of the National Government rather than abandon the cause of free trade. As late as the 1950s many rank-and-file Liberals were firmly on the economic right. Writing of this period, one Liberal veteran recalled that 'experience of the Liberal Party ... leads me to guess that in both 1945 and 1950 (and even more so at earlier elections) there were legions of old-style free-traders going to the polls under a Keynes/Lloyd George/Beveridge policy that they neither understood nor really supported'.[7]

In fact the rump of the party in the 1950s was definitely to the right of the Labour and Conservative Parties on economic matters; so much so that there was an exodus of the more leftish Liberals to the Labour Party, and the Radical Reform Group was formed in 1953 to resist the laissez-faire trend. Many of the party's old guard had stuck with the Liberals because of their loyalty to free trade – but many of the younger figures who kept the party going in the 1950s were also libertarian in their outlook. After 1951 all the members of the tiny parliamentary party leaned towards the economic right. Party intellectuals such as Elliott Dodds and the Unservile State Group were concerned with updating rather than replacing the party's traditional libertarian concerns.

There was also a vocal ideological libertarian faction led by Lord Grantchester,[8] Oliver Smedley,[9] S. W. Alexander and others, which attempted with some success to rally the party behind free trade and market economics. Grantchester was a key sponsor of Friedrich von Hayek's activities, including the Mont Pelerin Society, established in 1947 as an international network to promote economic liberalism on the back of his *The Road to Serfdom* (1944). Smedley has been described as 'fervent and obsessive in his belief in the beneficence of the free market'.[10] At Liberal assemblies in the 1950s he campaigned tirelessly for free trade and smaller government. In 1955, together with a Conservative, Anthony Fisher, Smedley set up the Institute of Economic Affairs (IEA), which was to become the intellectual powerhouse of the economic liberal counter-revolution. In the early days the IEA was strongly associated with the Liberal Party.[11] Arthur

Seldon, who, with Ralph Harris, was to be its driving force, had been an active Liberal since the late 1930s and continued to vote Liberal until 1970.

Given the Liberal Party's historic commitment to economic liberalism, and its ideological complexion in the 1950s, it would have been natural for it to position itself on the centre-right as it revived, targeting the Conservative vote. It was the shift to the left and the abandonment of economic liberalism that was surprising.

The Grimond revival

Jo Grimond was elected leader of the Liberal Party in 1956. The first glimmerings of the party's revival can be traced to the mid-1950s, but it got seriously under way with a series of encouraging by-election results in 1957–58, culminating in the victory of Mark Bonham Carter at Torrington. At the 1959 general election the Liberals won 5.9 per cent of the national vote, up from 2.7 per cent in 1955. It was the first clear reversal of the electoral decline of the party since 1929. A further run of good by-election and local government results in 1961–62 was crowned with the spectacular victory at Orpington in 1962. At the 1964 general election the Liberals gathered 11.2 per cent of the votes. This fell back to 8.6 per cent in 1966, and the exhausted and depressed Grimond resigned the following year, though he remained an MP and later Liberal peer until his death in 1993.

Jo Grimond's charisma, his injection of progressive new ideas and the influx of radically minded recruits he attracted, modernised the Liberal Party and overcame its greatest handicap, its old-fashioned and backward-looking image. He shifted the Liberals to the centre-left, and it might well be thought that the shift was inseparable from his leadership.

What is surprising is that this shift was strangely at odds with Grimond's personal views on economic policy. As Michael McManus's recent biography shows, for much of his career Grimond was on the economic right and was an early and outspoken critic of the post-war economic consensus. This was true of his initial years as an MP from 1950, when he was a lone voice in British politics (apart from other Liberals and a few maverick Tories) warning of the dangers of inflation and excessive public expenditure. The first quotation at the head of this chapter is representative of his usual line in speeches and writings at the time. It was also true of his views after he had ceased to be Liberal leader in 1967. It is no exaggeration to say that already, in the 1950s, he anticipated many of the core economic concerns and ideas of the Thatcherites. However, it is certainly true that during his leadership Grimond muted his economic views and that the party downgraded its traditional concern with free trade, competitive markets, low taxation and controlling public expenditure. By 1961 the party was calling for production targets for industry and ceilings on wages and profits.[12] The Liberals' 1963 economic policy called for a five-year plan with the establishment of national and regional planning bodies.

It is unlikely that Grimond intended the shift to go so far. In his *The Liberal Challenge* (1963), he seems to have conceived of economic planning as a coordination of economic and fiscal policies, not as any further encroachment on the private sector.[13] To some extent the party was swept along by the technocratic, corporatist mood of the time, by post-Orpington euphoria and by the logic of the radical realignment strategy. The party's economic policies were drawn up hastily and gave out conflicting messages.[14]

In fact there remained a significant undercurrent of economic liberalism in the Grimond party. An important part of the Liberals' appeal was as a protest party on behalf of the 'little man' against the political and economic establishment.[15] Liberal publicity continued to play up traditional concerns such as the need for action against monopolies in order to encourage competition. Free trade was not entirely forgotten, although it was largely eclipsed by new causes such as the Liberals' early support for British entry to the Common Market. This decision alienated some of the more right-wing economic liberals in the party, who saw the Common Market as a protectionist project.

If the decisive step was taken under Grimond's leadership, it was under his successors Jeremy Thorpe and David Steel that the shift was completed. Thorpe was an old adversary of the free-traders in the debates of the 1950s, and did not share Grimond's interest in policy issues. David Steel was in many respects a social democrat and steered the party towards the Lib–Lab Pact of 1977–78 and the SDP Alliance of 1981–87. He was by no means an instinctive economic liberal.

In practice it is unlikely that an old-style free trade party could have survived, and Grimond's modernisation was critical for the Liberals' revival. He was trying to update the party's economic liberalism, but lost control of the process which went further than he intended. Under Grimond the Liberals could have – and perhaps very nearly did – become the focus of the neo-liberal renaissance. But the opportunity was lost and by the late 1960s the Liberals were indistinguishable from the other two parties in their support for the post-war consensus.

The electoral landscape

So if the Liberals were destined to the centre-left neither by their history, their values nor their leader, were there electoral factors that gave them no choice? Perhaps the electoral landscape they faced in the late 1950s allowed no place for a centre-right alternative? Maybe the only space in which they could revive was on the centre-left?

This is not borne out by the electoral record.

First, the electoral ground gained under Grimond's centre-left strategy was very limited. A peak of only twelve seats was won and although the average Liberal vote per candidate increased from 15.1 per cent in 1955 to 18.7 per cent in 1964 (with many more candidates), by 1970 all these gains had been wiped out. Most of the

Liberal gains in local government of the early 1960s had also been reversed by 1970.

Secondly, the gains were heavily concentrated in areas of traditional Liberal strength in the West Country and the Scottish Highlands, and in the Tory suburbs and seaside resorts. Urban Labour Britain remained a desert for the party. Significantly, in the one urban area where the old Liberals had retained some traditional strength in the 1950s – the Yorkshire/Lancashire textile belt – they did well in 1959, but failed to advance in 1964. They also lost the two urban seats they held in this region when they broke local pacts with the Conservatives. The party's move to the left seemed to do little to strengthen the Liberals' challenge to Labour. A new feature at the 1964 election, absent in 1959, was the greater difficulty the Liberals had in increasing their vote much in comfortably Labour seats.[16] Nor did they have much success in squeezing the Labour vote in promising Conservative constituencies.

This pattern was to be repeated in later elections. In the 1972–74 and 1981–83 revivals the Liberals and the Alliance were unable to win more than a handful of seats, and were strikingly unsuccessful in winning seats in the Labour heartlands. During the period 1958–2001 the Liberals gained eighty-eight seats at by-elections and general elections, of which seventy-eight were won from Conservatives and only ten[17] from Labour. The gains from Labour have almost all taken place in exceptional circumstances, in the rare constituencies where the Liberals have survived as a traditional challenger to Labour, on the back of by-election advances, or in contests with far left Labour opponents – or thanks to a combination of these factors.

There is a similar pattern in local government, where the Liberal inroads into the Labour heartlands have been more impressive and the party has become the first or second party in many urban areas. But it is the Conservatives that they have replaced, not Labour.

Paradoxically the centre-left strategy may actually have weakened the Liberals' appeal in Labour areas. It is striking that the few parliamentary gains from Labour have been mostly achieved by traditionalist Liberals such as Richard Wainwright, Michael Meadowcroft, Cyril Smith or Wallace Lawler. It may well be that the Liberals would have fared better against Labour by accentuating the differences between the two parties rather than stressing their common ground with Labour moderates.

A major opportunity was missed in the 1960s. As Harold Wilson's Labour government lost popularity after 1966, disillusioned Labour voters swung in large numbers to the Conservatives, not the Liberals. This undid most of the electoral progress the Liberals had made during the Grimond decade and greatly reduced their capacity to exploit the electoral and political opportunities of the 1970s.

In sum, it is far from clear that the Liberals benefited electorally from their centre-left stance. As an electoral strategy it manifestly failed to deliver its main objective: regaining from Labour the old Liberal strongholds in industrial Britain. It is entirely possible that a more centrist/centre-right platform would have paid electoral dividends.

Realignment of the centre-right?

The breakdown of the post-war Keynesian consensus in the mid-1970s exerted enormous strains on both the Labour and Conservative Parties. The Labour Party swung left and partially disintegrated as the SDP seceded, but ultimately regrouped under Kinnock, Smith and Blair to become the all-conquering New Labour. The Conservatives – and Britain – underwent the Thatcher Revolution, taking up the neo-liberal agenda of think tanks such as the Institute of Economic Affairs. This brought the Conservatives success in the 1980s against a divided left, but was to lead to a sharp decline in the 1990s as the party faced effective and concerted opposition. The Conservatives' conversion to neo-liberalism was at odds with their traditions, and gave Labour wide opportunities to assume the 'one-nation' mantle.

This radical shake-up and polarisation of British politics in the 1970s and 1980s was not inevitable. A more gradual adjustment to the erosion of the post-war consensus, and an earlier introduction of economic disciplines, would have put less strain on the political system. Why did this not happen?

One reason was that since 1945 there has been a profound weakening of economic liberal ideas within the political mainstream, accentuated by the British party system. Such ideas were forced out to the fringes of politics, in academia, think tanks, or among maverick Tories such as Nigel Birch and Enoch Powell. The traditional conduit of such ideas – the Liberal Party – could exert little influence in the 1950s and by the 1960s and 1970s, as we have seen, had joined the Keynesian consensus.

If they had continued to espouse economic liberalism as they revived, the Liberals would instead have become the focus of the intellectual opposition that was beginning to gather pace. Neo-liberals and perhaps dissident Conservatives would have been drawn to the Liberal Party. It might seem that the Conservatives would have been too powerful a magnet for the Liberals to play this role. However, the Tory Party was remarkably resistant to neo-liberal ideas. Ted Heath's brief flirtation, as 'Selsdon Man', at the beginning of his government in 1970–71 was rapidly abandoned. The Thatcherites converted to these ideas from the mid-1970s but remained a minority; it was only in the early 1980s that they wore down the resistance of the 'wets'. Many of the economic liberals drawn to Thatcher were, moreover, deeply ambivalent towards the Conservative Party.

The opportunity was there for the Liberals to champion such ideas in the 1960s and early 1970s. If they had done so they might have reintroduced them into British politics without the explosive shocks that took place in the later 1970s and 1980s.

Of course this would have depended on the Liberals gaining enough strength to make an impact on the other parties. But if instead of fruitlessly seeking to replace Labour they had targeted Conservative voters more effectively in the 1960s, it is quite possible that they would have expanded their electoral base further in 1959–66 and advanced beyond it in the 1966–70 period when voters were swinging to the right. They might have emerged from the 1970 election with between twenty and twenty-five seats, instead of six, and been in winnable positions in many more. This would have offered a far more solid platform to make further gains during 1972–74 when the pendulum swung strongly in their direction. This was by no means impossible. In 1966 the Liberals missed winning a number of Tory seats which were within range.[18] If they could have maintained their forward momentum in 1970 instead of falling back so badly, they might have picked up some more, possibly including Margaret Thatcher's Finchley, which was well within their sights.

One can also speculate that such progress would have persuaded Grimond to stay on in the leadership beyond 1967, or in any case might have altered the political arithmetic that allowed Jeremy Thorpe to be elected in his place. Thorpe was only very narrowly chosen, and in the light of the disastrous 1970 election and the later scandal that engulfed his leadership it seems likely that any of the other candidates would have benefited the party's prospects in the long run.[19]

With a significant parliamentary contingent in the closely fought elections of the 1970s, the Liberals would have had greatly enhanced their possibilities to influence events and ideas. It is conceivable that the Conservative–Liberal coalition that Edward Heath attempted to form in the aftermath of the February 1974 election would have been feasible. In the real world, even had such a coalition been acceptable to the Liberals, the finely balanced parliamentary arithmetic militated against it; the two parties combined were still seven seats short of an overall majority – but with a larger and more politically weighty Liberal Party the dynamic of the election and its outcome could have been very different. The Liberals would have had to win a relatively small number of Labour seats to open this prospect. If, as argued above, a centre-right strategy had brought the Liberals greater success in Labour areas over the previous two decades, it is quite possible that enough Labour seats would have been within their range. A larger Liberal Party in the Commons would also have given a more even balance of strength between them and the Conservatives and might well have made a coalition or agreed programme of some kind more acceptable.

If the Liberals had held the balance of power they would have been in a strong position to negotiate with Heath. No doubt they would have insisted on a commitment to electoral and economic reform. The political climate in the aftermath of the world oil crisis, the miners' strike and rising inflationary pressures would have been challenging, to say the least. But with a presence in government and a distinctive, coherent and relevant economic platform increasingly in tune with the trend of public opinion, the Liberals would might well have advanced in the second half of the 1970s, a period when in fact they lost much ground.

The formation of such a coalition would also have prevented the meltdown of Heath's leadership in 1974–75 that allowed Margaret Thatcher to capture the succession. This would have altered the subsequent history of the Conservative Party, and may well have averted the historic shift that took place in its character and outlook under her leadership. A Conservative–Liberal coalition could have stimulated and eased the overdue adjustments of policy that were later forced on Britain in the 1980s, adjusting more gradually and less painfully to the world recession. The humiliation of the IMF loan of 1976 could have been avoided, and the severe impacts on vulnerable regions of the industrial decline of the early 1980s could have been mitigated in the absence of the more ideologically right-wing Thatcherite approach to regional policy. In turn, the reaction on the left might never have been so extreme, and the Bennite attempt to take over the Labour Party might have fizzled out much earlier. The Liberals might have lost the opportunity created by the Alliance with the SDP, but in any case the ultimate electoral gains from this proved to be very limited. It is quite possible that they would still have gained recruits from the Labour right if they had established their credibility as a significant political force in the 1960s and 1970s.

What is clear is that, if there had been a sizeable Liberal presence in the Commons in the 1970s and economic liberalism had continued to flourish in the party, the impact on British politics and economics would have been very significant. It would also have helped to avert the sharp and distorting shifts of ideology that overcame the other two parties. Whether it would have left the Liberal Party itself in a stronger position at the turn of the century than it actually occupies now is anybody's guess. But it would have given Britain a party of the centre-right combining economic, social and political liberalism: something which the Conservative Party, despite the hopes of some of its modernisers, seems unable to provide.

Notes

1 Quoted in Michael McManus, *Jo Grimond: Towards the Sound of Gunfire* (Birlinn, 2001) p. 120.

2 Quoted in Alan Watkins *The Liberal Dilemma* (Macgibbon and Kee, 1966) p. 91.

3 Samuel Brittan, *A Restatement of Economic Liberalism* (Social Market Foundation, 1990) p. 7.

4 For the sake of brevity, the term Liberal is used in this chapter to cover both Liberal and Liberal Democrat.

5 Rodney Barker, *Political Ideas in Modern Britain* (Routledge, 1997 (2nd ed)), p. 228.

6 Bernard Wasserstein, *Herbert Samuel: A Political Life* (Clarendon, 1992) pp. 312–13.

7 Tony (Lord) Greaves, *Liberal Democrat History Group Newsletter* 9, December 1995, p. 4.

8 Suenson-Taylor, Sir Alfred Jesse, 1st Baron Grantchester of Knightsbridge (1893–?), City banker. Liberal Party Treasurer and President of the London Liberal Party. President of Society for Individual Freedom and the Free Trade Union. Editor of the *Journal of*

International Liberal Exchange, later *The Owl*, quarterly journal of international thought. Helped fund Hayek's activities and Mount Pelerin Society, 1947–, and participated in meetings. 1955–59 on Advisory Council of Institute of Economic Affairs.

9   Smedley, W. Oliver (1911–89) Vice-President of Liberal Party. Founder of Cheap Food League, etc. With Anthony Fisher founder of Institute of Economic Affairs, 1955. Resigned as Liberal candidate in protest at resolution supporting entry to Common Market, 1962. Founded the 'Keep Britain Out' Campaign, later 'Get Britain Out' and the Free Trade Liberal Party, 1979–. 1964 founded Radio Caroline.

10 Richard Cockett, *Thinking the Unthinkable: Think-tanks and the Economic Counter-Revolution, 1931–1983* (HarperCollins, 1995), p. 125. This is an excellent source on links between Liberals and the economic right. It is worth noting that when he wrote *Serfdom*, Hayek regarded the Liberal Party as the natural repository of his brand of liberalism; ibid., p. 96.

11 Ibid., p. 137.

12 Watkins, *Liberal Dilemma*, pp. 110–11.

13 McManus, *Jo Grimond*, p. 417.

14 Ibid., p. 189.

15 Malcolm Baines, 'The Survival of the British Liberal Party 1933–59', in Gorst et al., *Contemporary British History 1931–61* (Pinter, 1991), p. 27.

16 David Butler & Anthony King, *The British General Election of 1964* (Macmillan, 1965), p. 347, table 6.

17 Colne Valley (66, 74F), Birmingham Ladywood (69), Rochdale (72), Cardigan (74F), Liverpool Edge Hill (79), Bermondsey (83), Leeds West (83), Greenwich (87, SDP), Chesterfield (2001). This excludes four seats where former Labour MPs held their seats for the SDP in 1983: Woolwich, Caithness & Sutherland, Plymouth Devonport, Stockton South.

18 They gained Cheadle and Aberdeenshire West on larger swings than they needed to capture several other seats that stayed Conservative.

19 The other candidates were Eric Lubbock and Emlyn Hooson.

Chapter 5

What if Gaitskell, not Bevan, had died in 1960?

Anne Perkins

Labour's long internal debate over how to adapt to affluence – or whether to adapt at all – was unresolved when Harold Wilson came to power in 1964. The balances and compromises he made in government as he tried to reconcile the party's rival interpretations of what was desirable discredited his premiership and he never recovered from devaluation in 1967. But what if Hugh Gaitskell, not Aneurin Bevan, had died in 1960?

~

Labour's fourth consecutive election defeat, in the summer of 1964, provoked first a stunned silence. It was not the silence of surprise, for in truth the result was not unexpected. It was more the silence of eye-witnesses to some public catastrophe, a plane crash perhaps, a slow-motion silence where the brain endlessly replays the final images, willing a different, happier outcome. But there was no way of putting different votes in the ballot boxes, and no way of turning the clock back to the moment, nearly a year earlier, when Aneurin Bevan had made defeat all but inevitable.

For weeks, the polls had been predicting a historic Tory victory. In the final few days, there had been a gnat's breath of optimism, and in the end the 100-seat majority of 1959 was cut back to twelve. But still the Conservatives returned to power.

The Labour right, long appalled that it had allowed Bevan to be elected party leader, was well prepared. This time there would be no mistake. Unity around a fudge was too high a price to play: four years posthumously, Gaitskell's passion for provocative clarity was to be vindicated. The right was prepared to fight for its convictions, and the left was hungry for battle. The final round of the long, grinding conflict between Bevanites and Gaitskellites, the utopian left and the radical right, was about to begin.

~

The origins of the bloody, sometimes savage, contest for the soul of the Labour Party go back to the foundation of the party itself, that first fudge which established a broad front of middle-class brain and industrial brawn, intellectuals and trade unionists, against the bosses and, sometimes, against capitalism too. In the good years, each was prepared to respect the other while continuing to argue for its own perspective. In the bad years, mutual loathing often exceeded detestation of the political opposition.

But the essence of the distinction between the two perspectives remained constant. Was the purpose of the Labour Party to bring about a socialist society as swiftly as possible, or was it a mirage, a banner of hope around which to rally the dispossessed in order to lead them in a campaign not to overthrow capitalism, but to capture it and tame it for the masses?

In the first part of the 1950s, when the conflict was personalised, the argument coalesced, misleadingly, around the single issue of modernisation. The ex-miner from the Welsh valleys, Aneurin Bevan, became the embodiment of inspiring, demagogic, utopian socialism against the clever, cautious Wykehamist Hugh Gaitskell. Gaitskell, rationalist, economist and leading tamer of capitalism, was convinced that socialism was a doctrine that had to be radically modified in order to appeal to a new, more prosperous generation of voters. He believed that he had to bend to the aspirations of the age of unprecedented affluence, of a people who had become more self-reliant, a society more atomised, values more commercialised.

Bevan, the brilliant, idle, vain, erratic oratorical genius believed, in contrast, that socialism described a way of life that was independent of affluence. Of course, it precluded wide disparities of income, but economic growth and success were the prerequisites of a successful socialist society, a society whose purpose was to make people not merely better off but, indubitably, better. Changing society required sacrifice, and voters had to be educated that it was in their interest – moral if not financial – to vote for a government which might not make them richer but which would improve the lot of their fellow men and of society at large. The path to socialism, Bevan believed, lay not in listening to the voters, but in educating them.

Gaitskell beat Bevan for the leadership in 1955. It had seemed Bevan's last chance of political glory, and he – if not his wife, Jennie Lee – apparently accepted the defeat as an end to personal ambition. If he and Gaitskell remained on either sides of the ideological divide, over the next five years they found a way of working together. Bevan signed up behind Gaitskell in the internal battle of 1957 against 'shopping-list' nationalisation. Even more damagingly for his support on the left, he backed the leadership against some trade unionists and much of the rank and file by condemning unilateral nuclear disar-mament; to the wounded silence of his old fan club at the Brighton party conference, he dismissed unilateralism as 'an emotional spasm' which would send a Labour foreign secretary 'naked into the confer-ence chamber'.

In 1959, the two men, who had so vehemently loathed each other for so long, stood shoulder to shoulder in what looked like the last heave before they were returned to power. Instead, the Tories increased their majority to 100. At a notorious meeting in the immediate aftermath, Gaitskellite sympathisers led by Douglas Jay identified what they decided was a clear pattern behind the party's inability to attract votes. The party was too closely associated with the sacrifice, austerity, bureaucracy and economic incompetence of the Attlee years. The commitment to further nationalisation, only vaguely expressed in the party's manifesto, was considered a millstone, at least by the right-wing vanguard who gathered at Gaitskell's house in Hampstead the day after the election. In short, as Bevan bitterly observed when the opinions of the meeting emerged in an article in *Socialist Commentary,* Labour was unpopular for being Labour.

Gaitskell and the right resolved to redraft the party constitution, and rebuild the party's internal structure so that policy-making was centralised in the hands of the parliamentary leadership while trade-union and conference influence was minimised. It was a schismatic approach, perhaps deliberately so. Some Gaitskellites were beginning to wonder if the party was capable of reform. Privately, they contemplated permanent breakaway (as, faced with Gaitskell rampant, Bevan had in the early 1950s). Now it was the left that claimed to stand for unity, to be defending the party, and Gaitskell whose attacks on public ownership, as expressed through Clause Four of the constitution, who was isolated and vulnerable.

Bevan meanwhile trod a wavering line. A day or two before the 1959 election, he had told his good friend, Geoffrey Goodman, a left-leaning journalist, that if there was a defeat, 'There will have to be a showdown … I will quarrel with Gaitskell straight away. I refuse to belong to a party unless that party is the vehicle of principles in which I believe.'[1] But within the week, in the backwash of the gloomy result, he accepted Gaitskell's proposal that he become Deputy Leader. Gaitskell had even invited him to what was to become the infamous Hampstead meeting; Bevan did not bother to go.

And although the left took comfort from his words in the following week's *Tribune* – 'If the Labour Party decided to adjust its policy in accordance with these [Gaitskellite] ideas, it would be practically certain to wreck itself'[2] – he used his speech at the party's annual conference a few weeks later to shore up rather than undermine Gaitskell's position, welcoming the debate, and demanding unity only in the fight against the Tories.

It set the pattern for what followed. Buoyed up by unaccustomed support from the trade union members, Bevan used his strength on the National Executive Committee to inflict a total but carefully decent defeat on Gaitskell's ambitions to abandon the party's constitutional commitment to public ownership. There was to be a separate statement of aims, published without a vote, at the following autumn's conference. By early summer, Gaitskell had been forced to accept that the party constitution would not be changed, that year at least. Attention focused instead on a new battle, to be fought out at the autumn conference, which went to the heart of the rank and file's desire for an ethical foreign and defence policy: the Bomb.

Cancellation of Blue Streak – the rocket system which would have carried Britain's nuclear bomb – put the question of Britain's multi-million pound independent deterrent back into politics. Bevan, who had single-handedly defused it at the 1957 party conference, was forced to address the issue again as the young Campaign for Nuclear Disarmament led the demand that the independent deterrent be abandoned, unilaterally. This time, trade union conferences took up the cry. Soon, they drew a link between their support for a policy that the leadership opposed and the leadership's desire to exclude the rank and file from policy-making.

And then, in a matter of weeks in July, just as the nation packed for the beach, Gaitskell suddenly sickened with an unidentifiable virus. Within a fortnight, he was dead.

So intense was the subterranean battle between surrogates for Bevan and Gaitskell within the party – and so perilously balanced the Cold War raging outside – that at Westminster serious consideration was given by the right to speculation that there had been an element of foul play in their hero's sudden death.

There is never a good time for a Labour leadership election, but the summer of 1960 could hardly have been worse. Gaitskell's peremptory demands for reform had exacerbated the old fault-line of disaffection. Worse, there was no external pressure for party discipline: there would be at least three years until the Conservative Prime Minister Harold Macmillan, with his 100-seat majority, need think of a general election. Meanwhile, the party rank and file were enraged. Left and right were organising both at Westminster and in the constituencies. Gaitskell had often seen his own battles with the left, and especially with the man who had become his reluctant lieutenant, Nye Bevan, as a battle for the soul of the party. His premature death in the midst of internal controversy had the potential to launch the decisive round.

Overshadowed by Gaitskell, only fifty when he died, the right was now entirely leaderless: there had been no challenger of his generation, no one who could equal his high intelligence and integrity. From early in 1960, Gaitskell's acolytes had been preparing to launch a Campaign for Democratic Socialism, a bid to counter the influence of *Tribune* in the constituencies and build support for change. But it was still a fledgling.

George Brown, the clever, bullying trade unionist, was ambitious and determined. But many on the right regarded his bid for the leadership with alarm. His support in the trade unions did not make him so attractive that it could overcome either his reputation as a bully or his habit of drinking too much. If not Brown, though, who else? Jim Callaghan was still young and untried, Tony Crosland younger still, and with a capacity for making enemies. It was too soon for Roy Jenkins or Denis Healey, too late for Frank Soskice.

If the right had a paucity of candidates, the left had one too many. They loved Bevan, but his betrayal over the bomb was too recent a wound. They distrusted Harold Wilson, yet they were still prepared to regard him – unlike the more ostentatiously middle-class intellectuals – as one of theirs. Wilson was young, only in his early forties, but not too young to have resigned, with Bevan, from Attlee's cabinet in 1951. He was clever, he was good in the Commons and on the conference platform, and he was already a past master of the new art of television.

But the left was as fragmented as the right. The fundamentalists, backed by *Tribune* and Victory for Socialism, had publicly attacked Gaitskell. Another, more centrist, group, including Richard Crossman and Barbara Castle, served under him while simultaneously planning to engineer his downfall.

No group commanded a clear majority at Westminster. The left was unwilling to challenge Bevan, the right uncomfortable with the idea of supporting George Brown. They did not trust Bevan, but he had been a loyal lieutenant to Gaitskell, he had saved their man from humiliation and, at sixty-two, he could hardly expect to be in office long. So it was that in a contest which had more the air of a funeral procession, Aneurin Bevan defeated both George Brown and Harold Wilson in the first ballot of the party's 258 MPs, and the high-living high priest of a moral socialism, scourge of what he called the meretricious society, a society which elevated the vulgar at the expense of the good, was called upon to steer his party into the age of affluence.

The decision was warmly welcomed, a sign of how far the old sectarian was seen to have travelled since he had fought Gaitskell for the same prize five years earlier. Even the right-wing press was prepared, in the absence of any more obvious candidate, to offer something less than condemnation to a leader prepared to stand up to the unilateralists in the party, But, as the leader writers pointed out, given his age he would be little more than a caretaker leader, someone who could lead the battle against the Tories without feeling the need to tackle the party's more pressing problems over policy formation.

On the left, it was greeted as a final triumph. Where there were doubts, loyalty sustained enthusiasm. *Tribune,* the newspaper Bevan had once edited and on whose board his wife Jenny Lee still sat, produced a special edition to celebrate the dawn of a golden age. 'At last', wrote Michael Foot, burying the hatchet of the betrayal of the bomb in a paean of golden prose, 'the Labour movement has a leader whose genius is a match for its high ideals'.

Richard Crossman, the Oxford don turned politician and diarist who had run Harold Wilson's campaign, was less certain. 'Of course everyone is cockahoop at Nye's victory. I made sure Harold paid an immediate public tribute. Nye meanwhile is refusing to see any of us. I wonder, is he really up to the job? He remains a great phrasemaker, but he has little of the fire that made him so dangerous ten years ago. I fear it has come too late.'

Crossman was right. Whatever his own instincts might have told him, Bevan was heavily constrained in his new office, and not only by the support he had won from across the party. Five years at Gaitskell's right hand had encumbered him with an embarrassing backlist of public commitments on which he could hardly renege without compromising his own reputation for integrity. He and Gaitskell had agreed that rather than unilateral nuclear disarmament there should be an attempt to encourage a non-nuclear club, a kind of engine for world disarmament. Whatever the pressure from the trade unions – and it was building fast – he could not shift from the multilateralist position so painfully achieved three years earlier. He was saved only by the building of the Berlin Wall which turned the tide hard against the unilateralists and in favour of the hawks.

There were no victories for the left in domestic policy either. Although, at the conference after the 1959 defeat, Bevan had defended public ownership, the left had never supported the kind of nationalisation the Attlee Government had introduced, where the internal structure of publicly owned companies merely echoed those of private companies. There was no element of democracy, of worker participation or of the kind of planning which he believed was the key above all to future national economic success. Bevan had important things to say about nationalisation, and about the moral significance of private ownership, but they were not fully or even partially developed policies. He had also, if reluctantly, endorsed the party's cautious strategy described in the controversial *Industry and Society* party document of 1957. The man who had declared so ringingly at the 1959 conference that policies could not be changed just because the electorate did not like them could hardly order a wholesale review less than a year later.

Nor did Bevan have the energy, the inclination, or the intellectual discipline to sit down and focus on the need for policy development. Instead, over the next two years, as the government of Harold Macmillan spent its way to popularity, Bevan toured the country on a kind of extended workers' educational association lecture tour, repeating the speech he had first rehearsed at the 1959 conference when he had warned:

> This so-called affluent society is an ugly society still. It is a vulgar society. It is a meretricious society. It is a society in which priorities have gone all wrong … I have enough faith in my fellow creatures in Great Britain to believe that when they have got over the delirium of the television, when they realise that their new homes … are mortgaged to the hilt, when they realise that the moneylender has been elevated to the highest position in the land … then we shall lead our people where they deserve to be led.[3]

Bevan had lost none of his demagogic appeal: he could still fill a hall anywhere in the country, while his encounters in debate with the Tory Prime Minister packed the House of Commons. But as leader, he was expected to deliver more than a high standard of public debate. The honeymoon lasted for just as long as it took the press to understand that Bevan was as far from being a Gaitskellite as he had ever been, even if his commitment to party unity led him to moderate his publicly expressed opinions. And the newly affluent, the trade unionists buying their first car or their first TV set, were often resistant to the appeal of a less selfish society. In corners at party conference, in the corridors of Westminster, the hero of the left was increasingly referred to as a Welsh windbag.

In the end it was the political passion from which he had prospered for so long that finally did for Bevan. In the early summer of 1963 it emerged that the Conservative Minister for War, John Profumo, had lied to the Commons, as well as to the Prime Minister and leading figures in the Tory Party, about an affair with a call-girl. It was a private matter given a flimsy dressing of public interest because the woman, Christine Keeler, was simultaneously the mistress of a Soviet Defence Attaché.

Profumo was a popular figure, married to a celebrated film star: they were the Posh and Becks of the contemporary political scene and the long tradition of press restraint was soon shredded by the prurient excitement generated by the story. Politicians were, briefly, flummoxed by how to handle the affair. Wary of being seen to indulge in mere titillation, Bevan's friends advised caution. It was, they told him (remembering his own vulnerability on the issue of marital fidelity) a moment for statesmanship. Bevan however, was genuinely outraged, not by the minister's infidelity or even by his lie to the Commons, but by the evidence of the establishment's loyalty, the visible protection of the old school tie and the right connections – all the 'established power' most loathed by the ex-miner, the boy from the valleys.

He was also unsettled by the mutterings of criticism within the party, not least from *Tribune,* and a rattled Bevan had a long history of poor judgement. In the Commons debate following Profumo's resignation, he launched a vituperative attack, not on Profumo himself but on the system which sought to protect the privileged while continuing to fail the poor. It was a disaster. Instead of the rapier wit with which he had tormented Winston Churchill in the war years, Bevan appeared red-faced, savage and unsubtle. It was just the weapon the establishment needed to allow them to defend Profumo and attack Labour. If there was truth in his attack, it was lost in the ensuing press sneers, while the wider public felt vaguely that a man who was already down should not be kicked again, however shockingly he had behaved. People suddenly remembered the 'lower than vermin' attack Bevan had made on the Tories during the 1950 general election, an attack which his enemies claimed had cost a million votes and Labour its working majority.

The charge was repeated again in the winter and spring of 1964 as the Tories bounced back with apparent ease from the Profumo scandal. Worse, as the economic situation deteriorated, Labour's failure to develop new policy initiatives left it unable to mount a credible attack. A demoralised party went into the 1964 election certain of only one thing – defeat. Even before all the votes were counted, Bevan announced his retirement. He and Jenny went to live quietly at Asheridge, their farm in the Chilterns.

This time, both left and right had had four years to prepare for the leadership campaign. Bereft of their leader, the Gaitskellite had regrouped much more effectively than the left, who were struggling under the nominal leadership of Bevan. But they could not agree a candidate. Both George Brown and James Callaghan, on the trade unionist rather than the Gaitskellite right, had supporters, while among the Gaitskellites themselves a discreet but increasingly bitter jockeying for position had been going on between Tony Crosland and Roy Jenkins, now at the head of a group of MPs swollen by the careful placing of sympathetic candidates in winnable seats by the Campaign for Democratic Socialism.

On the left, assiduously courting the Labour movement in the country, travelling from parish to parish to address trade-union conferences and constituency annual general meetings, Wilson stood alone. For the rump of the Bevanites, Wilson was the only possible candidate. A former cabinet minister, he alone in their ranks had stature with the public as well as support within the party. Yet there were plenty on the left who were uncomfortable with what they felt was an unprincipled willingness to cut a deal, a willingness which sat awkwardly with a party which had been lapped for the past four years in Bevan's moral certainties. The Victory for Socialism group, once Bevan's cheerleaders, had fallen silent as their champion had failed to fight their corner, but they had no illusions about Wilson as a possible successor. They preferred to find their own candidate, someone who could garner enough votes to be able to carry their unilateralist, anti-European, pro-nationalisation arguments into the heart of the next Labour leadership. Michael Foot would have been their choice had he not only just returned to the Commons after nine years of exile; instead, Tony Greenwood was mooted, with a few lone voices (not least, her own) for Barbara Castle.

The Gaitskellites, with their distaste for compromise and disdain for tactics, had no more time for Wilson than had the Victory-for-Socialism left. Gaitskell had himself habitually underrated his Shadow Chancellor, and even demoted him after the 1959 election, effectively making him carry the can for his own rash campaign pledge not to raise income tax. His followers discounted Wilson's studied loyalty to Gaitskell; they had heard rumours, before their hero's sudden death, that if there was to be a left challenge, he was most likely to be its source. Yet they had no obvious candidate of their own. George Brown was widely disliked, a bully with a drink problem, while Jim Callaghan was simply thought too lightweight.

Wilson, studiously trying to appear to be keeping above the fray, was kept briefed of opinion in both camps by his campaign managers, Richard Crossman and George Wigg. Barbara Castle, torn between an old friendship with Wilson and a romantic attachment to the uncompromising left, was showing some signs of being able to deliver some of the VFS, but at a high price: Wilson would have to stand on an openly radical (and in his view impossibly divisive) platform, in favour of more public ownership and against closer links with Europe. Wilson refused.

It was Crossman, the Oxford don who could talk with Roy Jenkins and Tony Crosland on their own terms, who saw the opening. The idea first emerged in one of his Sunday-morning dictating sessions with his diary early in 1964 as he contemplated the likelihood of another election defeat. The impact, he anticipated, could destroy Labour entirely: the right would demand a wholesale junking of the pre-war socialist agenda, and the left equally would call for a new and energetic crusade to be launched. How could the right be contained, prevented from demanding such radical change that the left and the trade unions were forced out of the Labour movement?, he pondered one frosty January morning at his farm in Oxfordshire. The answer, he decided, must be to find a way of tying Wilson, still just identifiable as a voice of the old left, to the Gaitskellites on the new right in such a way that both groups believed they controlled the direction in which the party was to travel.

The first criteria for the success of such a deal had to be total secrecy. Jenkins was (like Crossman) a gossip. Negotiations would therefore be conducted through Crosland, whose ambitions for the leadership, Crossman speculated, lay less in the appeal of being leader himself than in blocking Jenkins' ambitions. Only as an afterthought did Crossman consider discussing his ideas with Wilson.

Crossman was right to suspect the ambitions and the determination of the right in the face of a fourth election defeat. The Campaign for Democratic Socialism, led by Bill Rodgers and inspired by Crosland himself, with support in local government and the trade unions, was proving not only adept at political organisation, but a free-thinking ideas bank for the young right, the first generation of post-war grammar school and redbrick university graduates who had been drawn to politics by *The Future of Socialism*, Crosland's own prospectus for the left in an age of affluence. The Croslandites were uninterested in the old 'commanding-heights-of-the-economy' approach to socialism; ownership, in an age of managerialism and multinationals, was a peripheral matter. The central issue had become equality, not of some crude measure of outcomes, but of life-chances: schools and universities, professions and industries, must be open to all on merit alone. Welfare's purpose was to promote that equality and aid those unable to prosper from it.

The new right was impatient with the laborious policy-making processes of the Labour movement, and feared that prolonged debate of their ideas would result in more fudge and procrastination. The constitutional reform of the party that Gaitskell had first mooted was a necessary prerequisite, they believed, of ultimate success. In the columns of their in-house journal, *Socialist Commentary,* and increasingly in the *Guardian,* their arguments were developed. In the four years of Bevan's leadership, little effort went into countering them. In the aftermath of the 1964 election, the party was suddenly presented, through editorials and comment columns, with a blueprint for recovery for which it was entirely unprepared. All that was missing was a leadership candidate willing to stand on their platform.

Wilson, the tactician, was well aware of the way the right was thinking. But he was initially disbelieving of Crossman's proposal that some kind of deal should be sought, a trade-off between senior Cabinet appointments and a Wilson premiership. The man they had dubbed 'Nye's little dog' was unlikely to be an acceptable candidate to the neo-Gaitskellites. Nonetheless, he authorised Crossman to proceed.

Matters were brought to a head far more quickly than anyone had anticipated. Within days of returning to office, Macmillan and his Chancellor of the Exchequer, Reginald Maudling, stunned the country with the announcement of a massive devaluation of sterling and a sustained bout of deflation with immediate effect. The political landscape was transformed. The post-war certainties of growth and full employment suddenly looked, if not lost, then less certain. The Tory reputation for economic competence and political integrity was destroyed. The 'never had it so good' era was revealed to have been built on sand.

In the political uproar that followed it was Wilson, the economist who had himself steered the country through devaluation, who made sense of events, appearing as an authoritative and reassuring figure. Wilson commanded respect in the House and conveyed sanity to the electorate via the TV studios. The right, to their surprise, found themselves admiring him; Crosland professed both himself and – though he could not necessarily deliver them – his followers ready to do business. Negotiations, informal and off-the-record, were conducted in the Crossman house in Vincent Square, just down the road from Westminster. The right would support Wilson for the leadership in return for the portfolios key to delivering their agenda – education, health and welfare – and, of course, the Treasury, without which nothing else could happen. Wilson could balance those appointments with his own supporters, but he was to use his authority to smooth the path of the constitutional changes the right was determined to achieve. After all, as one bright young man pointed out, the left had argued since the 1930s for a diminution of the trade union block vote and the introduction of one-member-one-vote into constituency affairs.

When Labour was returned to power in May 1965, fourteen years after Attlee had left Downing Street, the foundations had been laid for an altogether new kind of Labour government. Wilson, the clever, classless iconoclast captured the public mood for modernity which he carefully presented as a cause around which they could unite: at his first party conference as leader, he had told a movement chastened by repeated election defeat that to meet the challenges of an uncertain era it was now called upon to rebuild itself in a different mould. There was no talk of wholesale nationalisation, and overwhelming support for an attack on privilege and discrimination, in education and at work.

As for constitutional reform, there was no appetite for a fight: after devaluation, the movement was confident that at last the Tories were beaten. Discipline and coherence were all that stood between them and victory. After all, as Wilson remarked to Crossman in the Downing Street study, on the day Barbara Castle joined the cabinet as agriculture minister some months after the victory, we're all middle class now.

Notes

1 Michael Foot, *Aneurin Bevan, A Biography, Vol 2 1945–1960* (Davis Poynter, 1973).
2 Ibid.
3 Ibid.

Chapter 6

What if the Liberal Party had disappeared in the 1950s?

Michael McManus

It wasn't until I was researching and writing a biography of Jo Grimond, who led the Liberal Party between 1956 and 1967, that it truly sank in for me just how close to extinction his party had come in the 1950s – or just how irrelevant it became. Looking at today's Liberal Democrats, participating in government in Scotland and Wales and running councils across Great Britain, it is hard to believe, but the party from which they emerged came within a whisker of perishing only half a century ago.

That the Liberal Party did not disappear into oblivion in the 1950s was thanks to a handful of fortunate factors. First of all, there were just enough parts of the Celtic fringe willing to stand by them even in those leanest of years. Then, even when its MPs really could all fit inside a single taxi, somehow the party still contained within its ranks someone who had the intelligence, the charisma and the ideas necessary to establish himself as a credible and attractive national fig-ure in the new television age: Jo Grimond. Most importantly of all, however, with all its history and sense of communal pride, the party somehow never lost the will to live. When it would have been easier to give up the ghost – opting either for oblivion or to be subsumed by the Conservatives, which would have amounted to very much the same thing – the party chose instead to live.

It is a remarkable and salutary tale, and one that today's Conservative Party has good cause to rue. Jo Grimond took over as leader of the Liberal Party fifty years after it had last won an election outright – the great landslide victory of 1906 – and that half-century had brought little but division, decline and despair. The party Grimond inherited in 1956 was virtually a shell, and certainly no longer a viable campaigning entity. In most people's eyes it was either an irrelevance or a laughing stock. Yet in 1962 the Liberals would win, at Orpington, what still rates as one of the greatest of all by-election victories, and they would go on, in the general election of 1964, to claim over 10 per cent of the vote and come tantalisingly close to holding the balance of power in a delicately poised House of Commons. A capricious and unrepresentative electoral system and the wiles of Harold Wilson denied them the national influence they craved, but the 1964 election still marked the first major staging post on the uneven but unmistakable return to the rude health that the Liberal Democrats enjoy today.

How ironic that when the Liberal Party lay gasping in the political intensive-care ward during the 1950s, of all people it was the Conservatives who provided the necessary life-support apparatus to keep the Liberals – just – alive. How today's Tory leaders must wish that their predecessors had slipped in when the matron's back was turned and put the patient out of its misery. At the time this merciful attitude seemed highly questionable. With the benefit of hindsight, to many people it may now look more like a catastrophic misjudgement.

Although this chapter is essentially about the Conservative Party's decision to spare the Liberals in the 1950s, that subject cannot be adequately dealt with *in vacuo*. The reasons for the parlous state of the Liberal Party – the factors that caused the stunning decline in its fortunes after 1906 – are all-important, so I here attempt to provide a (very) concise background sketch to the Asquith–Lloyd George split and its aftermath.

1906–31: From landslide to lameness

The decline of the Liberal Party began in the immediate wake of its greatest triumph, the landslide of 1906. The party had been routed in 1900, winning only 184 seats against 402 for the Conservatives, but succeeded spectacularly in turning around that substantial deficit in just over five years, winning 400 seats to the Tories' 157 in the election held in January–February 1906. On paper the new Prime Minister, H. H. Asquith, had a powerful mandate, but a new political force was already beginning to manifest itself in the traditional Liberal heartlands that would, in time, assimilate most of his party's support with astonishing ease. In 1900 only two 'Labour' MPs had been elected, but in 1906 this had risen to 30. That figure would go on rising steadily until Labour's 'breakthrough' elections of 1922 and 1929. In a quarter of a century, the number of Labour MPs rose from only 2 to 288. This happened largely for three reasons.

First of all, social change was rapidly eating away at the deference that had underpinned much of the working-class support for the Liberals: successive Education Acts (notably those of 1870 and 1902) had emancipated the children of the workers, making them not only more literate but also more questioning and openly rebellious. The forces that consumed Russia in revolution, and nearly did the same in Germany, were also at work, in their own rather more graceful and good-natured way, here in Britain. Secondly, the bitter split between Asquith and Lloyd George during the First World War led not only to the latter replacing the former; it left a legacy of recrimination and bitterness that was only intensified by the 'coupon election' of 1918 and then again by the three-way split the party endured after the formation of a National Government under Ramsay MacDonald in 1931. Thirdly, following on from these divisions, for many years Liberals endured a collective nervous breakdown and crisis of identity. They ran under a variety of different labels, supported by various leaders and party organisations and, confused themselves, they could hardly expect the voters to understand or forgive. By the early 1930s, only the most engaged and politically interested of voters would have known when a 'Liberal' was, or was not, a Liberal. Only with the emergence of Sir Archibald Sinclair as leader of the independent Liberals in 1935 did the party begin to reassert a clear, independent identity.

1945: Losing the peace

By the time war was declared in 1939, although the rancour between the factions had dissipated substantially, profound political and personal divisions remained even within a severely denuded Liberal parliamentary grouping. Liberals and Liberal Nationals were very much at each other's throats until the downfall of the Chamberlain Government in 1940. Even after that, although they could all generally be counted upon to support Churchill's war efforts, they were not necessarily always to be found in the same lobby when more mundane matters were voted upon. When a general election was held in 1945 between VE Day and VJ Day, even by their standards the Liberals were in a particularly confused and confusing state, with some candidates not sure in their own minds whether they wished to run as National Liberals or as independent Liberals under the banner of Sinclair, who had been serving as Minister for Air under Churchill.

Although Sinclair's party was able to fight only a minority of the 640 seats, it was hopeful of making some progress. The Liberal Party went into the campaign with nineteen MPs, of whom sixteen stood for re-election, and a rating in the Gallup opinion poll of 15 per cent. It met with disaster. Although the total Liberal poll, at around 2 million votes, was the highest since 1929, this only came about because there were 306 Liberal candidates, as against 161 in 1935 and 118 in 1931. The party won 9 per cent of the total votes cast, an average 18.6 per cent in the seats it contested. Ten seats were lost and only three gained, leaving the party with only twelve Members of Parliament.

Behind the headline figures of seats gained and lost, one finds an even more depressing picture for a party that had enjoyed a landslide victory less than forty years earlier. The bitterest blow came at Caithness, where, in a painfully tight three-way contest, Sir Archibald Sinclair had come third, only 61 votes behind the Conservative victor. In one of the few better results, unknown first-time candidate Major Jo Grimond had lost by only 329 in Orkney and Shetland. This was the story of the election for a painfully large number of Liberal candidates, thirty-four of whom came within 6,000 votes of victory.

Churchill still had a substantial number of the so-called National Liberals operating under the aegis of the Conservative Party, and he resolved at once to take over what remained of his old party if he could. With Sinclair out of the Commons, the 'chairmanship' of the Parliamentary Liberal Party fell to a talented but little-known and rather conservative Welsh lawyer called Clement Davies, the Member of Parliament for Montgomeryshire in Wales. He had served for a time as a National Liberal and his sole claim to fame was the important background role that he had played in the downfall of Chamberlain and his subsequent replacement by Churchill rather than Lord Halifax.

1950: Into single figures

The 1945–50 Parliament was predictably traumatic for the denuded independent Liberals. Even so small a group was grievously divided ideologically, containing a remarkable spectrum of opinion, ranging from Rhys Hopkin Morris, who regarded all and any manifestations of government as, at best, necessary evils, to David Lloyd George's daughter Megan, who was already halfway to joining Labour. The Liberals struggled unsuccessfully to assert an identity and lost two of their MPs during the course of the Parliament – Tom Horabin to the Labour Party and Gwilym Lloyd-George to the National Liberal-Conservatives. Liberal support in the polls nonetheless remained fairly steady, at a respectable if unexciting 12 per cent. In 1947, the Woolton–Teviot Agreement consolidated the assimilation of the National Liberals into the Conservative Party. The independent Liberals dissociated themselves totally, but many of the merged associations blithely went on to describe themselves as 'Conservative and Liberal'.

In the run-up to the 1950 general election, Churchill wrote to Clement Davies urging him to enter into some kind of anti-socialist electoral pact. Davies responded angrily and in the negative, attacking the Tories for their continued use of the term 'Liberal' in the name of certain constituency associations and election addresses. Churchill gave him short shrift, sending a patronising reply that Davies described as 'facetious and evasive'.

This robust exchange of views at the national level was largely for intra-party consumption: in some instances at least, the story at constituency level was rather different. The Liberals went into the general election of February 1950 defending nine seats. They lost three but offset that by gaining three others. Seven of the Liberal seats were won in three-way fights, but there were two notable exceptions – Carmarthen, where Hopkin Morris was returned by 187 votes, and Huddersfield West, gained by Donald Wade from Labour with a majority of almost 7,000 votes; in each case there was no Conservative candidate. It was no accident that the Tories gave Wade a free run. Huddersfield had been represented before 1945 by a National Liberal, but fell in that year to Labour. In 1947, the Liberals and National Liberals in the town had reunited, creating a substantial power base on the local council. A year later, Huddersfield was split into two constituencies, East and West. In the run-up to the election, Wade promised that he would not support a Labour government in a confidence vote; in return, the Tories resolved not to put up a candidate against him, and in Huddersfield East, the Liberals gave the Tories a free run. Although this arrangement delivered a much-needed reinforcement to the Liberal benches, it was regarded with dismay, suspicion or even outright hostility by left-leaning Liberals, who regarded the Tories, not Labour, as their party's natural enemies.

The 1950 general election returned Labour with a paper majority of only five seats. The party's morale was shattered, however, and everyone expected another election within a matter of months. Sinclair had lost again in Caithness, so Clement Davies was reaffirmed as leader of the parliamentary party. Frank Byers, who had replaced future defector Tom Horabin as party whip in 1946, had been narrowly defeated in his Dorset constituency and, within only a few days, Davies nominated new boy Jo Grimond to take over as whip. Even though Grimond's flock consisted of only eight other colleagues, it was to prove quite a challenge. By now it really was no longer clear that the residual Liberal Party served any useful purpose, and it was steadily losing members, including some of its highly limited supply of public figures. In particular, most of the leading left-wing Liberals had quit the party, generally to join Labour, and Megan Lloyd George seemed to be hanging on only for reasons of loyalty, sentiment and personal pride. As well as Lady Megan, nominally the Liberals' Deputy Leader, two other colleagues, Emrys Roberts and Edgar Granville, were increasingly inclined towards the Labour Party.

Nonetheless, the party did have its moments, for instance when Grimond symbolically – and unusually – served as a 'teller' (counter of votes) alongside a Tory in crucial votes on Europe in June 1950, after a debate in which Churchill declared that, in contrast with Labour, 'the Conservative and Liberal Parties declare that national sovereignty is not inviolable'. The Attlee Government, which wanted no part of the nascent process of European integration, defeated the Conservative motion by a majority of twenty. Four of Grimond's eight colleagues supported the motion, and none opposed it. The Liberals undoubtedly voted the way they did as a matter of principle, but their action did happen to coincide with a significant thawing of relations between their leadership and that of the Conservative

Party. Although Clem Davies had rebuffed Churchill's suggestion for an anti-Labour 'popular front', lines of communication between the parties remained very much open and, conscious that Churchill still felt a residual, sentimental attachment to his old party, his old friend and Liberal grandee Lady Violet Bonham Carter continued to nag him to do something about the electoral system, to give the Liberals a fairer deal. Most importantly, perhaps, despite their many travails, the Liberals had still managed to win almost 10 per cent of the vote, and the other parties both believed that the behaviour of Liberal voters could prove decisive in the next general election.

In April 1950, with Labour already hanging on by a thread, Churchill informed Jo Grimond and Lady Violet privately that, although the Conservative Party could not at this stage accept electoral reform, he was sure that most of its more thoughtful members would understand the advantages of sustaining a non-socialist third party as an extra bulwark against socialism. He had charged Rab Butler with preparing plans for collaboration with the Liberals along those lines. Butler was himself present at another lunch later the same month, held at Chartwell, at which these thoughts were developed further. Churchill ordered that the party's inquiry into electoral reform should be made public as soon as possible. Butler concurred, but warned both Grimond and Lady Violet on their way home that they should not overestimate Churchill's influence within the party he led. Churchill had recently put the case for looking at the electoral system to a meeting of the Conservative 1922 Committee, and the Committee's members had given him a hard time. Although Butler did not believe that Churchill could ever be in a position to deliver, Lady Violet and her allies refused to give up.

1951: And then there were six ...
In the event, at the national level at least, nothing concrete came of those tentative discussions in time for the next election. That was not

entirely the end of the story, however. At constituency level, certain Conservative Associations were coming to their own, pragmatic view. In Liberal seats that they had no prospect of gaining, and where the incumbent MP was not obnoxious to them, they demonstrated a new willingness to stand aside. In the Labour seat of Colne Valley, local Tories were prevailed upon by Churchill to stand down in favour of his old friend Lady Violet Bonham Carter, who was demonstrably on the right of her party; he even spoke in her support during the campaign. Meanwhile, in Bolton, a formal version of the Huddersfield arrangement was agreed, with the Liberals' Arthur Holt enjoying a clear run against Labour in Bolton West, and no Liberal fighting Bolton East. Without doubt, such arrangements were mutually advantageous at local level – it is safe to assume that the overwhelming majority of Conservative voters would have been willing to back a Liberal against a socialist. It was also estimated that, where the Liberals dropped out at the 1951 election, some 60 per cent of former Liberal voters switched to the Tories. Indeed, according to most analyses, in a clear majority of seats lost by Labour to the Tories in 1951, the withdrawal of the Liberals between 1950 and 1951 was the most decisive factor. This raises a deeper question: might it not have been far more advantageous to the Tories, in the long-term, to have driven the Liberals out of business altogether when they had the opportunity?

In general, the Liberal Party went into the 1951 campaign at a dismal all-time low. It was looking to defend only nine seats and its opinion poll rating had sunk from 10 per cent in August to a feeble 4 per cent in October. It managed to put up only 109 candidates, as against 475 in 1950. Only 45 of them were fighting the seat they had fought at the previous election. The number of full-time Liberal agents had fallen from 140 in 1949 to around 40. The decline in Liberal ambitions was reflected in the party manifesto, which offered no pretence that a Liberal government might be elected. Instead, it made the case for the party's very existence. Most of the MPs, notably

Grimond in Orkney and Shetland, had so little support from the party centrally that they marketed themselves more or less as independent candidates.

Unsurprisingly, the 1951 election was nearly fatal for the independent Liberals. Of the six winners, only Grimond had faced a Conservative opponent. The four other Liberal MPs from the 1950–51 parliament to face a three-cornered fight were all defeated, albeit narrowly, and there was only one gain, Bolton West, thanks to the controversial local pact with the Tories. Along with her two left-leaning allies, Messrs Granville and Roberts, Megan Lloyd George was defeated, largely because there was no love lost between them and their local Tories, who consequently saw no reason to stand down in their favour. Only forty-three Liberals retained their deposits by winning 12 per cent support, and only three non-incumbent candidates came within 5,000 votes of gaining a seat, two of whom had not been opposed by the Tories. An estimated 70 per cent of Liberal candidates in 1951 never stood again.

Shortly after resuming the premiership in 1951, with a narrow majority based upon fewer votes than Labour had received, Churchill made renewed overtures to Clement Davies. He offered him a cabinet post in charge of education, together with junior ministerial positions for two of his colleagues (Grimond and, presumably, Wade), as long as the six Liberals cared to follow the National Liberals, and Churchill himself, into the Tory fold. Davies had refused to help abolish his party on at least two previous occasions and, after what Grimond later described as 'a lot of ringing around', he rejected the overture of 1951 as well. His refusal of office, and of the proposition that the Liberals should be subsumed, was without doubt a remarkable act of political courage and statesmanship.

Violet Bonham Carter thought that he had made a dreadful mistake. When she said so to colleagues on the Party Council, however, she was generally execrated. It soon became clear that, had Davies been seduced by Churchill's gambit, it is unlikely that he could have carried more than a few of his party colleagues with him into a long-term arrangement with the Conservatives. His party may have been small and almost moribund across great tracts of the nation, but its surviving devotees were a proud and defiant group who intended to go down, if necessary, with the ship. It was this new parliamentary party of but six MPs – Davies, Grimond, Roderic Bowen, Hopkin Morris, Wade and Holt – that had to scuff out some kind of niche for a once-great political party. By the time of the Liberal Assembly in autumn 1951, Davies seems to have buried any regrets about this act of renunciation. 'In spite of all temptations', he told delegates, 'we still prefer our own doctrine and we are determined to maintain our independence'.

This was not the end of the story, however; the Liberals were now alive thanks only to Tory sufferance and, in February 1953, a group of senior party figures made a further visit to Churchill, again purportedly to discuss the voting system. Lady Violet, who led that delegation, warned Churchill that although local pacts along the lines of those in Huddersfield and Bolton were effective in keeping Labour out, they were not to the taste of many party workers and had a dispiriting effect on the party organisation. What was needed was a more representative voting system, under which such pacts would be unnecessary. Churchill knew only too well that electoral reform was a long-time totem for Liberals and, under pressure from this barrage, he agreed to look again at the findings of the inquiry he had set up into the likely effects of proportional representation, but still held out no real hope for progress. The measure just would not have the necessary support in the House of Commons. Churchill had in the past himself advocated electoral reform, at least within larger towns, and he could not disguise his frustration and sadness at being unable to deliver. Lady Violet perfectly understood that her old friend's hands were tied, however, writing in her diary that evening, 'what alarms me is that the Tory Party should still run so true to form'.[1]

1955: Stasis

The position of the Liberal Party did begin to improve barely perceptibly during the 1951–55 Parliament. There was no particular reason
for this; it just seems to be something that tends to happen to the
Liberals when the Conservative Party is in power. It certainly had little, or nothing, to do with the contribution of Clement Davies, who
was increasingly a sick man and spent much of the time incapacitated.
The parliamentary burden fell largely on but three sets of shoulders
– those of Grimond, Donald Wade and new Bolton MP Arthur Holt.
Measures were taken to improve the state of the party's finances and
organisation and, in December 1954, John Bannerman came within
a whisker of winning a by-election held in a snowstorm at Inverness.
Bannerman gained 36 per cent of the vote in a seat that the Liberals had not contested in 1951, running the Tories a close second in
what had been a safe seat. Sceptics pointed out, however, that this
was an obvious one-off: the seat was naturally fertile territory for the
Liberals – being far-flung and 'Celtic' – and turnout had fallen from
almost 70 per cent at the general election to below 50 per cent at the
by-election. Bannerman's near-breakthrough nonetheless provided a
rare shaft of light for the Liberals. 'Let us have more Invernesses!' proclaimed the *News Chronicle*.

The Liberals went into the 1955 general election with a Gallup
rating of only 2 per cent, a collapse from 8 per cent only two months
earlier. The election brought consolidation, but no real progress. All
six Liberal MPs stood for re-election and all six were re-elected. For
the first time since 1929 the party had not recorded a net loss of seats
at a general election; for the second election running, Jo Grimond
was the only Liberal victor to have faced a Conservative opponent.
Once again, this time under Churchill's recently nominated successor Anthony Eden, the Tories had stayed their hand when they might
easily have put at least three of the Liberal MPs to the sword. In every
other seat in Britain there was a Conservative (or allied) candidate,

and Labour fought every mainland seat. The total Liberal vote was a little over 700,000 – less than 3 per cent of the total, but over 15 per cent on average in the seats the party contested. For the first time, the Liberals targeted their resources and, in a handful of seats, saw the first fruits of concerted community campaigning at a constituency level. For the second time in the space of a year, John Bannerman came painfully close to snatching Inverness (losing this time by only 966) – and in five other seats the party was within 6,000 votes of victory. It should also be noted that the warning signs were now there for the Tories: it was almost exclusively in seats held by them that any serious Liberal threat was now beginning to emerge, particularly in the South-West of England.

From late 1955, the Liberal Party's position began to improve more perceptibly. At Torquay on 15 December 1955, Peter Bessell increased the Liberal vote by almost 10 per cent. Two months later, on 14 February 1956, at Gainsborough and at Hereford, the Liberals did rather well again, increasing their share from 25 per cent to over 36 per cent. The party went on to enjoy a number of unheralded gains in the local elections of May 1956. Senior Liberals, serious about restoring their party's fortunes, soon came to the view that their most pressing need was for a change of leader.

In the summer of that year came the first act of a drama that would in due course transform the political landscape: following the refusal of the Americans and British to finance the Aswan Dam in southern Egypt, the Egyptian President Nasser summarily nationalised the Suez Canal. A crisis ensued that would bring the British political establishment to breaking point, fundamentally changing many people's perceptions of the Conservative Party. A huge opportunity was about to be created for a re-energised Liberal Party.

As part of their building for the future, senior figures within the Liberal Party now took the difficult decision to initiate a change of leader. Although Clement Davies' position had never been openly challenged during the 1955–56 parliamentary session, he was now over seventy years old and, having played virtually no part in the 1955 election, could hardly be presented as a credible leader four or five years down the line. There was only one plausible successor: Jo Grimond. He was not only the most impressive performer in the parliamentary party; as whip he was also de facto deputy leader and he had an electoral independence that none of his colleagues enjoyed, as the sole Liberal MP to have defeated opponents from both other parties.

Grimond spoke to Davies in July 1956, at the beginning of the summer recess, and received not the slightest indication that he intended to call it a day. By the time the Liberals assembled for their assembly in Folkestone towards the end of September, however, everyone seemed to know that something was afoot. Even Davies' many admirers had apparently now realised that, with Suez threatening to engulf Britain in a national crisis, more energetic leadership was desperately needed – and Davies had taken the point.

Grimond's speech to the assembly was on the subject of industrial development. Taken at face value this was a peculiarly dull topic, but Grimond was masterly, stylishly leavening his remarks with characteristic humour and wit. At a meeting of the party's Executive Committee in July (before the Egyptians had nationalised the Suez Canal), Grimond had specifically turned down the opportunity to move the resolution on foreign affairs and opted instead for the automation resolution, 'provided he could include a general background of industrial conditions'. His choice of a non-controversial subject suggests that he wanted to avoid looking too much like a man indecently eager for the limelight. From the beginning of the assembly, however, there was no mistaking the warm, sometimes euphoric, response evoked even by the mention of Grimond's name.

When Davies entered the hall to deliver his leader's speech, he received a lengthy standing ovation and the words with which he acknowledged it confirmed that his renunciation was indeed imminent. 'Thank you for that wonderful reception', he said as the tumult subsided. 'Especially do I thank you this morning.'[2] After a traditional leader's *tour d'horizon,* Davies cut somewhat emotionally to the chase.

> It is time that the tiller were placed in the hands of a younger man, and a new voice should be calling upon the ship's company, rallying them to the great cause which we all have so much at heart ... Fortunately I can step down knowing that there is a worthy successor waiting, one who has fully earned his Master's Certificate. I step down from the bridge, and go below.[3]

In theory the choice of a new leader would be a matter for the six Liberal MPs as soon as they reassembled at the beginning of the new parliamentary session, but nobody doubted what they would do. When Clement Davies was interviewed later that day, he said that, although 'the question of leadership is always a matter for the Members of the House ... I am almost sure that my colleagues will choose unanimously Joseph Grimond'.[4]

Jo Grimond: New leader, new era

Most Liberals and Liberal Democrats still remember the Grimond era of 1956–67 with particular affection, as the time when the Liberals emerged from the shadows and re-established themselves as a credible national party. Ironically, things did not begin very well. A week after becoming leader in November 1956, Grimond had to put in an early appearance at a highly unpromising by-election, speaking at a rally in the City of Chester two days before polling day. This was not the kind of seat that he would have chosen for his first target as Leader: the Liberals had won only 11 per cent of the vote there in 1955, and the best that the party could hope for was to retain its deposit. On 15 November, its candidate failed to achieve even that modest target; the Liberal share of the vote rose by an infinitesimal amount, and the Conservatives held the seat comfortably. Compared with other by-elections in the previous twelve months or so, this was a dreadful result, seemingly an awful portent for the new regime.

Shortly afterwards, an even more dangerous by-election loomed for the Liberals when Liberal MP Rhys Hopkin Morris died unexpectedly at his home in Sidcup on the night of 21–22 November. Hopkin Morris had won his seat by fewer than 500 votes in both 1950 and 1951 and, although his majority had risen to over 3,000 in 1955, he had a sizeable personal vote and everyone knew that Carmarthen would be highly vulnerable. Then came a double bombshell: news that the Labour candidate was to be none other than Megan Lloyd George, and also that the local Liberals proposed to select as candidate one John Morgan Davies, who shared Hopkin Morris' pro-government views on Suez. The party leadership had to decide quickly whether it should disown a candidate with whom it disagreed on a matter of such national significance, or swallow its collective pride and principles by supporting Morgan Davies's campaign to retain the seat. In a decision that he apparently came to rue, Grimond decided to support the Carmarthen campaign, and encouraged his colleagues to do the same. On 28 February 1957 John Morgan Davies lost to Megan Lloyd George by 3,069 votes, a margin of 6.1 per cent. The whole business strongly affirmed the emergent view of Grimond and his close associates that the party needed to become more coherent and more professional.

Although the party now had only five MPs, a historic nadir never equalled before or since, it had now hit the bottom of the barrel. The standing of the Liberal Party would certainly wax and wane during the remainder of Grimond's time as leader and thereafter, but there would be no more Carmarthens. Between June 1957 and June 1958, the party would enjoy impressive near-misses in by-elections in North Dorset and Rochdale and, only a year after Carmarthen, Grimond's brother-in-law Mark Bonham Carter would gain Torrington from the Tories in a truly stunning victory.

1959: The end of crisis management?

At the general election of 8 October 1959, the Liberals again won only six seats, with Mark Bonham Carter losing Torrington narrowly and Jeremy Thorpe gaining North Devon, but there was no mistaking the sense that the party was now on the up. In eight seats (including Torrington) the party came within 5,000 votes of victory and, from 1960 onwards, notched up a series of tremendous by-election performances. There were sixty-two by-elections during the 1959–64 Parliament and the Liberals picked up many impressive second places, plus victories at Orpington and Montgomery (after the death of Clement Davies in 1962). The party's support in the opinion polls grew steadily throughout 1960 and 1961, briefly peaking at 30 per cent in March 1962, in the wake of Orpington. By choosing to contest the by-election at Bolton East in November 1960, the Liberals effectively drew a line under the era of pacts. This was to cost Donald Wade and Arthur Holt their seats in the 1964 general election, but in the long term it was a price worth paying. The Liberal Party was no longer beholden to anyone for its continuing existence.

The modern Liberal Party of Grimond had become a worthy successor to the party of Gladstone and Asquith. It had come of age, and was at last fully ready to stand on its own two feet.

What might have been

When, in 1955, the father of psephology Bob Mackenzie produced the first edition of his magnum opus, *British Political Parties,* the Liberals appeared only in a two-page appendix and in a brief explanatory note on the very first of the book's 600 pages. The book, explained Mackenzie, would not 'deal in any detail with the minor parties'. On that basis, 'the Liberal Party has been relegated to an Appendix … In view of the party's long and distinguished history, this may seem unnecessarily cruel … But there can be no escaping the fact that in the last election the Liberal Party received only 2 per cent of the popular vote'.[5]

If the Conservative Party had attempted to destroy the Liberal Party when it was at the lowest point in its fortunes, at the general elections of 1951 and 1955, it would probably have succeeded. So what would have happened if the Tories had not stayed their collective hand? What would have happened to the Liberals?

They would certainly have lost two or three of their seats, and the survivors would surely have been unable to maintain the pretence of being a national political party. It is safe to assume that Arthur Holt and Hopkin Morris would have lost fairly heavily and, although it is just about possible to believe that Donald Wade might have survived in Huddersfield West in the absence of his agreement with the local Tories, the evidence is not terribly convincing; after all, he did lose the seat in 1964, at the first election after the informal pact was abandoned. Of the likely survivors, Jo Grimond in Orkney and Shetland was impressive enough, but Clement Davies in Montgomery was already enjoying increasingly precarious health, and Cardigan's Roderic Bowen was, at best, a part-time MP, his legal practice accounting for the greater part of his energies. Either way, with three or four MPs the party would still have been very much down to the bare bones. It seems certain that the Liberal Party could have been obliterated in 1955 if that had been what the Conservative Party nationally – and locally in Huddersfield, Bolton and Carmarthen – had wanted to see. Yet the Tories chose to let the Liberals live. Why?

Sentiment undoubtedly played a part in the calculation, particularly when Churchill was still in charge, but the Conservative stay of execution was not undertaken entirely for idealistic reasons. Perhaps the main cause was complacency. The Liberals did not self-evidently seem to threaten Conservative interests or Conservative seats and, given the mixed voting record of Liberal MPs, they were certainly to be preferred to Labour replacements. There was also a good personal relationship between most of the Liberal MPs and their Conservative colleagues, and more common ground politically than might be readily understood today. As memories of the pre-war Conservative Party faded and the Cold War developed, a shared opposition to socialism became more and more important. After 1951 the old left of the Liberal Party was no longer represented in the parliamentary party, and Liberals such as Jo Grimond, Donald Wade and Arthur Holt were unlikely to give any succour to state socialism. Even after 1956 there was common ground: the leaderships of the two parties may have disagreed profoundly over Suez, but Liberal misgivings were shared by a significant number of Tory backbenchers; and Liberals and Conservatives worked closely together in response to the unconscionable and brutal Soviet suppression of the Hungarian uprising. Above all, however, too many Tories simply failed to apprehend the threat the Liberals might one day pose to them.

So the Liberal Party certainly *could* have been wiped out in the 1950s. *What if* it had been? My view is that its most significant player, Jo Grimond, would almost certainly have eschewed other parties. I do not believe that the likes of Gaitskell or Wilson, Macmillan or Heath would have enticed him into another party merely by offering the meretricious bauble of middle-ranking ministerial office. He could probably have continued for as long as he wanted as an independent MP for Orkney and Shetland and I think that is what he almost certainly would have opted to do, continuing to provide an engaging and dissident voice within a largely bipolar political system.

I am not convinced, however, that Grimond would have enjoyed the novelty value of being an independent Liberal MP indefinitely. Some worthy and suitably eminent public appointment – or even one in the private sector – would probably have lured him south eventually. There would have been no Torrington, no Orpington and, in all probability, no Warrington or Crosby either. By keeping alive the Liberal Party Organisation, even in virtual hibernation, Davies, Grimond and the others were incubating the necessary material for the third-party revivals of the 1970s and 1980s.

There is a distinguished and plausible school of thought within political science that believes that, as nature abhors a vacuum, so the party system must ultimately reflect the economic, political and social cleavages that characterise a society. On that basis, if the Liberals had been wiped out in 1956, almost as soon as they were obliterated they would have been needed again. Admittedly, in terms of shifting political loyalties, Suez had an effect mainly on 'elite' opinion, with the Mark Bonham Carters of the time detaching themselves from the Tories as a sign of their revulsion at Eden's tactics. On the other hand, this was not a wholly isolated realignment. By the early 1960s and the time of the great Liberal triumph at Orpington, there was a growing recognition that the 'old politics', based very much upon a pre-war class structure, was becoming outmoded. The monicker 'Orpington Man' covered a multitude of sins (and merits) but it encapsulated a sense that the old deference that had sustained the Tories might just be wearing thin, along with the class-consciousness that gave life and meaning to the Labour movement. The labour market was changing and, encouraged at least in part by liberal-minded politicians in the two main parties, society was beginning to change too.

Given the shifting sands of that historical background, therefore, is it really inconceivable that the Liberals might, somehow, have hung on at council and community level, in defiance of parliamentary obliteration, ready to prime the pump of a new liberalism that sprang not from the party system but from the irresistible social forces of the time? Frankly, it seems far-fetched – and we do not have to draw entirely upon the realms of fantasy to make the case. The SDP supposedly came into being not only because of the impossible and vicious divisions within the Labour Party, but also as a response to a new mood in the country, not only amongst the intelligentsia but far more widely. It was launched by four former cabinet ministers amidst a blaze of publicity and for a time it clearly caught the public mood. Within less than seven years, however, it was effectively defunct, crushed by tribalism and the voting system. This is not to belittle the SDP – far from it – but merely to indicate how difficult it is for a new (or reconstituted) party to establish a sustainable niche for itself under a first-past-the-post voting system. I have no doubt that, had the Liberal Party died in the 1960s, it would have stayed as dead as the proverbial parrot, and liberalism would have lived on within the two main parties instead.

It would also, in my view, have been infinitely more difficult for the SDP to come into being, assuming of course that other events had remained more or less on the tracks familiar to us. For all the froth of the SDP breakaway, it was the grafting on of existing Liberal organisation, manpower and expertise that unleashed the synergy that carried the Alliance and, latterly, the Liberal Democrats, through their by-election triumphs at Crosby and Hillhead, Portsmouth and Brecon, Eastleigh and Romsey and then, in 1997 and 2001, into significant parliamentary breakthroughs at general elections too.

If the Conservative Party had acted in its own cold and calculated best interests, and if the Liberal Party had indeed perished in the 1950s, given the harsh vagaries of the first-past-the-post voting system, there is in my view absolutely no reason to believe that it would – or could – ever have been resuscitated, even by the likes of Roy Jenkins, David Owen and Shirley Williams. So Liberal Democrats who really care about their history should elevate to the pantheon of Liberal heroes not only Winston Churchill, but also Donald Wade and Arthur Holt – and Anthony Eden and Harold Macmillan.

Notes

1   Mark Pottle (ed.), *Daring to Hope: The Diaries and Letters of Violet Bonham Carter, 1946–1969* (Weidenfeld & Nicolson, 2000), p. 117.

What if …

2   *The Times,* 1 October 1956.
3   *Coventry Evening Telegraph,* 29 September 1956.
4   BBC TV, 29 September 1956.
5   Robert Mackenzie, *British Political Parties* (Heinemann, 1955), p. vii.

Chapter 7

What if Lee Harvey Oswald had missed?

Simon Burns

Ask any adult over the age of fifty, and they will be able to recall what they were doing on Friday 22 November 1963, when it was announced that President John F. Kennedy had been shot and, half an hour later, died in Dallas, Texas.

The news was followed by an outpouring of grief and raw emotion that has been rarely witnessed over the death of a politician. The combination of four days of constant television coverage of the life, death and funeral of Kennedy plus the machinations of his widow, Jacqueline, aided and abetted by the journalist Theodore White, created the myth of Camelot which defined, for a generation, the image of a family and of a Presidency that lasted for only a thousand days.

This image was reinforced in a speech given by Bobby Kennedy at the 1964 Democratic Convention. Introducing a film about the life of his deceased brother he described him in heroic terms, borrowing a quotation from Shakespeare's *Romeo and Juliet* given to him by Jackie Kennedy:

> When he shall die,
> Take him and cut him out in little stars,
> And he will make the face of heaven so fine
> That all the world will be in love with night,
> And pay no worship to the garish sun.

The subtlety of these lines was not lost on his audience. By implication, the night that the world 'will be in love with' was his brother, and, in a stunning condemnation of John Kennedy's successor, the 'garish sun' was Lyndon Johnson.

The assassination itself, the hyperbole of the myth of Camelot created by his widow and the rhetoric of his brother, all powerfully established Kennedy's heroic status as the glamorous young father and dashing President, struck down in the prime of his career with so much potential unrealised. It is an image that still holds sway over vast sections of the American public and elsewhere around the world. The intriguing question is what would have happened if Lee Harvey Oswald had missed on that November morning in 1963? Would Kennedy have been re-elected in 1964 and been given the time and opportunity to realise the potential that so many people believed he possessed?

Would he have continued to commit America to the quagmire of Vietnam, or would he have withdrawn the American military advisers after the 1964 election, as he hinted to Walter Cronkite in an interview in Hyannis in September 1963? If he had taken the latter course the implications for the United States would have been awesome: no Nixon Presidency in 1969 and no Watergate scandal, with the devastating effects that it had on the American body politic for a generation.

~

At the time of his death, John F. Kennedy was in reasonably good political shape, though his popularity had dipped during the latter half of 1963. Throughout his Presidency his approval ratings averaged 70 per cent, reaching a peak of 83 per cent in April–May 1961, just after the Bay of Pigs fiasco, and a low of 56 per cent, in September 1963 following a summer of problems over civil rights in the deep south. By November 1963, his ratings had risen slightly to 58 per cent which, although twelve points below his average, was still fairly positive, being significantly above the 49.7 per cent of the vote he had received when he was elected in 1960.

More significantly for his chances in 1964, it seemed that the most likely Republican candidate against him would be the weakest that the party had to offer – Senator Barry Goldwater of Arizona.

Richard Nixon had virtually ruled himself out after his defeat in the 1962 Californian gubernatorial election and the disastrous and sour press conference he gave the day afterwards, when he turned on the press with a venom rarely seen publicly in American politics. Nelson Rockefeller eliminated himself from any chance of receiving the nomination when, following his divorce from his wife of over thirty years, he married Happy Murphy, a woman almost twenty years his junior who had signed away custody of her two children to her husband. The political fall-out was catastrophic: Rockefeller alienated both core Republican supporters and Bible-belt voters who were appalled by what they perceived as his gross moral lapse. His poll ratings plummeted and the main beneficiary was Goldwater.

Although Kennedy liked Goldwater personally, he relished the opportunity to face him in the general election of 1964. He regarded him as honourable but, given his views on states' rights, social security and the role of the state, too far to the right of the political spectrum to be acceptable to a majority of the American electorate.

Kennedy's first meeting to plan the 1964 campaign took place in the White House ten days before the assassination. The consensus at the meeting was that Goldwater would be the most likely Republican nominee and that it would be relatively easy to box him into a corner as the candidate of the far right. There is convincing evidence that this assessment was accurate. The Kennedy campaigning machine was formidable in its organisation; the President and his young wife and family were a public relations executive's dream product to package and sell to the American public.

Politically, Kennedy, with his urbane wit and soaring flights of rhetoric, had managed to establish himself as both a Cold-War warrior and a proponent of peace, the harsh rhetoric of his inaugural address and his handling of the Cuban missile crisis being tempered by his June 1963 speech at the American University in the pursuit of peace and the nuclear test ban treaty. In the field of civil rights, he was building up a strong body of support among blacks and liberals with his advocacy of the Civil Rights Bill in Congress – and he would easily have captured the vast majority of these voters if Goldwater had been his opponent. Goldwater refused to vote for the Civil Rights Bill in 1964, costing him dearly with some sections of the electorate. Ironically, against Kennedy, Goldwater would have picked up support for his views on civil rights in the South, eroding the Democrat stranglehold especially in the deep South. This is what actually did happen in his campaign against Lyndon Johnson in 1964, when he picked up five Southern states, including Alabama, where he captured 70 per cent of the vote, South Carolina (59 per cent), Louisiana (57 per cent) and Georgia (55 per cent). Despite this historic success, he only managed to win one other state in the Union, his home state of Arizona, and that by only one half of one per cent.

At a time when the Cold War was at its height, with the Cuban missile crisis fresh in peoples' minds, Kennedy would have campaigned as a peacemaker. In comparison, the hard-line views of Goldwater over Vietnam and Cuba, and his rhetoric on relations with the Soviet Union and nuclear weapons, would have frightened voters hoping for détente with the Soviet Union. Kennedy would also have benefited from a strong economy. Inflation was low, unemployment was negligible, the economy was expanding and the Kennedy tax cut was boosting the living standards of the average American. Despite the usual view that the Republicans were the more fiscally responsible party, Kennedy had neutralised their advantage by appointing the Wall Street Republican Douglas Dillon as his

Secretary of the Treasury; Kennedy's fiscally conservative approach to economic policy was more akin to his father, Joseph Kennedy, than to his liberal supporters such as John Kenneth Galbraith.

Kennedy would have campaigned as a charismatic and successful Chief Executive, a safe and steady hand on the tiller. In the 1964 election, Goldwater campaigned on the slogan of 'In your heart, you know he's right', which Lyndon Johnson and the Democrats deftly transformed into 'But in your guts, you know he's nuts'. Kennedy would have been equally keen to portray Goldwater as an extremist Cold-War warrior who could not be trusted as Commander-in-Chief.

There is one further key advantage that Kennedy would have had in 1964 which Lyndon Johnson did not enjoy. Kennedy was extremely popular within his own party; unlike Johnson, who was challenged in the primaries by George Wallace, he would have unanimously received the Democratic nomination without having to contest any bruising primary elections. Goldwater was not so lucky. He was challenged in the primaries by a number of candidates, including Henry Cabot Lodge and Nelson Rockefeller. Furthermore, it was known that the former President, Dwight D. Eisenhower, was not favourably disposed towards his candidacy.

The last primary of the season, in California, was particularly bruising as Rockefeller threw everything he could into the campaign to try and discredit Goldwater. Rockefeller abided by the elementary political principle that negative attacks were more effective than promoting issues; he believed that to win he had to ' destroy Barry Goldwater as a member of the human race'. The tactic failed, however, and Goldwater eventually gained the nomination – but at a terrible price. The party was scarred by the venom of the campaign as Rockefeller Republicans and Goldwater Republicans tore each other apart in public, much to the glee of the watching Democrats.

The problem was compounded at the Republican Convention which gathered at the Cow Palace in San Francisco to nominate

Goldwater. As Rockefeller began to speak, he was systematically booed, heckled and goaded into attacking the delegates, declaring that he had spent the last year defending the party from an extremist takeover. The delegates' response was venomous as their raw hatred of this perceived member of the liberal wing of the party was broadcast live on television all over the nation. It was as if the lunatics had taken over the asylum. In his own speech accepting the nomination of his party, Goldwater performed equally disastrously, declaring to an adoring audience: 'Those who do not care for our cause we do not expect to enter our ranks ... I would remind you that extremism in the defence of liberty is no vice. And let me remind you also – that moderation in the pursuit of justice is no virtue!' The crowd inside the auditorium may have gone wild with joy as pandemonium broke out but, in the real America, far from the Convention of right-wing zealots, there was revulsion at the extremism of Goldwater's language. It seemed to confirm all the accusations that moderate Republicans had been throwing at him during the primary elections and at the Convention itself.

Goldwater never recovered. Republicans seeking election, or re-election, deserted in droves; party workers stayed at home and fundraising for the campaign failed to materialise. From the outset, the campaign imploded and Lyndon Johnson was elected by a landslide, receiving over 60 per cent of the vote and carrying all but six states.

Kennedy would almost certainly have enjoyed a similar landslide victory and his coat-tails would have helped elect a Congress more sympathetic to his policies of the 'New Frontier' than its predecessor. This would have helped Kennedy immeasurably in his second term as he pushed harder for the extension of civil rights, voting rights for black Americans and the war on poverty that he was already drawing up before his assassination, and which Lyndon Johnson hijacked as his own in 1965 as part of his 'Great Society'.

Ironically, the greatest impact that a second-term Kennedy presidency would have had on the US would have been on an issue that barely raised its head during the 1964 election – Vietnam. When Kennedy became President in 1961 he had inherited a commitment from Eisenhower to provide about 500 military advisers to the South Vietnamese government; their function was to provide training and advice against the ever-increasing encroachment of the North Vietnamese. Without giving it much thought Kennedy accepted, in the early days of his Presidency, the Eisenhower domino theory, which predicted Communist control of all of Southeast Asia if South Vietnam fell. Inevitably, however, US advisers got drawn into combat; instructing South Vietnamese forces on anti-guerilla tactics meant accompanying them on field missions and getting involved in the fighting. In addition, as the Vietnamese lacked the facilities to train pilots to fly the latest planes and helicopters, US pilots were drawn into action, with the accompanying risk of deaths and injuries.

Despite these developments, however, and the fact that by November 1963 the number of advisers had increased thirty-two-fold to over 16,000, Kennedy was determined not to be drawn into a ground war. As early as April 1961 a memo from Theodore Sorensen, the President's close aide and speech-writer echoed Kennedy's thinking on the subject: 'there is no clearer example of a country that cannot be saved unless it saves itself – through increased popular support; governmental, economic and military reforms and reorganisations and the encouragement of new political leaders'.

It was quite clear that Kennedy had no immediate plans to commit American troops to fight a war in Vietnam. This decision took great moral courage; he was under tremendous and constant pressure from his military advisers to commit ground troops to fighting. By the spring of 1963, however, he was faced with a cruel dilemma. He became trapped in a deepening vortex of military escalation in which victory seemed ever more elusive. The illusion of success always required more advisers, more transport, more helicopters and more equipment to sustain them. Ironically, it was not that the American advisers had not done their job in Vietnam; they had done an extremely good job in training and advising the Vietnamese. The problem was that the South Vietnamese army was too small to deal effectively with the Vietcong; it was also badly organised and inappropriately trained to engage in counter-insurgency operations.

By the summer of 1963 the situation was spiralling out of control due to the political unrest in South Vietnam caused by growing disenchantment with the ineffective and corrupt Diem regime. Kennedy's predicament became a nightmare, complicated by the forthcoming US presidential election. He feared that the electorate would view it as a sign of weakness on his part if he withdrew the US advisers from Vietnam, as this would almost certainly lead to the collapse of the regime and victory for the Communist North. Kennedy had not helped his case over the previous two years by the confused signals which his administration gave to both press and public; he also failed to initiate a national debate over the *raison d'être* for the US presence in Vietnam. Part of the reason was the distraction of other, more pressing, problems such as the Bay of Pigs and Berlin in 1961, the Cuban missile crisis in 1962, the nuclear test ban treaty in 1963, and civil rights unrest.

By the summer of 1963, however, the deteriorating situation in Vietnam forced Kennedy to pay more attention to the developing crisis. He had become increasingly irritated by the different assessments of the situation coming out of Vietnam and in particular the over-optimistic reports of the military. As a counterweight, he sent Roger Hilsman, head of the State Department's intelligence division, and Michael Forrestal, of the National Security Council, to carry out an on-the-spot appraisal. Their report was mixed. They concluded that things were 'going much better than they were a year ago' and the Vietcong were 'being hurt'; but also that the negative side was 'still awesome' and that they expected the war to 'last longer than we would like, and cost more in terms of both lives and money than we anticipated'.

Part of the Kennedy strategy had always been to make optimistic public statements which did not necessarily reflect his more sanguine private thoughts. In December 1962, after a meeting held in Palm Beach on Vietnam, he told Kenneth O'Donnell, his long-time friend and appointments secretary, that 'I got angry with Mike [Senator Mike Mansfield, Majority Leader in the Senate] for disagreeing with our policy so completely, and I got angry with myself because I found myself agreeing with him'.

Robert Dallek, in his biography *An Unfinished Life: John F. Kennedy,* has argued with conviction that Kennedy's public conformity with optimistic appraisals in fact served a useful political purpose; if Kennedy was planning to withdraw, it was essential to encourage the notion that progress was being made in the war and that the US would thus be able to reduce its role in the fighting. That explains why Kennedy's public statements were generally so bullish, while at the same time he looked for, and took, any opportunities available to advocate a withdrawal when feasible. He was genuinely worried that the US would unwittingly get dragged more and more into what he regarded as South Vietnam's problem. He also feared that if he ever agreed to put in ground troops to fight, they would inevitably suffer losses, increasing the pressures on him to commit more and more troops to the fighting to guarantee success. So, in May 1963, when Ngo Dinh Nhu, Diem's brother, complained that there were too many American advisers in Vietnam and that at least half could be safely withdrawn, Kennedy responded by saying that whenever South Vietnam suggested troops should be withdrawn, they would be on their way home the next day.

In fact Kennedy and his military advisers went so far as to start to plan a withdrawal programme. He is reputed to have told Senator

Mansfield that he 'now agreed with the Senator's thinking on the need for a complete withdrawal' but with the proviso that 'I can't do it until 1965 – after I'm reelected'. In the 1970s, Mansfield confirmed the veracity of this conversation, adding that Kennedy had also told him that he felt that 'even then with 16,000 troops we were in too deep'.

As the summer of 1963 progressed, the situation in Vietnam deteriorated both militarily and politically; the regime tottered on the brink of collapse, suffering severe civil disobedience and a crisis provoked by the Catholic Diem, who was antagonistic to his country's majority Buddhist population. Diem's intransigence led Kennedy and his administration to arrive at the view that the only way to solve the problem was his removal, and until the coup at the beginning of November Kennedy pursued a dual policy of trying to pressurise Diem into reforming his regime and stopping the repression of the Buddhists, while also keeping in close contact with the military over the possibility of a replacement.

In September Kennedy gave a series of television interviews from his home in Hyannis. In his interview with Walter Cronkite, he made known his most forthright views on Vietnam:

> I don't think … unless a greater effort is made by the [Vietnamese] Government to win popular support that the war can be won out there. In the final analysis, it is their war. They are the ones who have to win it or lose it. We can help them, we can give them equipment, we can send our men out there as advisers, but they have to win it.

This was a significant departure from his previous policy of simply talking optimistically in public about the American role in Vietnam; it was the clearest indication to date of his deep disillusionment with the Diem regime and his determination not to allow his country to be dragged into an open-ended military commitment in Southeast Asia.

5

If he had lived, then, Kennedy was expected to have withdrawn some of the advisers from Vietnam during the course of the Presidential election in order to influence liberal voters fearing that the US was becoming bogged down in a hopeless conflict. It is likely that he would have tried to justified this at least partly by claiming that the war was being won, thereby avoiding alienating more conservative voters.

This policy is in very sharp contrast to the approach adopted by his successor, Lyndon Johnson, after November 1963. Johnson allowed himself to be unduly influenced by the gung-ho attitude of his military advisers and was inexorably sucked into committing American ground troops to a ground war where they did most of the fighting. Within two years of Johnson becoming President there were almost half a million US troops in South Vietnam and the numbers were still rising. Eventually, the war destroyed his Presidency and forced him to retire from the 1968 election rather than be defeated by the challenge to his leadership from Bobby Kennedy and Eugene McCarthy.

Not only did the war devastate Johnson's Presidency; it also tore American society apart. The divisions that opened up between supporters and opponents of the war deeply divided the nation, and the lack of military success caused a crisis of confidence within American society. Johnson's inability to tell the truth over Vietnam led to a credibility gap where few people believed anything he said, deeply undermining the body politic and the institution of the Presidency itself. The glamour of Camelot was replaced by an unpopular and, in many quarters, deeply despised President who was a prisoner in his own White House.

The irony is that in many areas of social policy, particularly in the field of civil rights and the war against poverty, Johnson's record was superb – but it was all subsumed by the debilitating impact of the Vietnam war. A legislative record that was the finest of any President since Franklin D. Roosevelt was discounted because of the damage the war caused to the nation.

~

If John F. Kennedy had lived, the history of America in the 1960s would have been completely different. The evidence that is available strongly suggests that, after re-election in November 1964, he would have used his renewed political mandate to pull out of the quagmire of Vietnam. Despite the rhetoric of Kennedy's 1960 inaugural address, when he proclaimed that the United States would 'pay any price or bear any burden' for freedom around the world, he had reached the conclusion that in reality the price was not worth paying in the case of South Vietnam.

By deftly extricating the US, Kennedy would then have had the opportunity to pursue the three key policies that had come to the forefront of his thinking in the last few months of his life – a more peaceful world, through détente with the Soviet Union, greater civil rights for African-Americans and the war against poverty.

He would have sought to build upon the success of the nuclear test ban treaty of August 1963 in order to promote a greater rapprochement with the Soviet Union, as heralded in possibly the finest speech he ever gave, at the American University the previous June. In it he signalled his commitment to genuine, lasting peace: 'Not a Pax Americana enforced on the world by American weapons of war ... not merely peace for Americans, but peace for all men; not merely peace in our time but peace for all time.'

Kennedy challenged the American public to re-examine the Soviet Union and the Cold War and to put past conflicts and prejudices behind them, concentrating instead on the common interests shared by both powers. His message was that 'our problems are man-made; therefore they can be solved by man', and his solution was based on the premise that:

We [America] must conduct our affairs in such a way that it becomes in the Communists' interest to agree on genuine peace …to … let each nation choose its own future, so long as that choice does not interfere with the choice of others. If we cannot now end our differences, at least we can help make the world a safer place for diversity. For, in the final analysis our most basic common link is the fact that we all inhabit this planet. We all breathe the same air. We all cherish our children's future. And we are all mortal.

Within two months the Soviet Union had signed the nuclear test ban treaty; there is a convincing argument that this move was only a first step towards a more positive attitude in general to working with Kennedy.

In the field of civil rights, Kennedy's record had initially been timid, but the events of the summer of 1963 in the deep South led to a reappraisal. It would be unrealistic not to accept that, if he had lived, he would have had difficulties in getting his Civil Rights Bill through Congress; in reality it was his death and the efforts of Lyndon Johnson that achieved that. He would, however, almost certainly have successfully passed some form of civil rights legislation as the mood in America (outside the South) began to turn to outrage at what was, in effect, a system of apartheid in the southern states. After his re-election, with the freedom of never having to face the electorate again, it seems very likely that he would have pressed further and faster for more civil rights legislation.

He would also have waged a vigorous war on poverty. As a wealthy man, immune to the suffering of many, he had been genuinely shocked at the poverty he had found in West Virginia during the 1960 election; before his death, his administration was already drawing up plans to eradicate poverty. As a more fiscally conservative politician than Johnson, Kennedy would not have made the mistakes that his successor did in seeking to solve the problem by throwing unlimited sums of money at it, with little accountability. This approach was always bound to fail once the taxes necessary to finance it began to bear too heavily on the middle classes and business – exacerbated in Johnson's case by the cost of the war in Vietnam.

Kennedy would certainly have poured money into the anti-poverty programme – but he would also have sought to involve the private sector in order to spread the burden of the costs, as Bobby Kennedy did so successfully in New York in the mid-1960s when regenerating the Bedford-Stuyvesant area. Kennedy would also have been far less grandiose than Johnson in his vision of how to tackle poverty, recognising the need for checks and balances and detailed achievement targets to ensure real returns on the investments designed to regenerate poor housing and inner-city areas and raise standards of living and the quality of education.

This twin approach to civil rights and poverty, without the divisions and distractions of a war in Vietnam, seem likely to have minimised, if not avoided entirely, the rioting and tensions within American society that did so much between 1965 and 1969 to make the US such a deeply divided and difficult society. As a result, America on the eve of the Presidential election of 1968 would have been a very different place. It would not have been in the middle of a political civil war, with the occupant of the White House imprisoned within its gates, the Democratic Party would not have been tearing itself apart over Vietnam, and Richard Nixon would never have had the opportunity to rise politically from the dead to become the next President of the United States.

The implications for the US of Nixon never becoming President would have been far-reaching. Without Nixon, there would have never been the Watergate scandal and the poisoning of the American body politic. The destructive influence of Watergate on America cannot be underestimated; it destroyed trust in politics and politicians for a generation. After the illegal excesses of the bugging of political opponents' telephones, the burglary of a private citizen's psychiatrist's office, the use of the tax authorities to pursue political opponents and political dirty tricks, there was a melt-down in confidence and trust in the institution of government and politicians.

This would all have been avoided if Kennedy had not been shot and America had withdrawn from Vietnam. The optimism of the early 1960s would never have turned into the deep cynicism and distrust of the 1970s. There is even the outside possibility that the popular quip of the early sixties might have come true and that John F. Kennedy would be President from 1961–69, Bobby Kennedy from 1969–77, Ted Kennedy for two terms from 1977 ... and then it would be 1984.

Chapter 8

What if the Conservatives had won in 1964?

John Barnes

The following extracts from the memoirs of the late Lord Maudling of Barnet relate to the successful 'dash for growth' engineered by Maudling when appointed to the Exchequer by Harold Macmillan. I have omitted a number of passages in order to provide a continuous narrative.

Some may think that Maudling dwells a little too much on the U-turn performed by the Labour Opposition. It is true that electoral expediency led it to highlight the large balance of payments deficit that had occurred as a result of Maudling's expansionist strategy, even though they had supported both the strategy and the idea that the deficit should be covered by borrowing. But it is surely asking too much of politicians en route to an unexpected electoral defeat to expect them not to play up a heavy balance of payments deficit. In their defence, it could be said that the figures were rather higher than anyone had anticipated.

In the end the U-turn mattered little because the Conservatives held on to win the 1964 election and to see the strategy through to success. These remarks, therefore, may well have more to do with the defeat of the Maudling Government in the wake of the 1974 oil shock than with events a decade earlier. Nevertheless we may well consider that had Wilson's gamble paid off with an election victory for the Labour Party, the price paid might have been steep. Almost certainly the incoming government would have been in deep trouble over the pound and while Wilson might have chosen to devalue and blame the previous Conservative government, there would probably have been some expectation that a government which had devalued once might do so again. Almost certainly, therefore, the dash for growth would have been aborted, not least because a devaluation necessitates a measure of deflation if it is to work, and the economy might have lurched on from crisis to crisis. If so, it would have been in a weaker state to cope with the aftermath of the oil shock of 1973/74. But might have beens, while interesting, are unprofitable territory for the historian if carried too far.

~

The concept of the 1963 Budget was to stimulate output on a basis that could be continued in terms of domestic inflationary pressures. It was, on the whole, well received, not least by those who came subsequently to criticise it. I well remember a summing up by the *Economist* in a leading article, 'Damn the torpedoes, half-speed ahead'.

The dangers were clearly twofold. The first was cost inflation. Spare capacity in the economy was sufficient to permit a large expansion of output and, as unit costs of production fall when output increases from the same equipment, this should have been helpful. However, it was easily nullified by excessive wage increases, hence Macmillan's innovative National Incomes Commission, which he described as the 'open-air cure'. We believed that we could get broad agreement within NEDC on the general level of wage increases, but there would always be a 'special case' to be made, and some could actually be justified. We sought a system whereby the exceptions could be identified and the reasons why they should be treated as exceptions clearly defined. In this way we hoped to kill off the mischief involved in comparability. I did a great deal of spadework with Vic Feather, which was to pay off after the election, but George Woodcock, the TUC's

General Secretary, resented the fact and that undermined our efforts. In any case the TGWU was opposed to the whole idea and the trade unions were easily persuaded that they should not cooperate with a dying government and its creature. Before the election the Commission was never the force it should have been, and I was at pains later to reconstruct it and place in charge a figure more acceptable to the unions than Sir Geoffrey Lawrence.

The second danger was the balance of payments. The British economy had shown ever since the war an alarming propensity to import manufactured goods and semi-manufactures. If you bring in your raw materials and components, it is obvious that you run up the import bill before reaping the benefit of the exports that follow. It was inevitable, therefore, that there would be a temporary strain on the balance of payments, but my calculation was that the period of strain would be relatively short and that we had adequate borrowing facilities to tide over any difficulties. If it was then thought unorthodox to plan deliberately to cover the current account deficit from overseas credit facilities – and it was – that did not give me pause. The facilities were there to be used and in my judgement this was the best possible use that could be made of them. I made it perfectly clear that this was what I was going to do and when I gave the reasons why I thought it justified, I found a good deal of support, not only from younger economic commentators like Sam Brittan and Nigel Lawson, but more importantly from the Labour opposition.

In January in an important speech at Swansea, Harold Wilson made it clear that the policy that the government was pursuing had cross-party support. 'If balance of payments difficulties arise in the next few months, as the Government has always said they must be met by using reserves', he told his audience. 'We should not be afraid to use them, nor, in an emergency, to use our very substantial drawing rights under the International Monetary Fund, to say nothing of other sources that can be mobilised in case of need.' That was helpful, but it would have been still more helpful if his trade-union allies could have brought themselves to accept voluntarily some restraint in wage increases. The memories of Selwyn Lloyd's pay pause were perhaps too vivid at that stage for them to do so. My efforts to bring them to cooperate with Neddy were rebuffed and I decided that it would be better to defer any fresh attempt to enlist their aid until the general election was behind us.

Since we were still behind in the polls, I accepted that a March date for an election was out. May and June were still possible and I knew that many of my colleagues, particularly the younger ones, were of my view that we should fight a summer election. Older heads like Rab and Selwyn Lloyd wanted – perhaps because they were older – to leave the election to the last moment. When asked by colleagues about the effect on the economy if we did so, I told them that it was difficult to make firm predictions. The current economic trends were durable, but there were unseen dangers for the summer. I did not anticipate a crisis, but if the situation did become dangerous we could go to the IMF.

In private, however, I warned Alec that there were major risks to our economic strategy if we delayed. Perhaps I ought to have thumped the table, but that was never my style. Instead I urged him to call an early election, fearing, as all Chancellors must, that delay would breed uncertainty. That was an even more threatening prospect than usual because I knew that the policy we were pursuing was likely to lead at some stage to balance of payments difficulties. I had made no secret of the fact, but my growing concern was that the difficulties would coincide with the election. Uncertainty about the result when combined with the normal wild exaggerations of party argument might give foreign opinion a fit of the vapours. I could hope that the Opposition might see the wisdom of biting their tongues lest they inherit the storm whipped up by their election rhetoric, but to be candid, I never expected them to do so. If the period of maximum strain on sterling coincided with the election, the consequences could be disastrous.

Alec did not reject my advice, and I suspect that his own instincts were to go early. However, the election professionals were unanimous in applying plenty of cold ice to his feet and, not unnaturally, he wanted to keep his options open. He even began to joke about the choice whenever he spoke, talking about when the election comes in June (long pause) or October. Although at first I shared in the genuine amusement, I felt that by April the joke was wearing a bit thin. In the end I was grateful that the approach of the first elections for the Greater London Council forced him to make up his mind. We had hoped to do well, but it was becoming clear that Labour might well win this trial run for the general election. In Central Office, Oliver Poole was taking a very pessimistic line on London, but neither he nor the party chairman thought that the general election was yet lost. Wait until after the summer, they counselled, and we could see the Conservative recovery, clearly under way, take us back into government. My worries were overridden and Alec announced before the polls closed on 9 April that the general election would be in October. My dismay was palpable, but the results of the GLC elections went far to justify those whose advice Alec took. Not only did we lose the GLC, but Labour captured boroughs like Enfield and Bexley that we ought to have held.

My budget on 14 April had as its main purpose a slight check to the rate of growth, bringing it back down to what I had indicated as the sustainable long-term rate of 4 per cent. I allowed myself the wry comment that although my previous budget had been 'described as timid and cautious, it has been followed by an expansion at the annual rate of at least 5 per cent'. My advisers had indicated that an increase in taxes of somewhere between £100 million and £225 million would do the trick, adding that if my choice was at the lower end, I might be forced to take further action in the summer, but that if I took too much, I might undermine business confidence. In my television broadcast, I was absolutely frank about the risk I was running in taking out only £100 million, but I reiterated my guiding philosophy: 'Provided that the worsening of the balance of payments is temporary, this should give rise neither to alarm or dismay and it would be very foolish of anyone to proclaim that it should. It is the predictable accompaniment of a vigorous rate of growth which all of us are committed to seek. We have very large first- and second-line reserves ...'.

In debate Wilson could not resist the gibe that I had timed my election boom for the autumn, but that because of the warning signs that were now appearing, I was having to put on the brakes. He did not urge further disinflation, however, apparently believing that nothing I had done or could do would have the slightest impact on the 'import gap'; it was Britain's industrial shortcomings that were 'at the heart of our nagging balance of payments situation'. But although he was clearly seeking to undermine Alec's argument that the economy was sound, it was equally clear that he was not advocating any change of course. Nor did the production index indicate any need to do so. There were even experts who thought the economy was not expanding fast enough, and some of them were to be found on the Labour benches.

The trade deficit for April was a considerable disappointment, a deficit of £55 million, and the figure for June was worse. It was evident that we were in for a long hot summer, and hot it certainly was. Britain basked in sunshine; the temperature was continually up in the seventies and eighties. Good weather brings good temper and contentment can follow. That certainly seemed to be the case in 1964. There were four by-elections in May and two in June. We were defending four seats and, slightly to my own surprise, lost only one.

Robert Roosa, the American Treasury's Under-Secretary, visited London early in May. He was worried that the uncertainties surrounding sterling could be aggravated by the forthcoming election, fears that were all too real, but it was also evident that he thought he would be dealing with a Labour Chancellor at its conclusion. At that stage I thought he was right. I explained my strategy in some detail. The economy had been enfeebled by a series of credit squeezes and I was determined not to repeat the dose. Provided that I could pull the economy through the early phases of expansion, when there was bound to be strain, I was confident that it would break through to a new plateau of expansion and that exports would accelerate to bring the economy back into balance. In the mean time there were reserves to cover the deficit and once productivity improved, we would be embarked upon a virtuous circle, replacing the vicious circle engendered by past deflation.

Roosa's strongest point was the absence of wage and price stability, but there too I knew the score. I could only say that I would hope to make headway with the unions once the election was behind us. In the mean time I could point to the undeniable fact that funds were accruing to the sterling balances and the reserves were actually increasing. I arranged for Roosa to see Callaghan – I think he was considerably impressed that I should do so – ostensibly so that he could explain the Anglo-American swap arrangements that underpinned sterling, and Callaghan duly reassured the Americans that a Labour government would not devalue the pound. Roosa scarcely needed to tell me that he thought we should make similar swap arrangements with the European countries, but I knew the Bank of England was not keen on the idea. The Governor, Lord Cromer, felt that he could do better for us if his hands were not tied. It was not until 16 July that the pound fell below $2.79, the first time it had done so since 1961, and the Federal Reserve stepped in, buying $54 million worth of sterling, and it bought again in August to help the spot rate against European currencies.

The first sign that the strategy I was pursuing might face political trouble came with the TUC conference. Characteristically, when speaking to them in Blackpool, Harold Wilson tried to have it both ways. Quite erroneously he announced that the trade gap 'means a deficit on our current balance of payments of £500 million a year'. Quite wrong, it was never thought more than £400 million, and even that figure was later revised downward. But, more helpfully, he then went on to say, 'This does not mean that I believe that we are necessarily facing an immediate financial crisis – a crippling run on sterling.' It remains a curious reflection on the consistency and good sense of the Opposition that in the debates on the budget, Jim Callaghan made the case that I was being too cautious, but a very different story was told when we came to the election.

The problem was clearly not with the economy but with the Conservative recovery that had accompanied the success of my economic policies. That recovery took us into the lead in the opinion polls for the first time since 1961 and it did so just at the moment when the election had to be called. For the first time I began to believe that we might achieve victory and be the party that broke free from the shackles that had hitherto prevented the country from achieving a faster rate of growth. It was scarcely a surprise, however, to find that the Opposition did not look forward to that prospect with undiluted joy.

The first sign that they might use the balance of payments to scare the electorate came with a speech by Harold Wilson at Ipswich. It was little noticed and I began to hope that we might get through the election unscathed. But George Brown had other ideas in mind. I did not see his broadcast myself – politicians in elections are far too busy to watch their opponents on television – but my aides told me that it was devastating. Not for the last time I reflected that George Brown half-cut could be more devastating than Harold Wilson sober. Our upward surge was halted. The election hung in the balance.

Alec was having a good campaign, however. Wisely he had decided to concentrate on subjects that he knew well and while arguments about the deterrent were not likely to swing many votes, he gave out a convincing aura of confidence. Only once was he rocked by hecklers and even then the occasion turned to our advantage; neither the press nor the public liked the thought that an election could so easily be turned into a bear garden. I have often thought that if the coup against Khrushchev in Russia had come only a day sooner, Alec would have positioned himself to reap full electoral advantage. As it was, we had one of the most thrilling election races of all time, rivalling, perhaps surpassing, the election at which I was first returned to the Commons in February 1950.

The first result that flashed up on the television screen in the Savoy, where I was watching the results at Lady Pamela Berry's party, came as a shock. We had held Cheltenham, but with a sharply reduced majority. But then came Billericay, an immense Essex seat full of new housing and middle-income suburbanites, just the kind of seat that Labour had to win. There was a recount, but at 10.30 came the news that we had held it comfortably, by 1,592 votes. It was then clear that we were in the race. There was a sorry trail of Conservative defeats to come, but we had much fat to lose and there were some dramatic, if narrow victories. In Central London Lena Jeger failed to retake her seat from Geoffrey Johnson Smith and just before midnight came the shock news of Patrick Gordon Walker at Smethwick, evidently but unfortunately the result of our candidate's controversial stance on race. This was not altogether welcome news, but it was the first of a series of results from the West Midlands that spelt out bad news for Labour. Dr Wyndham Davies took Perry Barr in Birmingham and we held on to both Yardley and All Saints in the same city. On the edge of the Black Country, Philip Lugg captured Oldbury and Halesowen. South East Derbyshire was another closely fought contest in which we hung on after several recounts, and early the following afternoon we learnt that Gordon Matthews had held on to Meriden. That, and Brecon and Radnor, were the final crushing blows that ensured us a narrow, but as it turned out a decisive, victory. Churchill had told me before the 1951 election that one was enough, but we had worried then about a majority of seventeen. Now we had to survive on a majority of six.

Alec had not taken anything for granted, but the work of a Prime Minister goes on. There were arrangements to be made for the transition of Northern Rhodesia into the independent state of Zambia and telegrams were speeding to and fro between Downing Street and Salisbury about the future of Southern Rhodesia. Sandys and Dilhorne, who were deeply involved in the discussions, stayed on afterwards for a celebratory drink. I joined them since I was anxious to take stock with Alec of how best to deal with the slight run on the pound that had developed as a result of Labour's campaigning.

By four that afternoon, it was clear that we had won and that the Labour Party's gamble with the country's future had failed. Confirmed in office, Alec's first thought was to invite me to continue at the Treasury and, almost in the same breath, he asked whether we could still deliver on our dash for growth. We had both been told that the deficit was running abnormally high, although I had forcibly rebutted the idea put about by the Labour Party that when considering the deficit on the balance of payments, the deficit on the capital account should be added to that on current account. Hence the charge that the problem we faced was an £800 million gap. We were doubly unlucky that both accounts had moved into deficit together and there were some quite fortuitous elements – the sale of Montecatini Oil, for example – which had worsened the picture. It was not until after the election that my advisers actually mentioned so high a figure for the total deficit. Inevitably there was some discussion of whether we should resort to import controls or even float the pound. Sir Donald MacDougall was in favour of doing the latter, but he was alone amongst my advisers in suggesting such a step. Since we had financed the deficit without difficulty so far, I saw no reason to abandon the growth strategy prematurely. Armstrong and Cairncross agreed, although the latter pointed to the need to address the strain being put on the balance of payments by the government's determination to maintain its defence commitments east of Suez.

I took the point. The most rudimentary comparison of our position in 1964 with the crisis Rab had faced in 1955 suggested that there was no sign that the pound was in fundamental disequilibrium. If one takes the years 1953–55 and compares them with 1962–64, there was no worsening of the trade position, nor any increase in net private long-term investment abroad. What had gone wrong was the increase in the government's net current expenditures and loans abroad, and that was the problem we needed to tackle. It had been masked in 1962 and 1963 by unusually favourable figures for the balance of trade and private investment. But it did not seem to me that there was any sign of a worsening trend in the relation of imports to exports, and I was still confidently expecting the latter to rise in response to the expansionary course I had set. There was no case that I could see for an early resort to import controls, and none at all for devaluation. My only worry was the figure for currency withdrawals in September. While it would be right, therefore, to send a signal to the markets about our determination to defend the value of the pound, it was equally important not to suggest any sign of panic. In the end it seemed best to prepare a White Paper setting out the facts – that there was no sign that the domestic situation was getting out of hand – and to preface it with a rise in Bank Rate that would be announced on the following Thursday. When Alec asked whether it would not be best to act immediately, I replied that I thought it important to adhere to the convention that such changes were always made on a Thursday. Anything else would imply a degree of nervousness that would give the markets the jitters.

Callaghan had offered during the election campaign to join me in a statement ruling out devaluation. Although I admired the patriotism that inspired the gesture, I thought it might be counterproductive and told him so. I was somewhat surprised, therefore, when, in the debate on the Address, Wilson sought to charge us with running an £800 million deficit. No doubt he felt that we might be forced to go to the country sooner rather than later, although he might have remembered that Attlee had been able to govern for nineteen months with a majority no larger than ours. In reply I was able to point to his own words earlier in the year, correct his figure, and demonstrate that there was no sign of overheating in the economy to justify us in reversing our course. I argued that it would be right to raise Bank Rate a point as a temporary measure, but I was confident that export growth would soon show and that we would be back on our way to the black. A White Paper, skilfully put together by William Armstrong, suitably reinforced our case and I was fortunate, perhaps, that a searching examination of trade statistics revealed that they were in error and that we were in a rather better position than either I or my Labour opponents had thought.

More important still, the return of a Conservative government, rather than the Labour government the markets had anticipated, was in itself sufficient to ease any strain on sterling, and thanks to the efforts of Lord Cromer and his fellow central bankers, I was able to announce that if we needed to borrow temporarily to sustain sterling, they would ensure that we could do so. The announcement was enough to scare off any speculators – they were not then either as numerous or powerful as they have since become. Any incoming Labour government would have been in a much worse plight. However skilful they were in handling the economy, there would have been suspicions that many in their ranks would be happy to devalue the pound, and the slight run on sterling that had developed as the result of the election campaign, instead of being checked, might have become far worse. It may be unfair, but a Conservative government has always reaped the benefit of being trusted to maintain the value of the pound. We had had no difficulty in financing the deficit in the first nine months of the year and we anticipated rightly that we would have few problems in doing so until the balance of payments came right.

I was determined, however, to tackle the strain that we, as a government, were putting on the balance of payments. Many of our loans to the Commonwealth were tied to exports. The problem therefore lay with defence expenditure overseas, and I was determined to reduce and eventually eliminate our commitments east of Suez. Not for me Wilson's vainglorious boast, when there was trouble between India and China, that Britain's frontiers were no longer to be found on the Rhine but on the Himalayas! That was the language of opposition. Of course the Conservative Party was uncomfortable with the reductions I proposed for the Navy, more particularly my decision not to proceed with a new carrier. The RAF proved staunch allies in that fight, however; in fact they were so keen on my policy that I was warned that they had, more than once, bent the geographical facts in their favour.

The timing was a little awkward. We had first to bring the Indonesian conflict to an end, but I then took drastic action to cut back our forces. Somewhat to my surprise I had backing not only from Duncan Sandys, who had wanted to do something similar when at Defence, but of Enoch Powell, not normally an ally of mine, although a good friend.

It was a policy that might well have been taken amiss by the United States but for the good relationship that Alec had built up with Dean Rusk. I was able to make the point that our contribution to the stability of the Bretton Woods system, which had served us so well since the war, was of much greater value than our presence east of Suez. Reluctantly the President and his advisers conceded that if that was genuinely the choice, I was right; while they contested the necessity of making such a choice, promising massive assistance to maintain the pound, they did not in the end press their point. Perhaps they hoped to draw us into supporting their defence of southern Vietnam, but Alec was too shrewd to see any value in being drawn into that quagmire. Peter Thorneycroft, who might well have opposed the moves I was making, was briefly out of the House. However, if he had continued at Defence, I would have taken some pleasure in reminding him of the arguments he had used against Sandys when Chancellor in 1957. I had no need to do so.

Not altogether to my surprise, I found a good ally in the Foreign Secretary. Duncan Sandys and I had fought some bruising battles over Africa and were on opposite flanks of the party; nor did I share his enthusiasm for European unity. I also felt for Rab when Alec despatched him ruthlessly to the Mastership of Trinity College. It has proved a congenial occupation, but one that scarcely stretched his talents. Nevertheless I had to admit that Rab's indiscretions during the campaign might have cost us victory. Alec had no difficulty in identifying his successor. Heath was committed to regional development and had no wish to move. Duncan Sandys had been a possible choice when Alec was appointed and his knowledge of the European political scene was very considerable.

Duncan had long been conscious, first as Minister of Supply and then as Harold Macmillan's hatchet-man at Defence, of the burdens placed on the British economy by our overseas defence commitments. While he argued the case with the Americans, his close friend, Geoffrey Rippon, who took Thorneycroft's place at Defence, was a staunch ally in my fight to rein in naval expenditure. I was left to reflect on the chance that only a few votes at Norwich South had prevented him from following Thorneycroft into temporary political exile. The decision cost us a Navy minister, and I cannot say that our backbenchers were happy, but our majority was too small for them to risk much, and the Navy themselves took some consolation that they were now the vanguard of our nuclear strategy.

If this was a major feature of my life in the run-up to Christmas 1964, it did not distract me from my central concern with the economy. Fortunately I had no need to take any further action. The deficit had peaked in the third quarter at £192 million. When the figures for the fourth quarter became available, the deficit had fallen to under £100 million and in the spring the long-expected upturn in exports began. The deficit began to shrink markedly and by the second half of 1965, the balance of payments was in surplus. 1966 was even more successful. With growth still running at 4 per cent, we were able to contemplate the expansion of public expenditure that had taken place in the run-up to the 1964 general election with comparative equanimity.

More to the point, the trade unions began to see sense. Although their defeat had been narrow, the Labour Party found a good deal to squabble about, and the continued economic prosperity made it likely that when we next took the verdict of the electorate, we would increase our majority. I had made overtures to the unions about a voluntary incomes policy shortly after the election, but it was not until our success with the balance of payments was apparent that they began to see the virtue of coming to terms. Frank Cousins did his best to resist the idea, but we managed to draw them into round-table discussions and eventually negotiated a voluntary agreement between both sides of industry in the autumn of 1965. It covered both pay and prices, and was the very move that Harold Macmillan had wanted to make nine years earlier. Within the framework of NEDC, I created a pay and relativities board to look into cases referred to it. In a climate of growth, I anticipated its success, although I have to admit that I was surprised at how quickly its prestige built up. Perhaps that had something to do with my inspired choice of George Brown to head it.

I had long seen a successful incomes policy as the answer to the problems posed by the success of Keynesian policies in creating conditions of full employment, although I have to admit that I did not foresee the boost that it gave to trade union power and arrogance. When at the end of my Prime Ministership, the whole world was plunged into chaos by what has since been described as the great oil shock, politics became very difficult. I have to confess that I was reluctant to see the need for very different economic policies, but I came to the conclusion that it was necessary to bring the trade unions within the ambit of the law. However, that story and its consequences must be left to the second volume of these memoirs.

For the moment I have to record that the government's record of economic success enabled it to go to the country in June 1966 with every prospect of winning a crushing victory. It was a triumph made still more certain by Alec's brilliant conduct of the negotiations with Ian Smith. The decision to ask the Duke of Edinburgh to take post temporarily as Governor was a master stroke, and I have never admired the Queen more than I did when she agreed to the step. What might have been a serious and costly crisis was averted. No Rhodesian servicemen would contemplate an act of rebellion, whatever Smith might have hoped, and he saw the wisdom of settling for a suitably modified version of the 1961 constitution.

For my own part, I could plan the budgets of both 1965 and 1966 with the certainty that I could achieve that unique four-hander: reductions in direct taxation; increases in public expenditure on housing, schools and health, with the prospect of a major expansion in higher technical education; a growing surplus on the balance of payments; and the prospect that I might begin to ease the country towards the virtuous circle of debt reduction.

Not surprisingly, I was at the peak of my form and popularity. I could look forward with confidence to the time when Alec would call it a day. I had agreed with my close friend, Iain Macleod, that we would not fight one another for the succession, and while I knew that both Heath and Powell would put their hats into the ring, I was rightly confident that I was now Alec's heir-apparent. From time to time, Enoch would grumble that he had thought we were the party of economic liberalism and that the economy would eventually be strangled by the corporatist arrangements I had made. There was perhaps more force in his case than I cared to acknowledge at the time. But in Cabinet those arguments made no headway against the obvious success of my policies and Enoch busied himself with the task that Alec had given him of reshaping Whitehall.

I have often reflected in retirement on how, if a few votes had been cast differently on 15 October 1964, there might have been a very different outcome for both the country and the Conservative Party, and I suppose it is possible that it might have prevented me from succeeding Alec as leader of the party and Prime Minister. Our success justified the turn towards planning that Macmillan engineered in 1961–62 and made it inevitable that the corporatist arrangements so common on the continent would become the norm here also. Instead of lagging behind the European economies, we began to compete on level terms and that lessened the pressure to enter the EEC.

Although I was never myself the most enthusiastic of Common Marketeers, I accepted that it was right, once de Gaulle had gone, to resume the negotiations broken off in 1963 and to entrust them to Duncan Sandys' successor, Edward Heath. But that is a matter for the next volume of my memoirs. Had Macmillan not asked me to preside over Britain's 'dash for growth', I might not be able to look back at the years in which Britain achieved continental rates of economic growth with the degree of personal satisfaction that I now feel. It is only fair to attribute the shaping of the strategy to him and to my ill-fated predecessor Selwyn Lloyd. It was left to me to implement the strategy and to steer it through the inevitable bumpy period of pressure on sterling before we could move into the calmer waters of the late sixties.

Chapter 9

What if Harold Wilson and the unions had agreed *In Place of Strife*?

Robert Taylor

The day 18 June 1969 was the most important date in the transformation of British trade unionism. Thanks to the painstaking
work of Labour Prime Minister Harold Wilson, and his indefatiga-
ble Employment and Productivity Secretary, Barbara Castle, a historic agreement had been reached on that day with the Trades Union
Congress that settled the long-term modernisation of the trade union
movement. For the first time in its history, the TUC agreed to an
ambitious and visionary reform programme to transform industrial
relations in the country.

Moreover, the deal had been reached with the positive and whole-
hearted help of newly elected left-wing union leaders – the General
Secretary of the Transport and General Workers' Union, Jack Jones,
and Hugh Scanlon, President of the Engineering Workers. They
were as delighted as the Prime Minister at the outcome of the mara-
thon negotiations. With the genial assistance of Vic Feather, who had
recently taken over from the intellectual George Woodcock as TUC
General Secretary, a national understanding, or concordat, emerged
that promised to provide the unions with a constructive and powerful
but independent role in the management of the country's industrial
relations. A Special Congress of the TUC was held at the Fairfield
Hall in Croydon a week later to endorse what had been agreed, and

it did so unanimously. A programme for action was also endorsed, setting out a timetable for the implementation of the full contents of the *In Place of Strife* White Paper that Harold Wilson and Barbara Castle had announced six months earlier.

In many important ways the national deal that came to be known as the Social Contract undoubtedly sought to placate the trade unions . Its avowed aim had always been to 'improve and strengthen collective bargaining'. The unions were given new legally enforceable rights that would enable them to win recognition from employers for bargaining purposes. A state-funded trade union development programme was also agreed that provided substantial financial assistance in the training and education of shop stewards and union officials. The newly formed and independent Commission on Industrial Relations paved the way for assistance in the often difficult process of union mergers and amalgamations. Moves were also made towards the creation of industrial democracy. Trade union representatives were able to join company boards and gain rights of access to information and consultation from firms on their strategic plans. Workers themselves, whether union members or not, were able to seek compensation as well as reinstatement if a tribunal found they were unfairly dismissed. The Social Contract also promised further constructive measures to improve the position of workers and trade unionists. It looked forward to the legal enforcement of equal pay for work of equal value for women, as well as laws to deal with gender and race discrimination in the workplace. After generations of insecurity and low status, manual workers were promised a New Deal that would end the class divide that made so many of them second-class industrial citizens.

Belatedly Britain was moving into line with what most Western European countries had achieved in the social settlements that followed the end of the Second World War. The government and the unions also acknowledged the establishment of a social dialogue in the running of the economy, involving an annual assessment of what the level of wage increases should be alongside price, profit and dividend targets. The move to the coordination of collective bargaining brought a return of strong industry-wide and sector agreements but the trade unions and employers also agreed to the formation of an independent pay comparability commission for the public services, preventing any damaging divergence in wage claims and rises between public- and private-sector workers.

Of course, this reform involved most trade unions having to shoulder new responsibilities in return for negotiated advances in their power in industry. The TUC's leaders accepted that for their part they had to play an active and constructive role in resolving many of the country's intractable industrial problems: low skills, stagnant productivity, demarcation lines and other restrictive labour practices that had held back economic performance for generations. The emerging imaginative and equitable national incomes policy based on the planned growth of real wages was an integral part of the new arrangement, and it meant trade unions training and restraining their shop stewards in the national interest. The unions had to accept the need for the full cooperation of their shop stewards in a reform of plant-level pay determination that acknowledged that improved living standards had to come from genuine productivity deals and pay rises that reflected what the economy as a whole could afford. In addition, the unions agreed on the need for the negotiation of formalised rules and procedures to prevent unofficial strikes, and the creation of elected consultative works councils and other forms of employee participation. This acknowledged the growth of a genuine social partnership at workplace level between capital and labour .

It was a vital if added bonus that the country's employers' associations were also ready to sign up to the Social Contract. The Confederation of British Industry agreed to reform its own internal structures, accepting the need to develop a more centralising role in requiring its affiliate companies to work in harmony with the unions.

This meant that firms accepted that their employees should become actively involved in company decision-making. It involved a determination to end the old sterile 'them and us' divisions that had been a severe obstacle to improved workplace performance in Britain since the Industrial Revolution. For the first time, employers were ready to acknowledge trade unions and workers as social citizens with a recognised and legitimate role to play in the running of the economy.

Of course, the Social Contract of 18 June 1969 was just the beginning of what amounted to a transformation in the country's industrial relations – one that turned Britain into a democratic, advanced political economy that could develop and reconcile economic efficiency with social justice. Some admirers called this approach the 'Third Way'. Certainly it marked a clean break with old Labourism. Under Harold Wilson the Labour movement had modernised itself. Moreover, it had done so with the full and active involvement of the trade unions. Jack Jones and Hugh Scanlon argued that they had not compromised their socialist values; on the contrary, to them the Social Contract brought a new and progressive legitimacy to trade-union power. It guaranteed greater workplace equity as well as a positive role for unions and workers in the running of companies and the economy.

In addition, the national agreement enabled a Labour government to develop a dynamic and innovative industrial strategy that enabled state support to pick industrial winners and make Britain a cutting-edge economy in research and development. The nationalised industries were turned into world-beaters with high productivity levels and substantial profits. The old stigma of state control in industry was lost. Even the Conservatives under Edward Heath embraced an active role for government in industrial management. The Social Contract had brought a wide and accepted consensus to the running of the political economy.

The negotiations that led to the historic agreement were not trouble-free. Harold Wilson and Barbara Castle had wanted to rush through legislation in what they called a short, sharp bill to impress overseas financial interests. This would have outlawed unconstitutional strikes, made procedure agreements legally binding and forced trade unions – under threat of fines – to discipline their shop stewards. Compulsory strike ballots would also have been introduced and thirty-day cooling-off periods enforced before workers could take lawful industrial action, with the threat of a detachment from earnings on those who went on strike in defiance of a ruling.

Trade union leaders stood firm, however, against any legislation concerned purely with the use of state coercion to bring about a more disciplined approach to industrial behaviour. They argued that the unions themselves were quite capable of exercising self-restraint, and that they should be trusted to carry out their side of any nationally agreed arrangement. Both Jones and Scanlon insisted that their own members, especially the increasingly powerful shop stewards, would not accept such state intervention in industrial relations. Both men disliked ideas of corporatism and an over-mighty state seeking to force workers and unions to act against their own interests. They insisted that the reform of industrial relations could only succeed if it went with the grain of workplace attitudes, and this in turn meant the achievement of positive cooperation. What needed to be done, they went on, was to remove the fears and insecurities felt by many workers in a system which invariably treated them as second-class citizens.

Demands for industrial democracy were gaining ground all over Western Europe at the end of the 1960s. In France and Italy workers had mobilised in militant action. Even in consensus-loving Sweden the trade union movement was starting to prepare plans for buying into private companies through collectively organised wage-earner funds. In this radical atmosphere it would be a terrible mistake for a Labour government to try and coerce the trade unions through penal legislation. But the union leaders also acknowledged that voluntary tripartism was no longer enough. The half-hearted efforts of the 1960s to establish a voluntary system of coordination based on the National Economic Development Council had failed to achieve much success. Voluntary deals without any sanctions would not be enough to act against the self-destructive but insatiable tendencies towards sectionalism that divided workers. Moreover, the maintenance of full employment and rising prices, coupled with skill shortages and increases in direct levels of taxation, were troubling but also strengthening the labour power of many workplaces. The dangers of fragmentation and a self-destructive individualism based on a perpetual and illusory drive for higher money wages were a threat to the cohesion and authority of the unions. The resulting crisis of representation was further undermining trade union cohesion.

Union leaders were therefore keen to persuade the government that if all the proposals in the *In Place of Strife* White Paper were implemented together, it would provide a better balance of rights and responsibilities that would address their own genuine problems as well as those of the state. After some weeks of intense negotiation Wilson and Castle saw the sense of dropping their proposal for a short, sharp bill, and instead accepted the positive offer of the TUC to back the whole package and not just parts of it.

In fact, it was the ever-imaginative Jack Jones who proposed further advances. He called for the creation of an independent and tripartite Advisory, Conciliation and Arbitration Service to replace the state's own service to deal with disputes and improve industrial relations practice. In addition, the health and safety at work laws were to be modernised and new workplace representatives were to ensure the tougher legislation was carried out. It was also agreed to press ahead with a more enlightened and active labour market strategy through the formation of a tripartite Manpower Services Board to modernise the job placement service and introduce positive programmes to deal with youth and long-term unemployment. It was accepted that those without a job should go on well-funded training and learning schemes to improve their employability, in line with the Swedish experience. No longer were workers to be left to the tender mercies of the labour market or to exist passively on inadequate benefits. Under the Social Contract, workers were to become industrial citizens with responsibilities as well as rights.

The Social Contract also promised a gradualist strategy for the extension of industrial democracy. It called for the nurturing of worker cooperatives, the introduction of works councils, the establishment of a learning and training fund for workers in new skills, and experiments in co-determination in the nationalised industries enabling unions and workers to make joint decisions with managers for the well-being of the enterprise. In addition, it was agreed that the state must take the initiative, with the consent of employers and trade unions, in the introduction of more humane plans for industrial restructuring. Redundancy payments were seen as an inadequate way to encourage labour mobility or ease the pain of job loss; instead, it was agreed that workers who were facing redundancy through no fault of their own must be assisted by a generous and active set of measures to boost training and ensure job replacement. By reducing the resistance to plant closures and supporting the workers affected in moving into newly created innovative enterprises, the government and the union leaders believed rightly that they could better equip the workforce for the need to embrace, rather than block, necessary industrial and social change. Even more importantly, this would remove the deep sense of insecurity that had led so many workers to become defensive and backward-looking in their attitudes to changes in the workplace.

In the spring of 1970 the TUC and the CBI joined government ministers in a world tour of industrialised countries to sell the proven benefits of what was already being described as the British Model. Thanks to the Social Contract based on the *In Place of Strife* White Paper, the country had become the envy of the world. Needless to say, the Labour Party won a sweeping election victory in June 1970. It was called by Harold Wilson the natural party of government, and the results of the next thirty years seemed to justify his assertion. Looking back from the year 2003, it can be seen that Labour found itself in office for almost the whole of the second half of the twentieth century. Among centre-left democratic parties, only the Swedish Social Democrats were to enjoy such an impressive record of political achievement. Indeed, Britain had taken the lead in the modernisation of social democracy, showing the way towards the creation of a successful country where economic efficiency went hand in hand with social justice.

But it was not just Labour's electoral successes that flowed inexorably from the agreement of 18 June 1969. More importantly, it ensured a strong and lasting alliance between Labour governments and the trade union movement that transformed the living standards and rights of working people. Trade unions became popular institutions once again. Workers joined them in their millions in response to the new, positive, role they were playing. Union density climbed to nearly 80 per cent of the workforce as a result, in line with the rates achieved in the Nordic countries. Moreover, trade unions became engines of change. They won over young workers in the new science-based industries, and made strong advances in the rising private services sector. Even more significantly, small firms found trade unions provided an important added value to their own performance. Slowly but surely, the concept of social partnership began to gain ground in the workplace.

Unions were also to benefit from the state funding they called upon to rationalise their own structures. They did not embrace industrial unionism, but the number of unions dropped dramatically over the next thirty years through a sensible strategy of mergers and acquisitions. Unions became less concerned with inter-union competitiveness and more interested in mutual agreements involving joint activities in the workplace. They turned into highly professional associations providing new services to improve the labour value of their members. They were also successful in training and nurturing new cadres of workplace activists, well-versed in the mysteries of corporate governance.

To their relief, the unions did not turn into highly centralised and disciplined arms of the corporate state. On the contrary, the Social Contract and the rolling programme of change that followed, was to strengthen workplace activism. Instead of becoming obstacles to progress, trade unions came to be seen as vital by employers in improving productivity and company performance. Share-ownership schemes and profit-based financial arrangements proved highly attractive in strengthening worker commitments. At the same time, the public service unions were transformed into valiant champions of the public interest, able not only to ensure that the wages and benefits of their members improved but also keen to stress their commitment to the consumers of public services. This revived public-interest ethic was appreciated by most people, who saw the unions as their allies in improving services in hospitals and schools. There was no need to introduce private money or sub-contract out public-service functions to profit-making companies. It was widely agreed that the public services sector was impressive in its performance, thanks both to generous but necessary state funding drawn from a progressive taxation system and a renewed workforce that was proud of, and respected for, its dedication.

Perhaps even more importantly, the 18 June 1969 settlement transformed the attitude of employers. Although they were not directly involved in the negotiations, their representatives were brought in during the later stages to hammer out the workplace programme of change in industrial relations. Historically they had rejected the concept of employer solidarity, seeing themselves as competitors in a free-ranging capitalism and looking suspiciously at state involvement in their affairs. But now these old attitudes changed; employers agreed to modernise themselves. The Confederation of British Industry widened its membership, while at the same time strengthening its central authority over affiliate firms and sectors.

Its involvement was crucial to the success of the British Model. Now a growing number of employers accepted the idea of the social market economy, agreeing to remove the instabilities and concerns of their employees through concerted action. The results came as a welcome surprise. Companies enjoyed rapid growth in productivity and their competitiveness on world markets improved dramatically. They became more keen to invest in research and development as well as skills and learning. The high-value and high-quality goods and services they provided set a benchmark for foreign competitors.

The transformation of industrial relations made a remarkable impact on overall corporate performance. Employers had become more socially responsible. Pressures from trade unions and the government meant that they dropped their old negative attitudes; now they saw the value of trusting and listening to their own employees. A genuine partnership emerged in many workplaces as the old self-destructive class-war attitudes of the past died away.

The 18 June 1969 settlement also made it easier to win national acceptance of Britain's entry into the European Economic Community. Initially many in the Labour movement had feared that such a move would weaken collectivist values and undermine industry. Now most people agreed that the country was well-equipped to take advantage of the wider European market as its industries grew ever-more competitive. The British industrial miracle had strengthened national self-confidence and released a spirit of endeavour not seen for generations. Membership of the EEC was no longer seen as a way to stimulate the country into necessary change, but a means to demonstrate the success of the British way in continental Europe.

Perhaps even more significantly, the Social Contract convinced the sceptical international financial community that Britain was no longer a problem economy in a globalising world. Overseas confidence in sterling was boosted. The balance of payments moved into surplus. Inflation was kept down. Public spending was prudently handled. Exports boomed, not on price advantage but because they were of a proven high quality and competitive on performance. For most of the post-war period successive British governments had suffered from periodic balance of payments crises. Now the old stop–go politics were at an end. Britain may no longer have been the world's banker but it was also no longer an international economic problem country. Trade union leaders and employers were able to convince overseas creditors , especially in the United States, that the British economy had been transformed.

This remarkable transformation had begun all those years ago, in 10 Downing Street, on 18 June 1969 – thanks to the wisdom and vision of Harold Wilson, Barbara Castle and an inspiring generation of union leaders and employers who saw how they could transform Britain into one of the most prosperous and socially equitable countries in the world as long as they agreed to work together in a common cause with the help of a benevolent state.

The vindication of what happened over thirty years ago came in 2003. Under the leadership of Denis Healey and then Roy Hattersley, the Labour Party had remained a civilising, centre-left force of conscience and reform. John Smith had proved a worthy successor to Healey in 1992. But now Labour looked to a substantial figure who had played a key role in the implementation of the Social Contract after June 1969. As a young man he had joined the TUC in that year as an enlightened Social Democratic moderniser. After becoming TUC General Secretary in September 1984, after the retirement of Len Murray, in 1992 he moved into political life to serve under John Smith. Although he had once thought that he ought to move to a job in the European Union, John Monks was now the newly elected Labour Prime Minister.

As he walked into 10 Downing Street, he must have reflected on the what ifs of history. None of this would have been possible if Harold Wilson and Barbara Castle had pushed ahead with their proposed measures to discipline the workers, refusing to make a lasting settlement with the trade unions. The nightmare would have meant nearly thirty years in the political wilderness for the Labour Party, as relentless political civil wars and electoral defeats tore the movement apart and led to a dramatic collapse in trade union strength and membership. Thankfully both sides had recoiled from the prospect of such a dreadful future, signing the Social Contract in the warmth of the Number 10 garden on that sunny day, 18 June 1969.

Chapter 10

What if Labour had won in 1970?

Greg Rosen[1]

On a hot June day in 1970, the UK went to the polls. The choice was characterised by maverick Tory Enoch Powell as one between a man with a pipe and a man with a boat.

The man with the pipe was Prime Minister Harold Wilson. Twice an election winner, he was confident of victory in his third contest. The man with the boat (or rather an ocean racing yacht) was Conservative Leader Edward Heath. He had already been beaten by Wilson once, in 1966, when Labour had secured a landslide election victory and an overall majority of ninety-six. That had been excused by his party: Heath had only just become leader, Labour had performed reasonably well since defeating Alec Douglas-Home's grouse-moor Tory government in 1964 but had been constrained by a majority of only four; Wilson had asked the public to trust him with a mandate for real change and he had got it.

Labour was now, said Wilson, the natural party of government. And the opinion polls appeared to confirm his confidence. Having trailed the Tories in the polls since April 1967, sometimes by as much as 25 percentage points during 1968 and 1969, Labour had regained several hundred seats at the local elections on 8 May 1970 with a swing large enough to re-elect the government with a majority of fifty. On 13 May Gallup gave Labour a lead of 7.5 per cent, and by June, indicated that only 13 per cent of people thought the Conservatives likely to win the election (down from 54 per cent in March) and

68 per cent expected Labour to win (up from 27 per cent in March). Labour MPs in marginal seats were confident. Despite all the troubles that had beset the Labour government – enforced devaluation and consequent spending cuts, the abandonment of *In Place of Strife*, the government's attempt to reform industrial relations, and the fiasco over Lords reform – Wilson's Government seemed to have recovered. Roy Jenkins, Chancellor of the Exchequer, appeared to have turned the economy round and the title of Labour's manifesto reflected a strategy designed to play upon this: *Now Britain's Strong, Let's Make it Great to Live In*.

Many, if not most, Conservative MPs expected defeat. In reality, of course, they won. Surprisingly bad trade figures for May, which raised questions about the solidity of Britain's economic recovery, England's defeat in the World Cup quarter-finals and a sudden newspaper strike may all have contributed to Labour's shock defeat. Wilson himself claimed that the hot weather and complacency caused by the predictions of the opinion polls led Labour voters to stay at home on polling day.

It is possible that all the polls were simply wrong. But if they were right, if the solid opinion-poll leads that Labour enjoyed right up until polling day were real, then the result could easily have been very different. Heath seemed irredeemably wooden during the campaign and did not appear to be able to catch the popular mood. And a considerable chunk of Conservative television and radio airtime was being hogged by Enoch Powell, who had for years nursed the grievance that he was not Tory leader.

In attempting to keep the flame of his leadership ambitions alive and gain the attention and applause of the Tory grassroots, since 1964 Powell had taken increasingly to speaking out in public contradiction of Conservative policy over a range of issues, to the fury of his Shadow Cabinet colleagues. Heath had finally sacked him from the Shadow Cabinet in 1968 over his racist 'Rivers of Blood' speech.

Powell's antipathy towards Heath and the Conservative Shadow Cabinet (who had applauded his sacking and would in many cases have resigned themselves had Heath not wielded the axe) was almost as prominent in the public eye as his new-found role as boot-boy pin-up. If they lost, the Conservative MPs who would choose a new leader knew who to blame: Heath, for his seeming inability to develop a rapport with the public, and Powell, for indulging his own frustrated leadership ambitions in the full glare of the media spotlight, to the detriment of the party's election campaign. They had already tried to give Heath a personality transplant, but it just did not seem to be working.

Even during the heat of the campaign, plans were laid and discussions took place amongst the Tory 'big beasts' about replacing Heath. While Conservative Shadow Chancellor Iain Macleod denied to friends that he would have another shot at the crown, Chief Whip Willie Whitelaw and deputy leader Reggie Maudling quietly arranged to rendezvous the day after polling day at the Hirsel, Scottish grouse-moor seat of former Conservative Leader Alec Douglas-Home. Douglas-Home had remained in active politics, serving as Heath's Shadow Foreign Secretary and then from 1966 Shadow Commonwealth Secretary. The challenge would be to pre-empt a Powell leadership bandwagon. If Heath did not resign he would have to be asked to. Douglas-Home was sounded out as a caretaker leader (or 'undertaker' leader as one grandee wag put it). He was reluctant – or at least he claimed to be. Hence the planned visit of Whitelaw and Maudling to the Hirsel to discuss the way forward.

There were several anti-Powell candidates available. Iain Macleod was the charismatic and intellectually driven favourite of the liberal media. A powerful debater, his popularity amongst Tory MPs was nevertheless less widespread than it might have been. Some would not forgive his refusal to serve under the newly elected party leader and Prime Minister Alec Douglas-Home in 1963, and his subsequent attack on the 'magic circle' of Tory grandees that had decided the leadership and kept the crown from Macleod's mentor Rab Butler. For others he was too liberal (particularly on issues like immigration, homosexuality, hanging and divorce) or simply too clever by half. The weakness of his base amongst Tory MPs, who made up the electorate, was perhaps the main reason that he ducked out of the first and only proper leadership election the Tories had had: the July 1965 three-way contest between Heath, Maudling and Powell. Macleod had backed Heath, who had polled 150 votes to Maudling's 133 and Powell's minimal 15.

Reginald Maudling, the deputy leader and Shadow Foreign Secretary had ballast and, while Heath's public persona was all too wooden, Maudling came across as a reassuringly comfortable armchair figure. The trouble was that Maudling's relaxed attitude to politics was becoming ever more so. Not the most energetic campaigner, he had accepted several City directorships and was said to be spending more time indulging a growing love affair with the bottle. Question marks hung over whether he had either the ambition or the stamina to be an opposition leader for a potential five-year slog. Quintin Hogg, Shadow Home Secretary, was colourful but had never quite recovered from his humiliating failure to secure the leadership in 1963. He was also ten years older than Heath and Maudling and would be nearly seventy by the end of another full parliamentary term.

Then there was Whitelaw himself, Chief Whip since 1964, with an avuncular personality and wide appeal across the party. He was close to Heath, who valued his loyalty, but he was also popular with the Tory Knights of the Shires who might have wanted Heath replaced with an acceptable non-Powellite Tory trusty. A wild card was Edward du Cann, former Tory Chairman and Trade Minister 1963–64; he was ambitious and lacked Whitelaw's ties of loyalty to Heath. Like Whitelaw he had no experience of serving in Cabinet, but unlike Whitelaw he and Heath enjoyed a mutual antipathy. Since

1967 he had been a backbencher, having stepped down as Party Chairman to spend more time pursuing his interests in the City. But he lacked Whitelaw's broad appeal: neither his City interests nor his anti-Common Market inclinations played well with leadership-loyal backbenchers.

There would be further issues too, in particular whether Heath would stand down voluntarily or whether a leadership contest would have to be forced, either by Powell or by Heath's allies to pre-empt Powell. This would probably depend on the scale of Labour's victory. A Labour majority of, say fifty seats, as polls were predicting, would ostensibly have enabled Labour to carry on for a full term and would have both encouraged Heath's resignation and Tory MPs to choose a younger successor. A Labour minority government, or one with a single-figure majority, could mean another election sooner rather than later. It would have made a leadership contest destabilising, and might have enabled Heath to carry on.

Whitelaw would have a crucial role in persuading Heath to fall on his sword. Much depended on him as the widely trusted Chief Whip; as Margaret Thatcher would later say about the man who had become by then her own loyal and trusted Deputy Leader: 'Everybody needs a Willie.' However, whether Whitelaw would have been prepared to force Heath out remains an open question. Time and again in later years he was deputed to communicate the collective concerns of the so-called 'Tory wets' in Thatcher's Cabinet to the Prime Minister and demand policy concessions. And time and again he would return to his colleagues having found himself unable to go through with it. 'The trouble with Willie is that he has no balls', recollected a despairing colleague.[2]

While the man with the boat tried to persuade his colleagues that it was not sinking, the man with the pipe prepared for another spell in office. Frustrating and exhausting as the office of Prime Minister could be, it did give Harold Wilson the opportunity to indulge himself in one of his favourite pastimes, Cabinet reshuffles, a hobby for which he believed himself to have a special genius. Wilson confided his intentions to a number of close colleagues as the anticipated election victory approached.

He promised his Chancellor Roy Jenkins the Foreign Office. Of all his Cabinet members, Jenkins had the pro-European pedigree closest to rivalling that of Heath. Wilson and his Government were committed to following through their application for EEC membership, and Wilson knew that the credibility of his previous attempt to sound out the Common Market over potential UK membership had been undermined by the Labour Party's anti-EEC record under not only himself but Gaitskell and Attlee. He did not want to suffer the humiliation of a further French *non*. Even with the departure of de Gaulle, it was by no means certain that a French veto might not recur – a risk that having Jenkins as Foreign Secretary would help minimise. It would also appeal to Jenkins' sense of his own place in history. He would be the Foreign Secretary who realised his European dream; and, moreover, with Rab Butler and John Simon, one of the few twentieth-century politicians to occupy all three traditional great offices of state (Treasury, Foreign Office and Home Office). In the event it would be Jenkins' great rival Jim Callaghan who would manage this feat, on top of securing the premiership itself.

Moving Jenkins meant moving the existing Foreign Secretary, the able but unflamboyant Michael Stewart. Now aged sixty-three, Stewart had already been Wilson's Foreign Secretary twice, brought in to mind the shop on the resignations of Patrick Gordon Walker and then George Brown. A pro-NATO and pro-European Gaitskellite like Jenkins, and indeed like Gordon Walker and Brown, Stewart lacked their leadership aspirations, having instead a commitment to team-play uncharacteristic of Labour Cabinet members of that era. Stewart had always been prepared to let Wilson take the limelight and Wilson calculated that he would loyally put up with being shunted

from the Foreign Office yet again, perhaps encouraged by a promise of becoming one of Britain's first European Commissioners once
EEC entry was secured.

He planned to make Stewart Leader of the House of Commons
in place of the Euro-sceptic centre-right Wilson loyalist Fred Peart,
whom he planned to shift to defence. Defence, he told Jenkins, had
experienced a strong minister for sufficiently long (Denis Healey
since 1964) that it could do with a weak one who would please the
generals. Healey himself, whose real ambition was to be Foreign Secretary, was to replace Jenkins as Chancellor. Wilson also suggested he
considered recalling from the backbenches his bright young protégé
Dick Marsh, whose uneven performance in Cabinet and penchant
for witticism at the expense of his chief had got him sacked in 1969.
Further changes would have resulted from Dick Crossman's decision
(of which Wilson had yet to be informed) to retire as Secretary of
State for Health and Social Services after the election and take the
editorship of the *New Statesman*. The seventy-year-old Lord Chancellor, Lord Gardiner, was also unlikely to have wanted to continue
in post much longer. The fact that Stewart and the Gaitskellite Treasury Chief Secretary Jack Diamond would both turn sixty-five by
1972–73 hinted at further vacancies in the future. This would have
meant an early Cabinet debut for Elwyn Jones as Lord Chancellor,
and potentially for the popular Shirley Williams, for talented young
Gaitskellite Treasury minister Dick Taverne, or for Reg Prentice, then
thought of as a centrist figure, who in opposition was to top the poll
in the 1972 Shadow Cabinet elections.

Had Labour won, Jenkins would have been in an incredibly strong
position. As the Chancellor who had turned the economy around,
who had rebuilt Labour's economic credibility, and thereby underpinned Labour's election victory, he would have become Wilson's
heir-apparent. Jenkins craved the premiership. Wilson knew this and
played on it when he told Jenkins that he would retire either at the

Labour Conference in October 1972, or shortly after 14 June 1973, by which time he would have been in office longer than Asquith, and the longest-serving Prime Minister of the twentieth century.

Whether Jenkins would have succeeded to the crown remains one of the great unknowns of history. Undoubtedly the great Euro-split and his rebellion over the Common Market vote and resignation as Shadow Chancellor and Deputy Leader in 1972 did irreparable damage to his chances when Wilson eventually did resign in 1976. For all his talents, Jenkins became tarred with the brush of splitting the party and voting with the Tories (or, as his supporters argued, keeping true to his principles and Labour's manifesto). Some said it cost him a good twenty to thirty first-preference votes in the eventual leadership election, votes that instead went to Callaghan as a unity figure. Although as Foreign Secretary Jenkins would still have been seen as a partisan figure in a Labour Party by no means homogeneous in its views on Europe, he would have been in a far better position to apply the charge of disloyalty to his critics than they to him.

Nonetheless, Jenkins was already seen by some MPs as aloof, as being more at home amongst the leather chesterfields of Brooks's Club in St James than amongst the workers of, say, Chesterfield, or even amongst Labour MPs in the Commons Tea Room. This perception might have been increased by a spell at the Foreign Office. His admirers included earthy trade unionists of the calibre of Frank Chapple and independent-minded maverick MPs like John P. Mackintosh. But his social circle became increasingly a devoted band of invariably Oxford-educated and London-based intellectuals (dubbed the FORJ – Friends of Roy Jenkins). For Labour MPs of socialist conviction it was also a matter of suspicion that the book of which as an author Jenkins was proudest was his elegant biography of the Liberal Prime Minister H. H. Asquith, rather than his biography of Attlee, to whom his father had been Parliamentary Private Secretary. His potential undoing amongst fellow Labour Parliamentarians was not so much the impression that Jenkins was not 'one of us' but the feeling that he didn't quite want to be. When a fellow MP suggested to Nye Bevan that Roy Jenkins was lazy, it is said that he replied: 'No boy from the valleys who has cultivated that accent could possibly be called lazy!'[3]

Many MPs on the pro-European social-democratic right of the party, such as Roy Mason or Joel Barnett, although they admired Jenkins' abilities, warmed far more to James Callaghan as a potential leader (or in Barnett's case to Denis Healey). In 1972 Callaghan was a weaker figure than in 1976. He had undergone a prostate operation at the beginning of the year and, although popular with the unions and secure as Party Treasurer, his reputation had still not fully recovered from his troubled time as Chancellor. And as Home Secretary (assuming he had not been moved) he would have been having a tough time dealing with Northern Ireland. Nevertheless, his popularity amongst Labour MPs was sufficient for him to top the poll in the 1970 and 1973 Shadow Cabinet elections.

Denis Healey, the other likely candidate of the social-democratic right, had admirers but lacked the cultivated Parliamentary base of either Jenkins or Callaghan. A loner by instinct, he simply did not nurture one. When he did run in 1976 his key supporters were essentially his Treasury team and his PPS. Moreover, the ability of his pugilistic personality to give affront to potential supporters did not help. He would also have suffered from having been Defence Secretary during Vietnam: he lacked both the support of liberal, pro-European MPs (and the liberal media) enjoyed by Jenkins and the traditional trade-union right enjoyed by Callaghan. As Chancellor, his profile would have grown, but in the troubled economic circumstance that were the reality of the early 1970s, it might not have enhanced his popularity either with the public, the unions or Labour MPs. Tony Crosland, not then yet a heavyweight Cabinet figure and enjoying a far lower public profile and popularity than Jenkins, Callaghan or Healey, would hardly have got beyond the starting blocks.

The other challenge to a Jenkins premiership would have been from the left. In 1972–73 Barbara Castle might well have stood (by 1976 she was sixty-five), but with her popularity heavily damaged by the fiasco over *In Place of Strife*, she would undoubtedly have lost. Peter Shore, still operating very much in Wilson's shadow, was not yet a heavyweight figure. Michael Foot was still a backbencher; only after Labour's 1970 election defeat did he stand and secure election to the Shadow Cabinet. He had hitherto declined office and the collective responsibility it implied, enjoying the freedom of the backbenches to campaign for unilateral nuclear disarmament and against government support for the war in Vietnam and potential UK membership of the EEC. After 1970 increasing age helped him reassess his position, but the fact that Labour was in opposition made things easier; he could secure election to the Shadow Cabinet on his own terms. If Labour remained in government after 1970, the likelihood is that in 1972–73 Foot would still have been a backbench rebel, vocal, passionate, but not a credible leadership contender. Labour MPs at that time would never have made Prime Minister someone entirely lacking in government experience. The bottom line was that had Labour won in 1970, the majority of its MPs would have backed a loyalist Gaitskellite candidate to succeed Wilson such as Jenkins, Callaghan or Healey, rather than a candidate of the left. And whatever the views of Jack Jones, Hughie Scanlon and left-wing constituency activists, it was the MPs who had the power to make that choice.

The power of Jones, Scanlon and the left-wing constituency activists was nevertheless considerable – and it was growing. Jack Jones had led the giant Transport and General Workers' Union (TGWU) since 1969 in succession to the left-wing and pro-CND Frank Cousins. With more than 1.5 million members, it was Britain's largest union and as its leader Jones had the largest block vote at Labour Party

Conference. Scanlon became President of Britain's second largest union, the 1.2 million strong Amalgamated Union of Engineering Workers (AUEW) in 1967. A former Communist, Scanlon got swiftly to work in changing the political stance of the union. His predecessor, Bill Carron, had been a notably loyal supporter of the Labour leadership. In an oblique reference to the Prague Spring, Wilson was soon forced to demand: 'get your tanks off my lawn, Hughie'.[4] Dubbed the 'terrible twins' by the right-wing tabloids for their role in torpedoing Labour's attempt to reform industrial relations in *In Place of Strife,* Scanlon and Jones were powerful advocates of their members' aspirations for better wages and conditions. And aspirations their members had by the bucket-load, for the 'New Britain' that Harold Wilson had promised that the hundred-seat majority the electorate had given him in 1966 would enable him to deliver.

The trouble was, they hadn't got it and they weren't getting it. The economic mess that Labour had inherited from the Conservatives in 1964 had led to a currency crisis, consequent stringency with the public purse, a botched devaluation in 1967 and further cuts. In the private sector, decades of under-investment, poor management and outdated working practices meant inadequate productivity, and often inadequate products, in the face of growing foreign competition. Labour had sought to improve the situation but it was an uphill struggle. Too often the mergers and reorganisations sponsored by the Industrial Reorganisation Corporation replaced small loss-making companies with larger loss-making companies. And that meant jobs facing the axe.

Even the success stories risked running into trouble. Rolls-Royce would still have needed bailing out by a Labour government in November 1970 and early 1971, not because of governmental failures or lack of British enterprise but because of the immense cost of developing new high-tech products and the protectionist attitude of America, the main potential market for its superb new engine, the

RB–211. The RB–211 eventually lived to become an extremely successful British export, but to break into the US market had required Rolls–Royce to sign a contract with Lockheed on punitive commercial terms which threatened Rolls–Royce with bankruptcy when the revolutionary technology the new engine utilised took longer to develop than had been allowed for. Rolls–Royce employed 80,000 workers, and a further 20,000 British jobs outside the company depended on the RB–211. Collapse and mass redundancy was unthinkable, and a multi–million pound bail–out or nationalisation were the only alternatives.

Everything was compounded by the confrontational culture of UK industrial relations, so effectively caricatured in the seminal film *I'm All Right, Jack*. The well-upholstered boss class had grown fat on the seed–corn it had eaten rather than invested during the 1950s. The workers wanted their share too and were often equally reluctant to embrace the modern technology that would have replaced workers' jobs in the short term but preserved the remaining jobs in the long term. Containerisation at the ports was resisted by the dockers for just this reason. This meant that demands for better wages were often linked to a reluctance to improve productivity, making industry less competitive and potentially driving it to the wall.

Pay increases without productivity increases were also potentially inflationary, and the tendency for rising consumer prosperity to suck in imports did nothing for the balance of payments situation, adding further to inflationary pressures. But pay restraint was difficult to achieve. For a start, between 1967 and 1970 the threshold for paying income tax at the standard rate was lowered by a third, squeezing take-home pay. Differentials in a number of industries were being eroded by technology; disputes could break out over relative pay rates and conditions between different trades within an industry. Militant union activists could and did tell the rank and file that more could be squeezed out of the bosses if only they squeezed hard enough. There was no legal requirement for unions to hold a secret ballot before strike action; there was not even a legal requirement to hold a secret ballot before electing a trade union's leader. Power rested with the activist shop stewards, a role that could too easily be hijacked by the militant minority. The opportunity to reform industrial relations had been thrown away with the badly handled debacle of *In Place of Strife*. No Labour Leader wanted to go through that again. A post-1970 Labour government would have done what the 1974–79 government sought to do, building a 'social contract' with union leaders to enlist their support for future pay restraint (though it is likely that both Jones and Scanlon would, at least initially, have rejected an incomes policy) and against pressure from the left both in their own unions and on Labour's NEC for more nationalisation.

However, economic conditions risked creating the same vicious circle for a post-1970 Labour government as they did in reality for Heath. Likewise, the problems with Chrysler, with Upper Clyde Shipbuilders, with dollar devaluation, with the shock quadrupling of oil prices in 1973 and the increase in commodity prices would have hit Britain, and a Labour government, as hard as they hit Heath. A Labour government might even have used the petrol rationing coupons that under the Heath Government were merely printed. Inflation, growing unemployment and balance of payments problems would have been the lot of a Labour Chancellor in 1974 just as it was for Heath's Chancellor Anthony Barber, though probably not quite so badly (Barber's tax-cutting budgets and his removal of restrictions on bank lending made things worse by stoking up a credit boom which went largely into property and imported consumer goods).

Even moderate trade union leaders had difficulties restraining their more militant activists, and containing the frustration of their members who felt that they risked losing out in the wage-price spiral if they did not make a grab for their share of the pie. The miners, for example, were led throughout this period, indeed until 1982, by Joe

Gormley, a pillar of the trade-union right wing. During the miners' pay disputes of the early 1970s, support for industrial action was solid across the pits, giving 'flying pickets' the opportunity to leave the pits and picket the coke depots. And it was in orchestrating the flying pickets that Arthur Scargill made his name – undoubtedly he would have done so under a Labour government too. Likewise, the rail union pay claim in 1972 that brought such trials and tribulations to Heath's Government would have given the same problems to Labour. It was not led by militants but by the moderate-led Transport Salaried Staffs' Association (TSSA) and National Union of Railwaymen (NUR) as well as the traditionally more truculent Associated Society of Locomotive Engineers and Firemen (ASLEF). Pay bargaining was becoming, as NUR leader Sid Weighell bitterly characterised it, 'the philosophy of the pig trough: those with the biggest snout get the biggest share'.[5]

Labour would have appeared at war with itself – just as it was to appear during the 1978–79 Winter of Discontent. Its economic and industrial policies would have appeared to be failing, just as Heath's did. And the Labour left would have been in full cry. After victory in 1970, the credibility of Labour's election slogan, 'Now Britain's Strong, Let's Make it Great to Live In', would have rung hollow. And the left on Labour's NEC, the Tribune Group of backbench Labour MPs and left-wing constituency activists would have argued for a different strategy – an alternative economic strategy. The hard left would have had its cheerleaders in Ian Mikardo, Frank Allaun, Norman Atkinson and others. But it would not yet have had Tony Benn.

Anthony Wedgwood Benn, who as 'Wedge Benn of MinTech' personified the white heat of Harold Wilson's technological revolution, probably would eventually have come to the same conclusion he reached after the 1970 defeat, that the strategy was not working. But had Labour won in 1970, it is unlikely that he would have politically redefined himself quite so quickly. He would still have been in government, constrained by collective Cabinet responsibility, and busy with his department. It is unlikely that he would have resigned, more likely that he would have tried to save his projects, Rolls-Royce, Upper Clyde Shipbuilders, Concorde and the rest. The left would not (yet) have seen him as one of their own, and the right would have continued to see him as a charming if slightly eccentric Wilsonian technocrat; 'Nothing wrong with [Tony Benn] except he's a bit cracked',[6] his old Oxford tutor Tony Crosland once said. As such he would have lacked the base to be a credible leadership candidate in 1972–73 (which he lacked amongst MPs in any case, even when he stood in 1976). And nor would Benn have been so likely to have embroiled himself in a campaign for a referendum on Europe. Referendums were alien to Britain's parliamentary traditions and were opposed in principle not just by the pro-Europeans who would have been leading the Labour Party but also by key anti-EEC figures like Peter Shore and Michael Foot, who remembered the plebiscite as a favourite device of the European fascist leaders of the 1930s.

Though as yet lacking Benn as a figurehead, there would have been no lack of potential Bennites; the late 1960s had seen a profound disillusionment amongst Labour activists with the Wilsonian Labour Party. The ageing loyalists were getting ever older and the student radicals who replaced them were radicalised by the perceived failure of social-democratic solutions, the panaceas of Marxism and the anti-Americanism of the Vietnam generation. A host of Trotskyite organisations, including the Revolutionary Socialist League (popularly known as the Militant Tendency) and Tariq Ali's International Marxist Group, sought to influence and infiltrate the Labour Party, capturing its policy-making machinery for their own agenda. Attempts to crack down on them were often frustrated by the Tribunite left who opposed what they called 'witch-hunts' of any whom they saw as allies in the battle for 'peace and socialism'.

One difference, however, had Labour won in 1970, would have been the likely attitude of Labour's headquarters at Transport House. In opposition, Labour appointed the disastrous Ron Hayward as General Secretary, over his younger, pro-European, rival Gwyn Morgan, on the casting vote of Tony Benn. Morgan was backed by both Jenkins and Callaghan (though he was also a great admirer of Healey), had a keen appreciation of the Militant threat and the energy and ability to regenerate Labour's tired and chaotic headquarters. Harold Wilson had, years before, been responsible for a report which characterised Labour's national electoral organisation as a penny-farthing machine in a jet-plane age, but as Leader he had done nothing about it, and nor had the elderly and tired party General Secretaries of the time. Morgan could have and would have tried. Since it was only Wilson's vote against Morgan that produced the tie and gave Benn the casting vote, had relations between Callaghan, Jenkins and Wilson been better, and had Wilson been planning to retire (rather than battling to hold the party together over Europe) it is likely that Morgan would have been chosen.

As General Secretary, Morgan would have had the respected Terry Pitt as his deputy. Pitt's Euro-scepticism balanced Morgan's Euro-enthusiasm and the excellent working relationship they had would have helped reduce party tensions over the issue. Morgan would have set about tackling the Militant threat, just as he had fought and defeated the Communists in his days as General Secretary of the National Union of Students in 1960–62. And he would have ensured that Labour headquarters stood up to the attempts to deselect social-democratic MPs such as Dick Taverne and Reg Prentice (which led both to quit the party and later encouraged the formation and growth of the SDP) for the crime of supporting the Labour government. Taverne, one of the rising stars of the 1966–70 Labour ministerial team, would almost certainly have been in a post-1973 Labour Cabinet, Prentice would have remained a valued member of it and

Derek Hatton, Tony Mulhearn, Dave Nellist et al. might have never gained the foothold in the Labour Party that they did.

On the other hand, however, the disillusionment with the government amongst non-Militant Labour activists was real. Many believed that Britain's economic troubles stemmed from the failures of capitalism, and that planning, workers' control and nationalisation offered a better way forward. It was a time when it was still possible to believe that the Communist bloc was an economic success story (at least in terms of ball-bearing and tractor production). Many did, even if they felt uneasy at the fate of dissidents and, indeed, the fate of the Hungarian government of 1956 and the Czech government of 1968. Anyway, they said, even if the Soviet Union could be heavy-handed, was not the US murdering innocents in Vietnam in its efforts to prop up an undemocratic and oppressive regime in South Vietnam?

The belief that the Labour government was not listening to activists and was ignoring conference resolutions was widespread. It was this that facilitated the growth of such left-wing groups as the Campaign for Labour Party Democracy and the Labour Coordinating Committee, and in the end secured victory for the campaign for mandatory reselection of MPs in 1979. Benn was to provide an inspirational figurehead for their cause, but even without him, their demands had a degree of resonance with the constituency activists, whose representatives on Labour's NEC provided a focal point for dissent and were increasingly locked in battle with Labour's leadership.

The tragedy was that whilst Gwyn Morgan and his team could have helped mitigate and contain the onslaught of the extreme left, the structure of the Labour Party at that time, with the big union block votes and the constituency general committees already in the hands of the activist left, made it virtually impossible to secure the reforms needed. These included one-member-one-vote (OMOV) secret ballots amongst party members for choosing MPs, rather than just amongst the left-wing activists of constituency management

committees. When Frank Chapple's electricians' union, supported by
David Owen, George Robertson and precious few others, sought to
introduce an OMOV ballot for party leader in 1981, they were overwhelmingly defeated by the left. Not until the Thatcher trade union
reforms of the 1980s would, on the advice of the electricians union,
all trade unions have a legal requirement to hold OMOV ballots for
their leaders and executives. Not until that happened did a sufficient
number back OMOV for Labour Party elections to get it through.
And after *In Place of Strife,* no Labour leader was going to touch trade
union reform.

Which brings us to the question of what a post–1970 Labour government would have tried to do. The 1970 manifesto was remarkably
bland, perhaps seeking to avoid the mistake of promising too much
and failing to deliver that had so damned Labour in office in 1966–
70. The economically irresponsible tax cuts promised by the Conservatives would have been avoided. So would the less irresponsible
but tragically flawed attempts by Heath to reform industrial relations;
appeasement would have been the order of the day on the industrial
front. Foreign policy would have been dominated by the attempt to
join the Common Market. Legislation to promote equality at work
and outlaw discrimination, of the kind taken through in 1974–76,
would have been attempted. Other priorities included a state earnings-related pension scheme, greater support for the sick and disabled,
including an earnings-related invalidity benefit, and more motorway
building.

The replacement of grammar and secondary modern schools by
comprehensives would have continued apace under Education Secretary Ted Short (though in the event more grammar schools were
comprehensivised under Margaret Thatcher as Education Secretary in
1970–74 than under any single Labour Education Secretary), and free
school milk would not have been further cut back – somehow, 'Ted
Short, milk snatcher', lacks a certain ring. Labour would also have

sought to reduce all class sizes to thirty. Selective Employment Tax, which discriminated against service sector employment in favour of jobs in manufacturing industry, would have been retained (the Conservatives were pledged to abolish it) while to join the EEC, Labour would have had to abandon its pledge of opposition to VAT. Another attempt to reform the Lords was a possibility, but ministers would have lacked enthusiasm for a repeat performance of the last fiasco. Local government would have been reformed on the bigger-means-better principle and aldermen abolished (as they were under Heath).

Whether Select Committees would have been extended and Scottish and Welsh devolution pursued in the wake of the Kilbrandon Commission's report of 1973 would have depended largely on the deployment of Cabinet personalities. Constitutional reform was not a particularly left versus right issue. Indeed the most successful Cabinet champion of Parliamentary Select Committees turned out to be Norman St John-Stevas in Margaret Thatcher's Cabinet in 1979–81. The fact is that few of the likely 1970 Cabinet were particularly interested in Select Committees and increasing backbench power. Only Cledwyn Hughes of the likely 1970 Cabinet was an actual enthusiast for devolution (Crossman had been, but he had retired).

The key to change lay with some of the people who Jenkins, Callaghan or Healey might have brought into Cabinet had they secured the leadership post-1972, and some of the people they would have sacked. Willie Ross, Wilson's Scottish *Gauleiter,* would have been replaced as Scottish Secretary by the talented Glasgow debater (and mentor to John Smith and Donald Dewar) Dickson Mabon, or, if Jenkins had been feeling adventurous, the brilliant maverick John P. Mackintosh. Mabon and Mackintosh were devolution and EEC enthusiasts both. George Thomas, the prickly and fiercely anti-devolution Welsh Secretary, would have been replaced, probably by his predecessor Cledwyn Hughes, brought back from Agriculture. Other rising stars such as Dick Taverne and David Owen, recognised the importance of constitutional reform, but most other ministers saw it as a distraction from bread-and-butter issues. Shirley Williams, for example, whilst the Home Office minister in charge, blocked the introduction of proportional representation in elections for the Ulster assembly in case the Liberals sought to capitalise on it. Indeed the unfolding situation in Ulster would have brought further difficulties to the government when it least wanted them.

Other potential new Cabinet members would have included the key lieutenants to whoever had become the new chief: Bill Rodgers, had Jenkins become leader, and Merlyn Rees had Callaghan secured the crown. Edmund Dell, regarded as having one of the most powerful brains in the Parliamentary Labour Party, was admired by Healey, Jenkins and Callaghan alike. The promotion of new faces required old faces to go. Had Callaghan become Leader, Barbara Castle, with whom he had clashed so bitterly over *In Place of Strife*, would have been vulnerable to enforced retirement. Had Jenkins won, those most vulnerable to the sack would have been, in addition to Willie Ross and George Thomas, the likes of John Silkin, Peter Shore and Fred Peart. All were regarded as Wilson trusties and passionately anti-EEC. Silkin and Shore were at the time widely regarded as over-promoted, although Shore was later to develop considerable stature.

Whether a post-1970 Labour government would have weathered the election following the 1973–74 economic storm remains an open question. It would not have been in quite as great a mess as Heath's Government, having avoided the consequences of injudicious tax cuts and credit booms. But having failed yet again to create the New Britain it had promised it would nevertheless have been in severe difficulties, both with its own supporters and with the electorate.

The Conservatives, meanwhile, would have had a very tough time in the wake of defeat in 1970. Assuming Heath had been forced to fall on his sword, Alec Douglas-Home would only have wanted to serve briefly as a caretaker leader. Iain Macleod's poor health was such that had he not died in the leadership election he would almost certainly have died shortly afterwards from the strain. 'Politically, he was our trumpeter', said his colleague Robert Carr[7] and, indeed, his loss would have been a grievous blow to the Shadow Cabinet. Had Maudling been elected, he would undoubtedly have resigned by 1972 amidst the furore of the Poulson scandal. Quintin Hogg was a long shot; Du Cann too anti-EEC and lacking in support. The likelihood is that the Conservatives would have ended up with Whitelaw, but that the defeated Powell would have refused to accept that he had been beaten, and would have been a continuing thorn in the party's side. Thatcher would have been a loyal middle-ranking member of the Shadow Cabinet. And the man with the boat? Had Labour succeeded in taking Britain into the EEC, Heath might well have sailed off to Brussels to become President of the European Commission.

The Conservatives would, however, have had a key weapon: the British electorate's support for industrial relations reform and an end to the rash of strikes crippling export industry and public services. Even during the 1970 election campaign, a print workers' strike had kept newspapers off the streets for four days. And as the 1970s progressed it got worse. By the time of a 1974–75 election, the slogan of the eventual 1979 campaign, 'Labour isn't Working', would have struck a chord with the electorate. So despite the difficulties described, the likelihood is that by 1974 the Conservatives would have been on the up, and Labour facing defeat.

Had the Conservatives won in 1974–75, remaining in office would have depended on making a success of trade-union reform and holding the economy together until the revenues from North Sea oil came on stream in. Had they done so, had they avoided the unpopularity that the Thatcher Government was to court via dogmatic monetarism, extreme deflation and consequent mass unemployment, and had a defeated Labour Party embroiled itself in civil war, they might have been in for two to three terms. But they would have been led from the centre and left of the party rather than from the right. It would still have been a Conservative government, prioritising income-tax cuts over investment in infrastructure and social services; but monetarism and the cult of Milton Friedman would have remained a subject for the political fringe. There would have been no poll tax and no rail privatisation.

Leading Conservative Cabinet members would have included Robert Carr, Geoffrey Rippon, Ian Gilmour, Peter Walker, Norman St John-Stevas, Jim Prior, Francis Pym, Alick Buchanan-Smith and Lords Carrington and Soames. Geoffrey Howe would probably have adorned the Woolsack. By the mid to late 1980s it is conceivable that the Conservative Party might even have been led by Iain Macleod's protégé Nick Scott; other rising stars would have included Michael Heseltine, Chris Patten, David Hunt and Kenneth Clarke. Those who were to become most associated with Thatcherism, such as Nicholas Ridley, John Nott, Cecil Parkinson and John Moore, would have been less likely to prosper.

If Labour had lost in 1974–75, its internal battles would have worsened: the left would have blamed both the man with the pipe and whoever had succeeded him for the defeat. Benn, liberated from the shackles of office, would have joined those calling for a 'socialist alternative' and sought to become a standard bearer for the left. Roy Jenkins, had he been the defeated Leader of the Opposition, bereft of a Prime Minister's power to hand out ministerial jobs, would have had the unenviable task of uniting a party riven by internal warfare.

The idea that he would have been able to found a golden age of Labour social democracy is highly questionable. Without doubt he would have faced a Labour Party at war with itself, just as Callaghan and Healey did in 1980. The defeated leader would have been forced to confront profound disillusionment within the party at the government's failure to build the 'New Britain', and the growing strength of the left in the union movement, the constituency parties and on

Labour's National Executive Committee. Jenkins, despite his formidable intellectual strengths, would not have relished the long-drawn-out battle that would have been necessary to rebuild a united and electable Labour Party. As Bill Rodgers, one of Jenkins' closest lieutenants, recollected in his memoirs: 'He had no great taste for narrow party politics or the messiness of internal party warfare. If the Labour Party was fast becoming ungovernable, Roy, as a potential leader, was already out of time.'[8]

Notes

1   I would like to thank for their kindness in sharing their insights and memories of the period: Andrew Adonis, Dr Lewis Baston, Tam Dalyell MP, Lord Donoughue of Ashton, Rt Hon. Lord Gilmour of Craigmillar, Rt Hon. Lord Graham of Edmonton, Joe Haines, Dianne Hayter, Rt Hon. Dr Dickson Mabon, Lord McNally, Gwyn Morgan, Rt Hon. Lord Rodgers of Quarry Bank, Lord Sawyer, Charlie Turnock, Gerry Wade and Phillip Whitehead MEP.

2   Private information.

3   Interview with Tam Dalyell MP.

4   Cited in Philip Ziegler, *Wilson* (Weidenfeld & Nicolson, 1993), p. 308.

5   Speech in economic debate, Labour Party Conference, Blackpool, 2 October 1978 (Conference Report, p. 224).

6   Cited in Susan Crosland, *Tony Crosland* (Cape, 1982), p. 204.

7   Cited in Phillip Whitehead, *The Writing on the Wall* (Joseph, 1985), p. 54.

8   Bill Rodgers, *Fourth Among Equals* (Politico's, 2000), p. 157.

Chapter 11

What if Ted Heath had gone to the country three weeks earlier in February 1974?

Mark Garnett[1]

The general election of February 1974 is conventionally (and conveniently) remembered as the contest in which the Prime Minister, Edward Heath, asked the voters: 'Who governs?', and their answer was: 'Not you, at any rate'. Actually, the Conservatives won the largest share of the vote – 37.9 per cent, to Labour's 37.1 per cent. But Labour took more seats, by 301 to 297. The Conservatives could no longer rely on automatic support from the Ulster Unionists, and after prolonged negotiations it proved impossible to agree a coalition deal with the Liberals, who had won fourteen seats. For the third time, Harold Wilson was asked to form a government.

This general election had taken place in unprecedented circumstances. The Conservative Party manifesto referred to: 'great dangers both from within our own country and from outside'.[2] The danger from outside Britain was the worldwide increase in the cost of commodities, particularly oil, which quadrupled in price in the wake of the October 1973 war of Yom Kippur. The decision of Middle-Eastern producers to reduce supplies meant that governments across the developed world had suddenly to confront the possibility of life without the fuel on which their economies depended. Britain was not excepted from this threat, despite its long tradition of warm relations with Arab states; and since its economy had underperformed since 1945 in comparison to its major competitors, it was ill equipped to ride out any crisis on this scale.

The outlook would have been grim enough anyway, but it arose at a time when the country was bitterly divided. The 'danger from within our own country' was a reference to what the manifesto described as 'a small number of militant extremists', who 'can so manipulate and abuse the monopoly power of their unions as to cause incalculable damage to the country and to the fabric of our society itself'.[3] The chief target for these remarks was the National Union of Mineworkers (NUM), which on 12 November 1973 had declared an overtime ban in support of a pay claim, in defiance of the statutory prices and incomes policy which the government had been operating for a year. Power workers and railwaymen also took industrial action, but the miners hardly needed any help in turning the screw on the government. The oil crisis had transformed their bargaining position. They had already secured one major pay increase through a strike of January–February 1972. In response to the new overtime ban, the government declared a state of emergency. On 13 December, Heath took even more drastic action, announcing that a 'three-day working week' would begin in the New Year. Preparations were in hand for the rationing of fuel.

Superficially, these hardly seem the most propitious circumstances for a Prime Minister to call a general election; Heath was like a football manager asking for a vote of confidence from his board when his team was facing relegation. Even his warmest admirer would have to admit that his government had failed to deliver the promised transformation of Britain's prospects, and since the Labour opposition had pledged to hold a referendum on UK membership of the European Economic Community (EEC), the decision to fight an election was putting at risk his greatest claim to a positive legacy. But the Conservatives believed that the consequences of a Labour victory would be even more far-reaching for the country. Their manifesto predicted that if Labour should win a sufficient majority to carry out its full programme, the effect would be 'to wreck the economy, undermine the free society, and accelerate the present inflation beyond the point of no return'.[4]

In fact the economic crisis, and a precarious parliamentary position which was only marginally improved by the subsequent election of October 1974, saved Harold Wilson from having to implement the radical programme of nationalisation which his party had embraced at its 1973 conference. Nevertheless, it seemed that by the time of Wilson's resignation in March 1976 the Conservative warnings had been verified. Wilson and his successor James Callaghan used every weapon they could grasp to maintain the orthodox post-war policy framework, but despite all of their efforts, Britain could not escape its new reputation as the 'sick man of Europe' – an ungovernable nation and an economic basket-case.

By May 1979 the advocates of radical alternatives from left and right could claim with some plausibility that the whole 'Keynesian' settlement had been discredited. Callaghan and his Chancellor Denis Healey had turned their attention to the control of inflation, rather than the maintenance of full employment. This dramatic reversal of post-war priorities could be traced back to the events of 1973–74. Vernon Bogdanor has written that the February 1974 election 'destroyed consensus politics for nearly two decades in every part of the United Kingdom'.[5] The only quibbles about that judgement could emanate from 'New' Labour's critics, who argue that the ethos of the old consensus has never returned.

The fateful non-decision
Could it all have been different? Some of those closest to Heath certainly thought so in the December of 1973, and their hopes were mirrored by Labour MPs who feared that the Conservatives were on

the verge of securing a thumping election victory. The reasoning ran something like this. At times of crisis, there is a tendency for people to rally around an existing government. Wilson himself was aware of this, and had appealed to 'the Dunkirk spirit' when he encountered troubles of his own during his previous stint as Prime Minister. Even a government which was widely regarded as the chief author of its own difficulties could hope to benefit from the tendency of voters to 'cling to nurse for fear of finding something worse'. Only Labour's diehard loyalists could imagine that the Opposition was likely to pull Britain out of the crisis. The party was clearly disunited in late 1973, and its record between 1964 and 1970 had hardly been one to inspire confidence in its ability to deal with the key issues of the economy and the trade unions. So Heath could ask for a 'Doctor's mandate' in the knowledge that his main rival was widely regarded as something of a quack.

One serious complication in assessing the hypothetical results of an early election is the question of timing. The idea originated within the Conservative Research Department, whose Director, James Douglas, submitted a memorandum as early as 9 November 1973, when the likely consequences of the oil crisis had become apparent, but before the miners had declared their overtime ban.[6] The beauty of this idea was that an election at that stage would focus on general issues of competence, instead of being portrayed as a trial of strength between the unions and the government. For a 'one-nation' Conservative like Douglas – and Heath himself – a 'who governs?' election would be a disaster in itself, underlining the country's divisions instead of acting to heal them.

Unfortunately for Douglas, the merits of his plan were unlikely to register immediately with busy politicians who were naturally averse to the prospect of an early contest unless they saw no realistic alternative. It took the overtime ban to concentrate ministerial minds; but of course as soon as that occurred an early election could only be the kind of 'who governs?' contest that Douglas had been so anxious to avoid. And this was precisely the kind of battle which appealed to Conservative activists, who were spoiling for a fight with the unions.

Sustained press speculation about an early election began in December. If Heath had called the election on 17 December, he would have ensured that the campaign coincided with a blizzard of announcements which emphasised both the extent of the danger and the government's determination to meet it with robust measures. On that day the Chancellor of the Exchequer, Tony Barber, announced emergency cuts in public spending. Heath had introduced the three-day week on 13 December. The problem with this scenario – even if Heath had been ready to accept it – was the fact that the campaign would have been interrupted by Christmas and the New Year. The best alternative would have been for Heath to dissolve parliament in the first few days of 1974. After all, the three-day week would not come into effect until 1 January, confronting the electorate with the practical consequences of the miners' action.

The most important advocates of a January poll were the Party Chairman, Lord Carrington, and his Deputy, James Prior, who were well aware that grassroots Conservatives were appalled by the thought of another 'surrender' to the miners. By contrast, backbench MPs were almost equally divided on the question of an early election; but parliamentary foot soldiers had never enjoyed much influence over this government. Carrington and Prior had accepted the case for an early poll by 18 December, when Heath's political secretary, Douglas Hurd, noted in his diary that 'Slowly the bandwagon for an early election is beginning to roll'.[7]

Two days later the party's Steering Committee discussed a draft manifesto, which had been produced as a contingency by Nigel Lawson in his capacity of special adviser, along with a preliminary draft for a hypothetical election which might be 'fought in more normal circumstances'.[8] Comments were made on the tone of Lawson's draft, and it was clear that more detailed proposals would have to be fleshed out. Heath concluded by hoping that his colleagues would give thought to the matter over the Christmas break. But the supporters of an early poll were not prepared to let the matter rest for so long. Prior visited Heath at Chequers two days after Christmas, and was frustrated by the Prime Minister's refusal to discuss the manifesto. On 18 December Hurd had recorded that his boss was 'unconvinced', and despite the urgency of Prior and Carrington he moved no closer to a decision over the festive season.[9]

Heath's state of indecision might have been a symptom of tiredness. But he had good reason to hesitate, because those he trusted most were offering contradictory advice. The newly appointed Secretary of State for Employment, Willie Whitelaw, believed that a settlement with the miners could be reached without an election – indeed, he felt that the growing speculation about an election was a serious obstacle to fruitful negotiations. Furthermore, Whitelaw was rightly concerned that the Sunningdale Agreement for power-sharing in Northern Ireland would be jeopardised by an election which seemed certain to result in a serious setback for moderates on both sides of the debate in the province. His views were seconded by Francis Pym, formerly the party's Chief Whip and now Whitelaw's successor at the Northern Ireland Office. Heath scarcely needed reminding of the importance of Northern Ireland; he had thrown himself into the Sunningdale process which had concluded on 9 December 1973. This crushing addition to the routine burdens of office would fully account for any weariness that Heath might have felt during these crucial weeks.

During the first two weeks of January the divided counsellors rehearsed their arguments in a series of meetings with Heath. On 12 January 1974 several advisers who had helped with the successful 1970 election campaign were summoned to Chequers. Unanimously they pressed the Carrington–Prior case on Heath, but still no decision was forthcoming. Hurd thought that Heath was acting as Elizabeth I had done in the discussions leading up to the execution of Mary, Queen of Scots, hoping that the weight of rational argument would persuade him to take a step from which his instincts recoiled. If so, he was playing a dangerous game. That same evening Tony Benn reported in his diary that election rumours were growing 'at a fantastic rate'. The 'bandwagon' was gathering speed, and the people who had set it in motion were no longer giving much thought to its ultimate destination.[10]

Carrington and Prior knew that time was running out for their strategy. If the decision were delayed much longer the sense of national crisis would begin to dissipate. Also, a new electoral register would come into operation on 16 February. Historically, the Conservatives were much more efficient than Labour at keeping track of their supporters who moved to new addresses. So there was a clear advantage for the government if the election could be held with the old register still in force. For Carrington and Prior, Thursday 17 January was the last day for decision; with the minimum three-week campaign, this would mean an election as early as 7 February.

In line with this timetable, the advocates of a snap election raised the pressure on their leader still further as the deadline approached. On the evening of 16 January speculation reached fever-pitch. But Whitelaw chose to make a final appeal for delay, and this seems to have been decisive. Heath probably took no account of a widely publicised claim by Enoch Powell that an election held in these circumstances would be 'fraudulent', but this was a worrying portent. Whatever the reason, 17 January passed without the fateful order being given.

Prior's reaction was to tell Heath that 'all the Labour Members are coming up to me in the tea room to tell me that we have let them off the hook'.[11] One prospective Conservative candidate, Alan Clark, was dismayed by the 'total reversal', feeling that the voters of Plymouth

Sutton would have relished an 'anti-union platform'.[12] As James Callaghan was to find in the autumn of 1978, Prime Ministers rarely earn much gratitude when they act belatedly to quell such speculation. As a tactician it seemed that Heath had emulated the Grand Old Duke of York, marching his troops to the top of the hill then halfway down again, without convincing them that they would not have to turn around and launch an assault after all. But Heath had always despised electoral opportunism; and if his troops had begun to march, it was not because of any order he had given. As he told Prior during their angry exchange on 17 January, 'It's all your bloody fault. If you hadn't allowed Central Office to steam this thing up, we would never have got into this position.'[13]

An ill-starred campaign

The Heath Government was consistently unlucky, and its fortunes did not change after this anticlimax. But the next few weeks were also marked by some inexplicable moves by ministers, who seemed unsure whether to continue playing up the crisis or to act as if it were 'business as usual'. On the day of Heath's non-decision, Carrington suggested that it might soon be possible to ease the restrictions of the three-day working week. This, together with more optimistic noises about the level of coal stocks, could only inspire speculation that the sense of emergency had been exaggerated for electoral reasons. On 24 January, the government's Pay Board reported in a way which apparently endorsed the NUM's argument for a generous deal. Whitelaw was inclined to seize on this report as a means of resolving the dispute, but he felt that the Prime Minister had not given him the authority to settle.[14] Five hours of talks with the NUM on the same day produced no new offer. The union immediately organised a ballot on an all-out strike, which resulted in an 81 per cent vote in favour of an escalation. When this verdict was revealed on 6 February, Prior told reporters that: 'The miners have had their ballot, perhaps we should have ours'.[15] The decision to go to the country was taken later that day, and Heath asked the Queen for a dissolution of Parliament in the early hours of 7 February. To the end it was clear to his closest associates that he had no appetite for a contest of this kind.

Prior characterised the ensuing campaign as 'a nightmare'. It began with a new blunder. On the same day that the election was called, the government showed new interest in the Pay Board recommendations which had been ignored when they could have been used to settle the dispute without an election. Predictably, the economic figures released during the campaign merely illustrated the extent of the crisis, without rallying the public behind the Conservatives. Then, just two days before the general election, Campbell Adamson, the Director-General of the Confederation of British Industry, called for the repeal of the government's Industrial Relations Act. As a final twist of the knife this could hardly have been more deadly. It seemed that even the government's closest allies had finally lost faith in what had been the centrepiece of its industrial strategy.

Could it have been different?

In retrospect Douglas Hurd maintained that the Conservatives would have won the election if it had been held on 7 February:

> It would have taken place against the background of an overtime ban, not a strike. The three weeks which we lost brought with them, as we predicted, a steady ebb of the government's authority. The issues became blurred. Practical people began to long for a settlement which would put the lights on again and get the factories back to a full working week. The dangers of inflation began to seem less important. The government found the initiative slipping from its hand. The opposition parties had precious time to prepare themselves.[16]

An astute and well-placed witness like Hurd is always persuasive, and he certainly provides some good reasons for supposing that the

Conservatives would have performed better in early February than they did at the end of that month. Even on 28 February, with their additional handicaps, they outpolled Labour and won more seats. But in the unique circumstances of February 1974, the minimum requirement for a 'vote of confidence' from the public was an overall majority in excess of the thirty-seat cushion they had enjoyed at the previous election in June 1970. Even if the election had been held earlier, it is very doubtful that the Conservatives would have jumped that hurdle.

Hurd mentions two important opinion poll findings during this period. One, a *Times*/ITN survey published in December, showed a Conservative lead of 5 per cent, and the second a detailed, specially commissioned poll by the Opinion Research Centre (ORC), suggested that although the party could win an early election it was almost certain to lose at any other time. While Hurd thought that these polls strengthened the case for an early election, they were heartening precisely because they contrasted with almost all of the evidence taken during the course of the 1970–74 Parliament. Instead of enjoying a protracted honeymoon with the voters, the Conservatives had barely been granted a one-night stand. Even policies which ought to have been popular, notably Keith Joseph's generosity towards the elderly and the disabled, never filtered through to the voters; the Industrial Relations Act, and entry into Europe, were controversial in many quarters. As a result, over its lifetime of three and a half years, Gallup found that approval for the government only topped 40 per cent in two months – April 1971 and April 1972. By contrast, although Labour's rating had been very poor during 1969, in each of the three months before its unsuccessful bid for re-election in June 1970 its rating was at least 40 per cent. In short, the polling position was not strong enough to justify expectations of a clear Conservative win at any time between November 1973 and the actual calling of the election.

Another problem for the Conservatives was the image of their leader. Heath had usually trailed Wilson in the popularity stakes, even before the 1970 general election. During 1973 the gap between them was relatively narrow, and many voters clearly did acknowledge Heath's integrity during the economic crisis. Yet the improvement in his position vis-à-vis Wilson arose from a decline in public esteem for the latter as much as a boost for himself. The image-makers had never persuaded him to court personal popularity, or even to counter unfounded accusations. While those closest to him were confident that his qualities would shine through if he came under unusual scrutiny, the ability of his enemies to portray him as a divisive figure was another good reason why the Conservatives were never very likely to exceed the 38 per cent of the vote they had secured in 1970.

It is commonly assumed that opposition parties have far less effect on the outcome of elections than the performance of government. But it also seems that on this occasion the Conservatives underestimated both Labour and the Liberals. After the speculation of January 1974, but before Heath decided to run for re-election, Harold Macmillan told Alan Clark that an election would be a disaster, because 'the working class will see it as a loyalty vote'.[17] In those days before class dealignment became a commonplace of academic commentary, a high level of unthinking support for Labour could be expected even if that party ran an indifferent campaign. And this it was unlikely to do, given the tactical acumen of its leader. Throughout the campaign, Wilson appeared to be hoping to minimise the margin of defeat rather than awaiting the call to return to Downing Street. Lord Donoughue has confirmed this impression, revealing that Wilson planned to go into hiding after what he expected to be a personal humiliation. Yet under any circumstances he probably would have conducted a defensive, highly tactical campaign – not least because he disbelieved in the policy proposals which his own party had forced upon him. His pose as a unifying figure played to his strengths – or rather, it played up

Heath's perceived weaknesses. In particular, Wilson was far too wily to allow the Conservatives to execute their plan of portraying Labour as the prisoner of the militant trade unionists. He was ably abetted by the miners themselves, who refrained from provocative gestures during the campaign. Almost certainly, all this would have come to pass if the election had been held on 7 February or earlier.

Equally, at no time during the run-up to the election did the Conservatives develop an adequate strategy for dealing with a potential surge in support for the Liberals. Subsequent research showed that the Liberals drew their extra support almost equally from each of the two main parties. But the rise in the Liberal vote, from 7.5 per cent in 1970 to nearly 20 per cent (if still only fourteen seats) in February 1974, was obviously damaging to a governing party which was seeking an authoritative mandate from the electorate. A significant rise in support (if not quite on this scale) ought to have been expected. On 8 November 1973 – the day before James Douglas floated the idea of an early election – the Liberal Alan Beith had taken the seat of Berwick-on-Tweed from the Conservatives. Heath's campaign message, that Labour could not be trusted on the economy or industrial relations and that the Conservatives needed a little more help to finish the job, could easily be translated into: 'So why not give the Liberals a try?' Judging by their manifesto, Conservative strategists did not entertain this possibility because they thought of their party as a would-be government of national unity without the need to form a coalition with other parties. This was of great credit to the integrity of Heath and his ministers, but it also proved their blindness to the extent of popular rejection of their 'one-nation' claims.

Then there was the Powell factor. Whatever his motives in declaring that he would not fight the election as a Conservative, and later that he had cast a postal vote for Labour, Powell would have taken identical steps whatever the date of the election. It seems indisputable that he cost his old party some seats in the crucial Midlands area, and his outburst must have acted as a general depressant on the Tory vote throughout the country.

Perhaps Powell might have attracted less attention – or more effective criticisms from party loyalists – had the election taken place when the country was coming to terms with the economic crisis. But he still would have had some negative effect. Powell's defection was not damaging simply because of who he was; it was also a matter of what he was saying. Whether or not the Conservative argument for the necessity of an election was really 'fraudulent', as he put it, was a matter of taste. But it was certainly open to accusations of opportunism, from objective observers as well as from people with an axe to grind. Of course, the 'electoral cycle' is always manipulated by Prime Ministers who enjoy the power of dissolving Parliament whenever it suits them. But Powell had exposed the government's guilty secret – its knowledge that unless it cut and run at the first opportunity, it could never hope for a second term of office.

Hurd might have been correct in thinking that the electorate would have been more willing to vote Conservative during a miners' overtime ban than in the fraught atmosphere of an all-out strike. But the constitutional case for an early election was certainly strengthened by the escalation of the dispute, which explains why not a single minister demurred when the decision to go to the country was eventually taken. The argument that the verdict of the people, rather than the will of Parliament, should settle the dispute was still fairly weak even after the NUM had voted for a strike. But before this it was only persuasive to people who had a personal commitment to the government's re-election. In other words, Powell's charges of opportunism would have been even more effective against an election at the beginning of February than they proved to be at the end of the month.

Finally, the government never gave an adequate response to the question of what it would do about the miners even if it did win a resounding electoral endorsement. Since ministers failed to deal with this problem before 28 February, there is no reason to think that they would have done any better if the election had been held earlier. Norman St John-Stevas remembered asking Whitelaw about the consequences of a victory. The Employment Secretary replied that it would mean 'a whole new ball game'. Understandably, given his continuing misgivings about the election, Whitelaw did not elaborate on the nature of this new game. Of course, a healthy renewal of the government's mandate would have strengthened its hand in negotiations with the miners. But the British people could not vote away the consequences of the Yom Kippur War, and the sudden vulnerability to fuel shortages which had made the NUM so formidable. Some senior union leaders were obviously keen to cut a deal with the government. Yet all the evidence of negotiations with the unions showed that the secret preferences of leaders were unrepresentative of the rank and file. Ministers could look forward to a terrible reckoning for the miners once North Sea oil came on stream, but in the short term they would still have had to deal generously with the union militants. They would also have to reach an accommodation with the unions on the reform of their own Industrial Relations Act.

Conclusion

The brief for this chapter was to explore the likely consequences if Edward Heath had bowed to his colleagues at Central Office and called an election before 28 February 1974. The answer is that he might have won outright, but the margin could not have been convincing enough to transform a depressing situation. An election on the old register would have helped the Tories, and the delay certainly helped the opposition parties to prepare for battle. Far from enjoying the usual advantages of knowing the election timetable in advance, continued uncertainty meant that the Conservative Research Department was unable to circulate a finished version of its invaluable *Campaign Guide* for candidates. Conceivably, ministers might have made fewer mistakes if the campaign had begun before their frayed nerves had been stretched even further by the arguments of January – which, ironically, were virtually the only Cabinet disagreements of the entire Heath era.

But none of these factors would have made the outcome radically different, given the problems which would have handicapped the Conservatives in any premature contest. The Douglas/Lawson plan for an election before the miners' overtime ban provided the best hope on paper; but in practice it would have been impossible to sell the idea to the electorate.

And what would have happened if the Tories had come back with a workable majority, but no more, at the beginning of February? The miners would have been bought off, with the kind of deal that Whitelaw had envisaged before the election. In the next Parliament the Conservatives might have managed the economy more success-fully than Labour proved able to do between 1974–79. But crises would have come, and at those times the voluntary decision to hold a premature 'who governs?' election would have been cited by the opposition parties as a precedent for another early poll. If the gov-ernment had refused to call a vote in the face of widespread public demand, the possible consequences would have been fearful. Alterna-tively, if Heath had caved in and held a second snap poll it is probable that he would have suffered a narrow defeat, thus ushering in a weak and divided Labour government which almost certainly would have encountered the same sort of problems that beset Callaghan and his Chancellor Denis Healey between 1976–79.

A narrow victory on 7 February 1974, followed by a deal with the miners, would not have endeared Heath to those party activists who had thirsted for an early election as a way of hitting back at the min-ers. The party's rules would not have been revised to allow a challenge to a sitting leader, as they were after the party suffered its two defeats in 1974. So Heath would have stayed in office. But it is difficult to see how he could have won the next election, whenever it was called, and at that point he would surely have resigned. Margaret Thatcher might not have been his successor – after all, one important reason for her victory in the leadership election of February 1975 was that her decision to stand was so unexpected, and if the Conservatives had served another term in government there would have been more time for the electorate of MPs to examine her credentials under persistent fire. But on balance the next leader of the party was likely to have come from her wing of the party, or at least to have presided over a Shadow Cabinet dominated by economic liberals. A leader with less reason to be insecure than Mrs Thatcher might have made Heath Shadow Foreign Secretary, but as a committed Keynesian he would have been excluded from economic policy-making. In short, under any conceivable scenario 'one-nation' Conservatism was doomed after Yom Kippur. The old familiar story – the destruction of 'consensus', the leftward movement of Labour and the formation of the SDP – would probably have happened, albeit with a different chronology.

But even if the ultimate outcome could not have been very different, this does not belittle the extent of the calamity of February 1974. The Conservatives ended up with the worst of all worlds. Faced with conflicting evidence from people he trusted, Heath allowed speculation about an election to grow, when he would have been better advised to make a quick decision one way or another and stick to it. Once the rumours started, the Prime Minister became a prisoner of a series of events which he had not triggered. He was sure to be stampeded into a premature dissolution as soon as a plausible pretext presented itself. As Heath himself has noted, the narrow defeat of February 1974 was the worst conceivable result.[18] The only surprise was that when Wilson called a new poll eight months later, the result was so close again. Even this rebounded against the Conservatives, since Heath was emboldened to stay on as leader and could only be removed after what was tantamount to an internal *coup d'etat*. Thus among the many distant consequences of February 1974 has to be numbered the fact that Conservative leaders are now even more insecure than England football managers.

Rather than speculating about the possible outcome if Heath had cut and run before 28 February 1974, one might ask: 'What would have happened if the government had stayed in office for its full term?' This was certainly the question which haunted Willie Whitelaw after the defeat. But by January 1974 Heath and his ministers were traumatised by their trials, and had become adept at creating their own bad luck. However much historians should resist the word – and how much the advocates of 'one-nation' politics will deplore it in this context – there was indeed a certain 'inevitability' about the course of events after the oil shock of 1973.

So the real 'might have been' is: 'What would have happened without Yom Kippur?' But it is still difficult to entertain a happier long-term outcome for 'one-nation' Conservatives. The Heath Government would have been asking too much had it hoped for a trouble-free run of any duration. According to the monetarist theory, the increase in the money supply associated with the Barber boom would in any case have condemned Britain to an inflationary nightmare before the 1970 Parliament had run its natural course. Whatever the truth of this, subsequent experience confirmed the lesson of the Heath years – that prices and incomes policies designed to contain inflation could work for an interim period, but would provide no permanent answer. The Industrial Relations Act would also have remained a running sore. This was a government which even managed to be damned for its good deeds – like its decision to offer refuge to thousands of Asians expelled from Uganda by Idi Amin.

Ultimately, it seems that 'consensus' government can only be sustained by a 'consensual' public. Edward Heath, whose ideas had been forged at a time when Britain really did approximate to 'one nation', was unfortunate enough to win the premiership at a time when his compatriots had surrendered to very different impulses. Probably Chris Patten gave the most appropriate verdict on those fateful weeks when he reported to a friend on 28 January 1974 that: 'I think we would all like an election to put us out of our misery one way or another'.[19]

Notes

1 My thanks to Jim Douglas and Nigel Lawson for reading and commenting on a draft of this chapter. Any errors of fact or interpretation which remain are entirely my responsibility.

2 *Firm Action for a Fair Britain: The Conservative Manifesto 1974*, p. 1.

3 Ibid., p. 5.

4 Ibid., p. 32.

5 Vernon Bogdanor, 'The Fall of Heath and the end of the post-war settlement', in Stuart Ball and Anthony Seldon (eds.), *The Heath Government 1970–74* (Longman, 1996), p. 373.

6 Ian Gilmour and Mark Garnett, *Whatever Happened to the Tories? The Conservative Party since 1945* (Fourth Estate, 1997), p. 284; David Butler and Dennis Kavanagh, *The British General Election of February 1974* (Macmillan, 1974), p. 28.

7 Douglas Hurd, *An End to Promises: Sketch of a Government 1970–74* (Collins, 1979), p. 122.

8 The phrase used by Sir Michael Fraser at the Steering Committee meeting of 20 December 1973; SC/73/25, Conservative Party archive, Bodleian Library.

9 Jim Prior, *A Balance of Power* (Hamish Hamilton, 1986), p. 91.

10 Hurd, *End to Promises*, p. 127; Tony Benn, *Against the Tide: Diaries 1973–76* (Arrow, 1990), p. 90.

11 Prior, *Balance of Power*, p. 92.

12 Alan Clark, *Diaries: Into Politics* (Weidenfeld & Nicolson, 2000), p. 39.

13 Prior, *Balance of Power*, p. 92.

14 See Mark Garnett and Ian Aitken, *Splendid! Splendid! The Authorised Biography of Willie Whitelaw* (Jonathan Cape, 2002), pp. 174–80.

15 Prior, *Balance of Power*, p. 93.

16 Hurd, *End to Promises*, p. 128.

17 Clark, *Into Politics*, p. 40.

18 Edward Heath, *The Course of My Life: My Autobiography* (Hodder & Stoughton, 1998), pp. 517–18.

19 Quoted in John Ramsden, *The Winds of Change: Macmillan to Heath, 1957 to 1975* (Longman, 1996), p. 374.

Chapter 12

What if Ted Heath had stepped down in 1974?

Matthew Bailey and Philip Cowley

But in politics, as in life, the 'ifs' offer no consolation.

Margaret Thatcher[1]

Nineteen seventy-four was not a good year for Edward Heath. In February he had gone to the country asking, 'who governs?' The response from the electorate was: not you, mate. Eight months. later, in October, campaigning on the merits of a government of national unity, he was once again to lead his party to defeat. In the meantime, personal tragedy had struck: his boat, *Morning Cloud III*, had sunk off the south coast killing two crewmen, including his godson Christopher Chad. And at the very moment when he would be required to be on top form in order to save his political skin, a thyroid deficiency which had been affecting him for some time began to get worse.[2]

Despite criticism following the February election, Heath's position had then been relatively safe; few felt they could dump the leader with another election due at any time. After October, however, things were different. In a party not renowned for its tolerance of losers his record was: played four, lost three; and it was increasingly certain that calls would be made for him to step down as leader. Following his *annus horribilis,* and with the prospect of bitter infighting ahead, it would have been understandable if Heath had made the decision to spend more time with his piano.

That he did not do so is often said to have been a crucial moment in British political history. By late 1974, there were plenty of Conservative MPs who wanted rid of Edward Heath. Some of his opponents were motivated by ideology, some were alienated by his brand of interpersonal skills – he had perfected a unique strategy of losing friends and alienating people – while yet others simply felt they could never win an election under his leadership. By refusing to go quietly, he forced his opponents to trigger a leadership contest.

As the only serious anti-Heath candidate – the others having ruled themselves out, shot themselves in the foot, or both – Margaret Thatcher received nearly all the anti-Heath votes in the first round of the contest. Aided by her skilful campaign team led by Airey Neave and William Shelton, she managed to lead the first ballot on 4 February 1975 by 130 votes to 119, a result that gave her unstoppable momentum in the second. With minor variations, therefore, almost all accounts of the 1975 contest argue that it was a negative victory: the Conservative Party, in Julian Critchley's words, 'did not vote for Margaret, they voted against Ted Heath'.[3] It was also said to be accidental. Conservative MPs did not intend to end up with Margaret Thatcher as their leader; her victory was merely the unintended consequence of removing Edward Heath.

But had Heath performed a swift and gracious exit following the October defeat, he could have ensured the smooth transition of power to a colleague much more congenial to his world-view: Willie Whitelaw. As it was, Whitelaw's chances were ruined by Heath's actions. Mindful of his duty to the party and loyalty to the leader, Whitelaw found himself unable to do anything but stand aside until Heath had been beaten, by which time Thatcher's momentum was unstoppable. By the time Whitelaw entered the race, he had already lost. Had he been in the traps from the beginning there would have been no need for all the anti–Heath forces to muster behind Mrs Thatcher. There would have been no need for anti–Heath tactical voting. There would have been no pro–Thatcher momentum. There would have been no Thatcher victory.

Rather than being one of the major political figures of the twentieth century, Margaret Thatcher would then have become but a minor footnote, remembered (if remembered at all) as an unpopular Secretary of State responsible for closing lots of grammar schools. Whitelaw would have been a far more conciliatory, consensual, 'one-nation' Conservative premier. For supporters of Thatcher, like John Nott, this would have been 'an unmitigated disaster ... there would have been no determined and radical attempt to solve the nation's problems. The management of decline would have suited William Whitelaw very well.'[4] For those less enamoured of Margaret Thatcher, Britain would have been spared her reign of terror. Either way, the story is simple: Heath's refusal to stand down in October 1974 gave us Thatcher and Thatcherism.

Counterfactual history, of course, turns on just this sort of simple twist of fate. The reader is asked to imagine that but for want of a nail, history may have been very different. Such twists of fate can range from the most trivial or freakish (a missed train here, a stray bullet there) to the almost inviolable.[5] Expecting Edward Heath to have behaved less obstinately falls at the latter end of the spectrum, but it is at least plausible. What follows is a critical examination of what would have happened had he done so. It offers a version of political history that is far less dramatic than either Thatcher's supporters or opponents would care to admit.

The leadership contest

The first problem with this conventional view of What Might Have Been is that it misunderstands the nature of the leadership contest by which Thatcher became leader. Although it is now usually portrayed simply as a cocktail of accidents, courage, manipulation and personality, to many of the protagonists at the time it was clear that real issues were at stake, and that the potential direction of the party rested on the contest's outcome.

Writing in 1985, Julian Critchley claimed that Thatcher was 'a zealot whose fundamentalist beliefs were not, at the time of her election to the leadership of the party, as widely known as they are today'.[6] But it is disingenuous to believe that nobody knew on which side of the fence Thatcher sat by late 1974. The party had, by now, already witnessed Keith Joseph's 'conversion' to true Conservatism. Having seen the light, he embarked on developing a critique not only of the failings of Heath's administration but of all the post-war governments, Labour and Conservative alike, who he accused of conniving in imposing a creeping socialism on Britain. Although less vocal, Thatcher was an identified member of Joseph's new think tank designed to convert the Conservative Party to the cause of the free market and a receptive audience member for Joseph's public *mea culpa*.[7]

Such events had not gone unnoticed on the left of the party. One of the very reasons Heath gave for remaining as leader following the October election defeat was precisely that he was 'determined to fight the right wing'.[8] Meanwhile, Ian Gilmour could be found neatly, if typically snobbishly, associating Mrs Thatcher's perceived suburban prejudices with the developing promulgation of an alien dogma, warning Conservatives against 'digging our trenches further to the right' and taking refuge 'behind a privet hedge'.[9] Writing in 1978, Gilmour observed that whilst the various wings of the Conservative Party were impossible to define with any certainty, '"right wingery" ... is, like the elephant, easily recognised when it is seen'.[10] By the mid-1970s Gilmour and his colleagues on the left of the party should not have needed to consult their *I-Spy Book of Mammals* to know what they were up against.

And whilst personality and Heath's unpopularity are important factors in explaining the outcome of the election in 1975, so too was ideology. Much of the voting in both rounds of the contest was determined by the ideological preferences of the MPs. There was a strength and depth to the right-wing hostility to both Heath in the first round and Whitelaw in the second. The right of the party had manifestly decided what it liked and what it did not. Equally, despite Heath's many failings, he was able to count on the support of the vast majority of MPs from the left. There were some from the left who backed Thatcher (either negatively and/or for tactical reasons), but they almost certainly amounted to no more than ten in total. The vast majority of the left – around 80 per cent – stuck with the incumbent in the first round and then moved on to support Whitelaw.[11] Chris Patten once summed the 1975 contest up as 'more the overthrow of the tyrant king than as a great ideological shift',[12] but in fact it was both: as well as being the result of a desperate desire to get shot of Edward Heath, the contest was also evidence of the growing strength and direction of the right of the party.

So, in any leadership contest fought in 1974, Whitelaw would almost certainly have found himself challenged for the leadership by a figure from the right of the party, eager to test the depths of dissatisfaction with the *ancien régime* and put down a marker for the new direction the party needed to take. That candidate might have been Keith Joseph, although his propensity to agonise in public, and in turn to put his foot in it (witness the infamous 'human stock' speech he gave at Edgbaston only nine days after the October election) makes this far from a certainty.[13] But be it Joseph, Thatcher or whoever, the crucial point is that although Whitelaw might have won, it would not have been a shoo-in. Whoever the candidate of the right, he or she would have produced a strong and significant showing.

Opposition

With the levers of power safely in the hands of a good one-nation Tory it is probable that the left would have a heaved a collective sigh of relief, and hoped that in defeat the ideologues of the party would see the error of their ways. If so, they would have been in for a shock. The right of the party were, and would have proved themselves to be, a force to be reckoned with.

A combination of their strong showing in the leadership election and Whitelaw's innate desire to balance the various wings of the party would have meant that many of the voices to the right of him would have been included in his Shadow Cabinet. These would almost certainly have included Geoffrey Howe, Keith Joseph, and Margaret Thatcher. If any of these had stood against Whitelaw in 1974 they would have had to have been rewarded for their strong showing with a senior position.[14] There is no reason to suppose that a Whitelaw-led party would have produced a less right-wing Shadow Cabinet than that chosen by Thatcher in 1975. The right would have had the platform from which to make their case.

And just as they did in reality after 1975, the left would have underestimated the threat facing them. Whilst there was initial shock ('the bitch has won', 'the party's taken leave of its senses' and so on)[15] and constant grumblings about the dogmatic turn the party appeared to be taking, the overwhelming view after 1975 was that one could simply sit back and wait for good sense to out. Once she'd been leader a little while, it was assumed that Thatcher and her cronies would come to recognise that the realities of political leadership required compromise and pragmatism, not messianic fervour. What the left of the party failed to grasp was the right's absolute belief in its depiction of past failures and its absolute conviction in its plans to arrest that decline.[16] In the year Thatcher entered Downing Street, a book was published entitled *Is Britain Dying?* She thought the answer was yes, and that she knew how to stop it. Indeed, in one of the more vainglorious parts of her memoirs, she comes close to claiming that she was the only person who knew:

> Chatham famously remarked: 'I know that I can save this country and no one else can'. It would have been presumptuous of me to have compared myself to Chatham [although, as you'll see, this wasn't going to stop her]. But if I am honest, I must admit that my exhilaration [at winning the 1979 election] came from a similar inner conviction.[17]

Building upon Joseph's critique of Britain's decline, the right had constructed its own identikit against which the experiences of the Heath years could be found severely wanting. Instead of adhering to the promised 'quiet revolution' supposedly ushered in at Selsdon in 1970, a series of noisy U-turns could be pointed to by which the Heath Government had run straight back to the failed policies of the past. Moreover, this failed template was the one to which the moderates were still attached but which had led them, while in government, to have to inquire just who ran the country. Indeed, the right's distrust of the left in the party cut straight to the bone. During a Shadow Cabinet meeting in 1976, Thatcher interrupted Gilmour in a discussion of a policy paper introduced by Keith Joseph, to ask, 'Ian, you *do* believe in capitalism?'[18] Given the alternative, the right could not afford to let up for a moment. Just as it battled to have its way under Thatcher's leadership, so the right would have fought just as hard under Whitelaw.

Simultaneously, events were working in their favour. The Labour Party had itself been forced into adopting both monetarist policy and rhetoric (albeit undertaken more through necessity than endorsement – what Nigel Lawson has termed 'unbelieving monetarism').[19] From as early as 1975 Denis Healey had been using the money supply to influence parts of the government's economic policy. In his 1976 conference speech, Prime Minister Jim Callaghan had explicitly renounced orthodox Keynesianism with the infamous exhortation that: 'we used to think that you could spend your way out of a recession … I tell you in all candour that option no longer exists …' Even Thatcher's tax cuts were pre-empted by Callaghan's promise to cut the 33 per cent rate to 30 per cent.[20] Nor was Callaghan's 'candour' limited to the field of economics. That all was in a state of flux was witnessed by his initiation of a 'great debate' on education, while in his first radio broadcast as Prime Minister he wondered: 'Do you, like me, think that perhaps we've been slipping?'[21]

The ground was crumbling beneath those who cautioned for a more moderate approach to the government of Britain. As the events of the late 1970s unfolded, consensus and compact were repeatedly dashed against the intransigence of the unions. The arch-wet, Norman St John-Stevas, lamenting 'the disappearing consensus', had noted:

> Britain has become much harder to govern in the second part of the twentieth century because of the pace of social and moral change for which our previous history provides no precedent. The consensus evolved over the centuries on what constitutes 'the good life' is in danger of dissolution into a welter of competing philosophies and viewpoints … The interior sanctions provided by an agreed moral and social outlook are disappearing at the very moment they are most needed.[22]

Such developments did not, these Conservatives felt, lend themselves to easy solutions (or at least solutions wholly within the government's competence), but without them they were left at the mercy of those who could advocate the simplicity of sound money and tough measures for the unions.

Against this background the right would have sunk its roots into distinctly fertile ground whoever the leader of the party had been. Just as they did in reality under Thatcher's leadership, a Conservative Party led by Willie Whitelaw would have carved out a series of policy documents in opposition which carefully sought to accommodate all parts of the party. But the combination of events and the growing strength and confidence of the right would have ensured that its pre-scriptions were far from marginalised.

Government: 1979–83

The 1979 election is a classic example of a government losing power rather than the opposition winning it. With such an unenviable record, it was small surprise that Callaghan should have suspected a 'sea change' in what the public wanted and was prepared to accept from its government. There is little reason to doubt that events would have been radically different in an election fought between Whitelaw and Callaghan than they were between Thatcher and Callaghan (if anything, given that Thatcher was no great electoral asset to the party in 1979, the election may even have been a more convincing Conservative victory under Whitelaw). The contest might have been more avuncular – like watching a good-natured argument between two loveable granddads – but the outcome would have been essentially the same.[23]

Would things have been all that different once the Conservatives were in government? There would, of course, have been differences between a Whitelaw Government and a Thatcher Government, but it is likely that these would have been far fewer than either Thatcher's supporters or detractors like to admit.

Take, for example, trade union reform. By the 1970s there was relatively little disagreement in the Conservative Party that something needed to be done about the unions. Most of those in a Whitelaw Cabinet would have rallied around Lord Hailsham's 1979 conclusion that the unions were 'selfish, short-sighted and narrow-minded' and had 'betrayed their membership, their country and their class'.[24] As they did under Thatcher, the left of the party would initially have had the more persuasive voice on the subject and, employing the lessons of Heath's abortive Industrial Relations Act, won the day in pressing for a cautious and piecemeal approach to any reform.[25] But, just as under Thatcher, the right of the party – vociferously so in the case of the parliamentary party – would have been consistently urging further and further reform. (In fact, even some of the wets thought Jim Prior was a little too cautious initially.)[26] While 'beer and sandwiches' would have been out for good following the excesses of the 1970s, trade unions may have received a little more tea and sympathy at the hands of Whitelaw than they did under Thatcher. However, while the manner and rhetoric might have differed, the policy outcome would have been remarkably similar.

Other policies usually credited to Thatcherism, such as the sale of council housing and privatisation, would also have found their way on to the statute book in the first term of a Whitelaw administration. The sale of council houses had been an idea of Peter Walker's, a figure from the left of the party; he had had to persuade Mrs Thatcher of its merits.[27] Privatisation was barely mentioned in the manifesto with which Thatcher had gone to the country in 1979, and the policy developed more by accident than design over the years, not least because it was a great money spinner.[28] Just as they did for Thatcher, so these measures would have been leapt upon by a Whitelaw administration as providing popular and eye-catching distractions from the harsh realities of government and its wider economic policy. Crucial as privatisation now is to the narrative of radical Thatcherism, it is difficult to see how, once stumbled upon, any member of the Conservative Party would have had immense ideological qualms with such a policy. Indeed, both council-house sales and the widening of share ownership could be – and were – seen in the light of Iain Macleod's desire for a 'capital-owning democracy' just as much as a central tenet of Thatcherism.

So far, then, so 'Thatcherite'. But what about economic policy? Surely here the 'moderates' could have expected to exert more influence in a Cabinet overseen by Willie Whitelaw? Part of the problem was that the so-called 'wets' were never a coherent group.[29] While the likes of Ian Gilmour, Jim Prior and Francis Pym were vocal critics of the monetarist policy undertaken by the Thatcher Governments, others, such as Lord Carrington and Christopher Soames, were prepared (having seemingly exhausted all other avenues in the search for a cure to the county's ills) to give this new approach a chance.[30] As Carrington recalled: 'I believed that there was … probably no alternative … Under the Conservatives other routes to salvation had in the past been tried and one had to admit that, at least in the particular circumstances of Britain, they hadn't worked'.[31] Norman St John-Stevas despaired: 'I don't know if it [monetarist policy] will work or not. Why is there no critique of it? Because no one has any alternatives. There is nothing else to try.'[32] As in opposition, this wing of the party not only lacked agreed solutions, they could not even rely on a united front with which to launch an attack.

The right would have certainly held the advantage in being more determined and engaged about economic matters than the 'wets', for many of whom the subject was not their strong suit. 'When practitioners of the dismal science descend on us, Lord Home is not the only one to reach for the matchbox', St John-Stevas confessed.[33] It meant that in large part the 'wets' had little else to offer by way of a convincing substitute. And in a Whitelaw Government one of the very men who admitted to having 'little natural aptitude' for the economic field would have been the man heading the government. Prime Minister Whitelaw would therefore have adopted much the same strategy as did Home Secretary Whitelaw in the Thatcher Government: 'having set out on a course of firm monetary discipline … it would be folly not to follow it through'.[34] Once Whitelaw had been persuaded of such a strategy the 'wets' would have been under pressure to fall further into line. As it is, many have since offered justifications of loyalty to both the party and the country as their motive for not resigning from the Cabinet of a leader they held in much lower esteem.[35]

This would not necessarily have produced complete rigidity in economic policy. Even under Thatcher, and despite the rhetoric, economic policy was lacking in doctrinal purity. Faced with what Andrew Gamble described as a more doctrinally pure 'Hayekian blitzkrieg' on entering office or an attitude of 'gradualism', Thatcher in practice opted for the latter. This, Gamble goes on to suggest, meant that it was difficult to 'maintain any strategic control' over the project as a whole'.[36] In fact, as the leading guru of monetarist doctrine, Milton Friedman, was to pronounce in 1982, monetarism came 'to cover anything that Mrs Thatcher at any time expressed as a desirable object of policy'.[37] Much the same would have occurred in a Whitelaw Government, perhaps with additional minor or symbolic victories for those concerned that the approach seemed too austere. Under Whitelaw such 'flexibility' may well have been seen as something of a virtue.

There may have been more noticeable differences in foreign affairs, not least because at the most fundamental level, international diplomacy is the part of government where style could be said to be as, if not more, important as substance.[38] It takes no great leap of the imagination, for example, to suppose that Willie Whitelaw may have been a little less rude to the French. Perhaps more importantly, it is also at least plausible to suppose that, with Whitelaw as Prime Minister, the UK may have avoided war with Argentina over the Falklands. This is not to argue that any easy answer would have been found to the problematic imperial legacy. Exactly as the 'leaseback' option appeared the most credible option in the Foreign Office under Mrs Thatcher, so it would have seemed to Whitelaw's team. But, just as that option ran into the recalcitrant foaming of parts of the Conservative backbenches, so it would have done under any Prime Minister. That mauling – described by Ian Gilmour as 'the silliest half hour that I ever heard in Parliament' (which, given that he'd clocked up thirty years in the place, is really saying something) – killed off the leaseback policy and any likely negotiations on it.[39]

What may have prevented war under Whitelaw, however, is the assumption that he would have been more willing to heed Foreign Office warnings over the seriousness of the Argentinean threat. Prime Minister Whitelaw might not have chaired a Cabinet willing to agree to the withdrawal of the only deterrent in the area, HMS *Endurance*, just at the moment it was most needed. But if he had, or had the Argentineans chosen to invade anyway, then Major William Whitelaw MC would have been just as likely to have sent the task force to reclaim the islands.

There would, however, have been one crucial difference between a Thatcher premiership and a Whitelaw one, one that has already been alluded to: their style. The policies pursued by his government might have been similar, but their presentation would not have been. There would have been more public agonising, more wringing of hands, more expressions of concern.[40] Equally, Cabinets would have been lengthier and more introspective under Whitelaw, as each minister was allowed to give full voice to their anxieties. Of course, such behaviour would have only further alarmed the right to the fact that things could be slipping. Accordingly they would have redoubled their efforts to keep Whitelaw on the straight and narrow. No doubt an entirely straight-faced Thatcher would have been heard briefing journalists that 'Willie's not stiff enough'. But the policies would have been essentially the same. Thatcherism without Thatcher as Prime Minister would have been Thatcherism, but with apologies. Britain would have faced an iron fist in a velvet glove, rather than the boxing glove that was the case.

Electorally, this would all have made little difference. Having (probably) avoided war in the South Atlantic – and with its generally apprehensive, and deeply concerned, tone – Whitelaw's Government would not have been able to go to the country in 1983 in quite the brazen way Mrs Thatcher did, but the Conservatives would still have won. Indeed, it is almost inconceivable that the Conservatives would have been able to orchestrate a scenario in which they were to lose the 1983 election. The impact of the Falklands victory on the result of the 1983 election was not as significant as is often believed,[41] and blessed with an opposition as equally divided and dire as the one faced by Thatcher, a Whitelaw second term would have been a certainty. It would have brought with it a large influx of less patrician, less privileged, Conservative MPs, many of whom were eager recruits to the right's flag.[42]

Maggie may

Had Edward Heath stood down in 1974, therefore, the nation may well have been denied (or spared) having Margaret Thatcher as Prime Minister. It would have been spared (or denied) the aggressive style of Thatcherism. But most of the policies known as Thatcherism would still have occurred. Indeed, it is even possible to envisage a scenario under which Heath stands down in 1974 and Margaret Thatcher still becomes Prime Minister. Just consider this:

Invigorated by their new and enhanced mandate, Willie Whitelaw's second administration would have been able to enjoy pointing to what it considered to be the first fruits of its labour. Soon after the election, inflation was down to its lowest level for fifteen years, and by September unemployment fell for the first time since 1979. It was – to use a famous Willieism – 'Splendid! Splendid!'

Noticeably less splendid, though, were the events of 1984–85, when Arthur Scargill 'led' the miners out on strike. But having learnt the lessons of their clash with the miners in 1973, Conservative politicians of all stripes were prepared to take them on this time, and to be properly prepared when doing so.[43] As Whitelaw was to reflect: 'Like all such confrontations, success for the nation in surviving this deliberate challenge was not achieved without unhappy strife and bitterness within communities and between families ... [yet] ... The confrontation of the miners' strike had to be met by the government and successfully overcome'.[44] As so often with Whitelaw, the manner and style were different – there was no talk of the enemy within – but the outcome was the same.

The biggest difference between Whitelaw and Thatcher, however, now became clear. Unlike Thatcher, Whitelaw had no desire to go on and on. From the beginning he had been a reluctant leader of his party – questioning whether he was really up to it[45] – and by the mid-1980s his health was beginning to fail.[46] So following his doctor's advice he informed the Queen and Cabinet that he had decided to resign as Prime Minister and Conservative Party leader, staying on until a replacement could be found.

On Thursday 11 July nominations closed for the first round of the 1985 Conservative leadership election. Three candidates threw their hats into the ring: Michael Heseltine (dismissed by Whitelaw as 'the sort of man who combs his hair in public') hoping to 'put down a marker for the future';[47] Francis Pym for the left, offering a policy of consolidation; and from the right, and urging the government to continue with its strategy for national renewal, the recently appointed Chancellor of the Exchequer, the Rt Hon. Margaret Hilda Thatcher MP ...

1   Margaret Thatcher, *The Path To Power* (HarperCollins, 1995), p. 328.
2   See for example, John Campbell, *Edward Heath* (Pimlico, 1994), pp. 568–69. Despite almost every observer claiming that the problem got worse during this period, Heath, whilst acknowledging that he suffered from it later, has claimed that he 'had no problems at all with it during 1974'; Edward Heath, *The Course Of My Life* (Hodder and Stoughton, 1998), p. 512. Perhaps he just got grumpier?
3   Julian Critchley, *Westminster Blues* (Futura, 1985), p. 121.
4   John Nott, *Here Today, Gone Tomorrow: Recollections of an Errant Politician* (Politico's, 2002), p. 169.

5   For the latter, see Carlos M. N. Eire, 'Pontius Pilate Spares Jesus', in Robert Cowley (ed.), *More What If? Eminent Historians Imagine What Might Have Been* (Macmillan, 2002), pp. 48–67.

6   Critchley, *Westminster Blues*, p. 122.

7   For Joseph's 'conversion', see Andrew Denham and Mark Garnett, *Keith Joseph* (Acumen, 2001), ch. 10.

8   James Prior, *A Balance of Power* (Hamish Hamilton, 1986), p. 98; William Whitelaw, *The Whitelaw Memoirs* (Aurum, 1989), p. 142.

9   Quoted in *The Times,* 31 January 1975.

10 Ian Gilmour, *Inside Right: Conservatism, Policies and the People* (Quartet Books, 1978), p. 12.

11 For a detailed analysis of the voting behaviour in both rounds of the 1975 contest see Philip Cowley and Matthew Bailey, 'Peasants' Uprising or Religious War? Re-examining the 1975 Conservative Leadership Contest', *British Journal of Political Science,* 30 (2000), pp. 603–29.

12 Hugh Young and Anne Sloman, *The Thatcher Phenomena* (BBC, 1986), p. 31.

13 See Denham and Garnett, *Keith Joseph,* pp. 265–69.

14 It is extremely unlikely that Whitelaw would have made Joseph Shadow Chancellor – because he was to argue strongly (and successfully) against Thatcher making exactly that appointment (see Hugo Young, *One Of Us: a Biography of Margaret Thatcher* (Pan, 1990), p. 104; or see Mark Garnett and Ian Aitken, *Splendid! Splendid!* (Jonathan Cape, 2002), p. 216) but a senior post would have had to have been given to the challenger, along with other posts for his or her soulmates.

15 The former is a Vice-Chairman of the party (quoted in John Ranelagh, *Thatcher's People* (Fontana, 1992), p. ix; the latter is Reggie Maudling (quoted in Kenneth Baker, *The Turbulent Years* (Faber and Faber, 1993), p. 44).

16 They may, at times, have taken their eye of the ball completely. Geoffrey Howe records Gilmour as being 'possibly the most committed champion of the incomes policy, yet always somehow semi-detached from the fray' and a 'less than regular attender' of the Shadow Chancellor's Economic Reconstruction Group; Geoffrey Howe, *Conflict of Loyalty* (Macmillan, 1994), p. 101.

17 Margaret Thatcher, *The Downing Street Years* (HarperCollins, 1993), p. 10.

18 Gilmour replied: 'That is almost blasphemy', but the point had been made.

19 Nigel Lawson, *The View from Number 11: Memoirs of a Tory Radical* (Bantam Press, 1992), p. 66.

20 John Vincent, 'The Thatcher Governments, 1979–87', in Peter Hennessy and Anthony Seldon (eds.), *Ruling Performance: British Governments from Attlee to Thatcher* (Basil Blackwell, 1989), p. 275.

21 James Callaghan, *Time and Chance* (William Collins, 1987), pp. 409–12; Phillip Whitehead, 'The Labour Governments, 1974–79', in Hennessy and Seldon, *Ruling Performance,*

p. 256; for an analysis of how such rhetoric aided the right see Stuart Hall, 'The Great Moving Right Show', in Stuart Hall and Martin Jacques (eds.), *The Politics of Thatcherism* (Lawrence and Wishart, 1983), pp. 19–39.

22 Norman St John Stevas, 'The Disappearing Consensus', in Anthony King (ed), *Why Is Britain Becoming Harder To Govern?* (BBC, 1976), p. 72.

23 Had Callaghan decided to go to the country in 1978 things may well have been different. But that, as they say, is another story – for which see Paul Richards' chapter in this volume.

24 Lord Hailsham, *The Dilemmas of Democracy* (Fount, 1979), p. 64.

25 See, for example, Geoffrey Howe, *Conflict of Loyalty,* p. 165. Indeed, despite his (cultivated) skinhead image, Prior's replacement, Norman Tebbit, also adopted a gradual, piece-by-piece, approach to union reform; Norman Tebbit, *Upwardly Mobile* (Weidenfeld and Nicolson), 1988, p. 184.

26 Ian Gilmour, *Dancing with Dogma* (Simon and Schuster, 1992), p. 80.

27 Peter Walker, *Staying Power* (Bloomsbury, 1991), pp. 141–42.

28 See Philip Cowley, 'The promise of reform', in L. Robins and B. Jones (eds), *Half a Century of British Politics* (Manchester University Press, 1997), p. 118.

29 Dennis Kavanagh, *Thatcherism and British Politics: The End of Consensus?* (Oxford University Press, 1990), p. 261; also Young, *One Of Us,* p. 201.

30 Gilmour, *Dancing With Dogma,* p. 35.

31 Lord Carrington, *Reflect on Things Past* (Fontana, 1989), p. 309.

32 Quoted in Young, *One Of Us,* p. 205.

33 Norman St John-Stevas, *The Two Cities* (Faber and Faber, 1984), p. 116.

34 Whitelaw, *The Whitelaw Memoirs,* p. 251; see also Young, *One Of Us,* p. 302, who notes that by late 1982 what all the Cabinet could agree on was 'that there could be no change of course'.

35 Gilmour, *Dancing with Dogma,* p. 33; Walker, *Staying Power,* p. 159.

36 Andrew Gamble, 'Thatcherism and Conservative Policies', in Hall and Jacques, *The Politics of Thatcherism,* p. 127.

37 Quoted in Peter Riddell, *The Thatcher Government* (Martin Robinson, 1983), p. 6.

38 See for example Harold Nicolson, *Diplomacy* (Oxford University Press, 1969), ch. 5: 'The Ideal Diplomat'.

39 Gilmour, *Dancing With Dogma,* p. 244. For a *mea culpa* by one of the participants, see Matthew Parris, *Chance Witness* (Viking, 2002), p. 308.

40 See, for example, the comments of Lord Carrington: having acknowledged that the policies pursued in the early 1980s were right, he wrote that 'if people are actually suffering, actually losing jobs … then I believe that a government – and its supporters – should show that the human side of the process is a matter of concern and should take care to use words which reflect that concern. I don't think we always did so.' (*Reflect on Things Past,* p. 310).

41 See, for example, David Sanders et al., 'Government popularity and the Falklands War: a reassessment', *British Journal of Political Science* 17 (1987), pp. 281–313.

42 See Martin Burch and Michael Moran, 'The Changing Political Elite', *Parliamentary Affairs* 38 (1985), pp. 1–15. The influx of 1983 are often described as 'Thatcher's children'. But they were not right-wing because of Thatcher, they were right-wing for the same reasons as Thatcher. Rather than Thatcher's children, they were the bastard offspring of Edward Heath.

43 Indeed it was again that figure from the left, Peter Walker, to whom many give credit for masterminding the tactical outmanoeuvring of the NUM.

44 Whitelaw, *The Whitelaw Memoirs,* p. 254.

45 At a lunch with the editor of the *Guardian* shortly after having lost the leadership to Thatcher, Whitelaw confessed that he was not sorry to have been defeated, adding that 'he probably didn't have the capacity to be a good Conservative leader'; The Hetherington Papers (22/7); for a more sceptical view of this position see Garnett and Aitken, *Splendid! Splendid!,* pp. 211–12.

46 In reality, ill-health did not force Whitelaw from government until 1987, but the pressures of the premiership are unique.

47 Garnett and Aitken, *Splendid!, Splendid!,* p. 311.

Chapter 13

What if Jim Callaghan had gone to the country in October 1978?

Paul Richards[1]

The period between James Callaghan's election victory in 1978 and Labour losing power twelve years later is considered by most people as the most successful in the British Labour Party's history. After a rocky start in the period 1974–76, Labour won three general elections, in 1978, 1982 and 1987, devolved power to Scotland, Wales, Northern Ireland and the English regions, managed a significant increase in spending on public services, oversaw a major programme of industrial democracy and 'socialisation' of the main public services and utilities, and kept Britain a leading voice in Europe and on the world stage.

Backed by the increased revenues from oil and gas production in the North Sea, the UK not only weathered the global recession of the early 1980s with the 'New Deal' programme for the unemployed, skills training and investment in the computer industry, but also became the only developed country to increase spending on health and education as a proportion of gross domestic product. Despite the unanticipated events that blow all governments off course, and the splits and divisions that seem to affect Labour governments in particular, James Callaghan's period in office remains a model of stable social-democratic government with rising standards of living, narrowing inequality, and improving public services. By the mid-eighties, politicians, academics and visitors from the US, Sweden, Australia and elsewhere were flocking to Britain to see at first hand the 'British model' of social democracy, and to write books, articles and pamphlets on Labour's success.

So how did Labour manage to sustain itself as the natural party of government over the period from the defeat of Edward Heath's government in 1974 to Conservative leader Michael Portillo's victory in 1992?

1978 – Labour's turning point

The choice of the date of the general election in the British system is the Prime Minister's alone. He may seek advice, listen to advisers, pore over opinion polls, but the final judgement rests with him.

For Prime Minister James Callaghan, in the job for less than two years after Harold Wilson's surprise resignation in March 1976, it was a decision of huge importance and one laden with the potential for catastrophe. The government had no working majority. The parliamentary party was exhausted from months of late-night votes, shabby deals with opposition parties, and the Tories' guerrilla tactics.

The trade unions were in an increasingly hostile and combative mood, especially after Callaghan and Chancellor Denis Healey had voiced their support for a 5 per cent pay settlement in the private and public sectors. Healey argued in a *Guardian* interview on 30 December 1977 that 'more and more people are coming to realise that no government can avoid having an incomes policy as far as its own employees are concerned. But of course to have a pay policy for the public sector and a free-for-all in the private sector can be very unfair to the public sector.'[2] In January 1978 Callaghan stated on the BBC *World This Weekend* that he linked pay increases directly with price increases and he wanted to see 5 per cent pay increases in 1978–79.[3] The unions demanded their right to free collective bargaining and at annual conference after annual conference rejected incomes policies in general and the 5 per cent policy in particular. The TUC General Council voted to reject it with only its chairman, Tom Jackson, of the Post Office workers' union, in favour. The union barons – Moss Evans, Clive Jenkins and Alan Fisher – lined up in opposition to the Labour government.

So with union discontent fermenting and Labour's parliamentary support hanging by a thread, Callaghan's judgement over the date of the general election would be crucial to his chances of winning. Cut and run, and Labour might have risked losing power; wait, and the political environment might have become even worse, heralding a Margaret Thatcher premiership. The industrial situation might have destroyed Labour's support amongst trade unionists and a series of public sector strikes might have lost support with the wider elector-ate. With a 'winter of discontent' looming, Callaghan needed to take decisive action.

James Callaghan made his mind up over the summer of 1978 to go for an election in October that year – a decision which as history records, proved extremely wise. Siren voices, including Leader of the House Michael Foot and Chief Whip Michael Cocks, had coun-selled Callaghan to delay the election until 1979. Arguments for delay included the worsening situation in Rhodesia, and forthcoming nego-tiations with Ian Smith and Joshua Nkomo (subsequently cancelled), the improving economic situation, and tactical considerations such as the need for an up-to-date electoral register and the desire to run down the Tories' election war chest by elongating the contest. Other senior figures, such as Harold Lever and David Owen, were also in favour of Labour hanging on until 1979. The party's pollster, Bob Worcester, warned that Labour might lose a 1978 election. Even Callaghan's own amateur psephology, as he studied polling data at his Sussex farmhouse in August 1978, pointed to the dangers of an early election.

But Callaghan was swayed by the weight of economic and psepho-logical evidence pointing the other way. As early as July 1978 David

Blake, economic editor at *The Times,* had argued that the economic factors – inflation at a low of 8 per cent, and incomes rising by 15 per cent – would make October most favourable for Labour's electoral chances.[4] In August Healey predicted a 3 per cent growth rate for the rest of the year. The balance of payments, which had been in deficit in the second quarter of 1977, showed a £483 million surplus in the third quarter and a £351 million surplus in the fourth quarter. By 1978, North Sea oil revenues helped the position even more, allowing the government to repay the final instalments of the IMF loan, balancing the books over the Parliament and jettisoning the crippling IMF interest payments.

Callaghan's senior policy adviser, Bernard Donoughue, prepared an analysis of polling figures and political factors which pointed to a favourable position in the polls by the autumn of 1978. The *Sun* journalist Roger Carroll was appointed as Callaghan's campaign speech-writer and was told to prepare for an autumn election. On 1 September 1978, on the eve of the TUC congress, senior trade union figures, including David Basnett, Terry Duffy, Moss Evans and Len Murray, joined Callaghan at his farm in Ringmer, near Lewes in Sussex, to urge an October 1978 election. After a good meal prepared by the Prime Minister's wife Audrey, the barons left, convinced their advice had been heeded.

On 5 September Callaghan gave an upbeat speech to the TUC in Brighton. Congress in 1978 was more like an election rally than the usual arcane procedures and wrangles. He delighted the union delegates with a rendition of Vesta Victoria's 'There was I, waiting at the church' (which he wrongly ascribed to Marie Lloyd). The knockabout performance was widely interpreted as a signal to the Tories that the election was coming soon, and Thatcher would be left standing.

On 6 September, Callaghan privately informed the Palace in writing of his decision. Alex Aitken, writing in the *Guardian* on 7 September, warned that if Callaghan failed to call an October election he would face the twin dangers of defeats in the House of Commons and the possibility of a no-confidence vote followed by an unplanned election, and the stalling and reversal of Labour's growing recovery in the opinion polls.[5] On the same day Callaghan, at the weekly Cabinet meeting at Downing Street, informed his Cabinet colleagues what they suspected: that the election would be held a little under a month later.

As Denis Healey recalls in his memoir, *The Time of My Life:* 'at Cabinet Jim told us that months of frustrating compromise and trench warfare were over. The news that an election was in the offing made us put our differences to one side and concentrate on winning the election. We felt like greyhounds finally released from our traps, and the hare we were chasing was Mrs Thatcher.' In his *Diaries* Tony Benn wrote: 'at last Jim has made a decision. Cabinet was not given the chance to discuss the election date. We were handed it by Jim like some feudal king addressing his court. But Labour's victory in October will give the left a real chance to fight for socialist policies.'

The 1978 campaign – Labour wins its mandate

On 7 September Callaghan broadcast to the nation on all three television channels, calling a general election for Thursday 5 October 1978. Labour's supporters were galvanised by the news that the election was coming within weeks. Labour's Transport House headquarters delivered an impressive campaign, projecting two key messages: that Labour needed a working majority to deliver its programme of jobs and public services; and that the 'new' Tories under Margaret Thatcher represented a 'new danger' to Britain. Labour moved seven points ahead of the Conservatives by late September, and by the final days of the campaign, in the first week of October, Labour enjoyed a ten-point lead. Callaghan's personal ratings were fourteen points ahead of Margaret Thatcher by the denouement of the campaign.

When the first results came in, it was clear that Labour had won a working majority and that Margaret Thatcher's Conservatives had been rejected. With a majority of fifty-eight seats, Callaghan had secured the mandate he needed. His gamble had paid off.

Margaret Thatcher and the Tories' travails

In politics there are winners and losers, usually in inverse proportion to one another. If the late 1970s and early 1980s can be seen as years of Labour success, for the Conservatives they were years of bitter infighting and discord.

There are many Conservatives who would prefer to forget Margaret Thatcher, and many voters who already have. Thatcher was chosen as leader of the Conservative Party in 1975, and immediately imposed her ideological and personal dominance on her party's policies and Shadow Cabinet. From the start Thatcher had an image problem. Her adviser Tim Bell remembers that: 'nobody liked her voice. Nobody particularly liked her. Her manner was a bit bossy, and a little bit school-marmish.'[6] Matthew Parris, then working in the Conservative Research Department, recalls 'the nickname we all used for her was "Hilda" … and it was not meant kindly.'[7]

Her short period of leadership from 1975 to 1978 is often cited as a telling example of the dangers of political parties conceding the centre ground in pursuit of ideologically extreme territory. Embarking on a 'policy review' fuelled by a range of obscure thinkers including Hayek, Adam Smith and the Chicago School of economists, she unceremoniously dumped a range of mainstream Conservative policies on Europe, the welfare state, and unemployment. The new approach, echoing British nineteenth-century laissez-faire and the economic liberalism being pioneered by the US Republicans, failed to connect with the swing voters Thatcher needed to persuade in 1978.

The Conservative policy platform was dismissed in Labour's 1978 manifesto as 'as dangerously out of their time as a penny-farthing on a motorway'.[8] The Tories' manifesto included pledges on the family, law and order, defence, restrictions on immigration, and selling off some sections of the nationalised economy. It promised:

> We will offer to sell back to private ownership the recently nationalised aerospace and shipbuilding concerns, giving their employees the opportunity to purchase shares. We aim to sell shares in the National Freight Corporation to the general public in order to achieve substantial private investment in it. We will also relax the Traffic Commissioner licensing regulations to enable new bus and other services to develop – particularly in rural areas – and we will encourage new private operators.[9]

The manifesto also promised a 'complete review' of the British National Oil Corporation (BNOC), which some saw as a sign of impending sell-off.

Margaret Thatcher was removed as leader of the Conservative Party in December 1978 after a vote of the parliamentary party. She resigned from the House of Commons in 1979 after two decades as MP for Finchley, causing a by-election which saw the Labour candidate, the young Liverpudlian lawyer and future Home Secretary, Cherie Booth QC, just squeak in. Her husband Anthony later became chairman of the Bar Council, and in 1989 a Labour peer. Margaret Thatcher established the Thatcher Foundation to promote her free-market ideas in 1979. It folded in 1984, amid accusations of financial mismanagement, and the untested ideas of 'Thatcherism' became no more than a historical footnote.

With coiffured blond hair, impeccable outfits and a no-nonsense style, the Conservatives' new leader shook up the old Tory establishment. One grandee complained that the 'estate agents have taken over from the estate owners' when Michael Heseltine won the leadership ballot in 1978. Tory MP Alan Clark complained that he was the sort of chap who had to buy his own furniture. Heseltine dragged the Conservatives through another policy review, which sought to reclaim the party to one-nation Conservatism and recalled the gentler times of Edward Heath and Stanley Baldwin. By the early 1980s the Conservatives had staked out their territory as pro-European, pro-business, pro-welfare state and pro-industrial democracy. Commentators argued that by becoming a pale blue imitation of the ideologically ascendant Labour Party, the Tories would remain in opposition for ever.

Labour's reforms 1978–82

With a renewed mandate and working majority of fifty-eight, backed by increased oil revenues, the Labour government discovered new vigour and purpose. James Callaghan had earned a strong position as Prime Minister, both with his party colleagues and in the country, and the government, and Callaghan personally, remained ahead in the polls throughout most of the Parliament.

With this renewed authority, Callaghan sacked his main opponents from the Cabinet (just as he had sacked Barbara Castle in 1976), notably Tony Benn MP, and renewed the government ranks with a series of inspired promotions. He had showed in 1977 that he was capable of making surprising appointments at Cabinet level when he appointed David Owen, then thirty-eight, to be Foreign Secretary, and the first Cabinet after the 1978 election, and subsequent reshuffles, showed a similar pattern. His governments balanced veterans such as Healey, Jenkins and Foot with new, dynamic ministers such as Shirley Williams, Bill Rodgers, David Owen, Neil Kinnock, Roy Hattersley, Gerald Kaufman, John Smith, Ann Taylor, Bryan Gould, Peter Shore and, after the 1982 election, Gordon Brown, Jack Straw, David Blunkett and Robin Cook. Callaghan deftly balanced right and left, England, Scotland and Wales, and the wartime generation with the baby boomers. Throughout the 1980s, Labour could deploy the talents of a generation of hard-working and skilful ministers.

In the 1978 reshuffle Callaghan kept Roy Hattersley, as Secretary of State for Prices and Consumer Protection, in charge of the government's pay negotiations. Hattersley ended the sectoral negotiations being conducted by individual ministers with one or two trade unions; often ministers lacked the stomach for tough rounds of negotiations with unions which they themselves belonged to, and were sponsored by. So Hattersley, with the support of younger colleagues such as Owen, John Smith and Bill Rodgers, met the union leaders one after another and imposed a series of tough pay settlements within the government's own secret negotiation range of 10 per cent. With a single point of negotiation, and with Callaghan's own renewed authority behind the scenes, further trade union discontent was avoided through the autumn and winter of 1978.

Oil

If Labour's successes in the 1980s were down to one factor, it was viscous, black, and came from beneath the North Sea.

In the mid-1970s, Labour ministers, including Tony Benn, Eric Varley, and Harold Lever, ably advised by Oxford economist Tommy Balogh, had established the British National Oil Corporation to secure some control over the oil resources, and a tax regime which brought maximum benefit to the Exchequer without penalising the oil companies. It became the accepted political view that whoever won the next general election would win the one after that, thanks to oil; either Labour would use it to invest in public services, or the Tories would use it to cut taxes.

The potential benefits of North Sea oil, however, had been subject to bitter infighting amongst Labour ministers. Benn and Healey favoured differing uses for the extra revenues, Benn seeking an immediate investment programme in social spending and Healey favouring debt reduction and long-term investment. A meeting in November 1977 attended by Healey and Treasury adviser Derek

Scott, and Tony Benn and his adviser Frances Morrell, for the Department of Energy, had resulted in impasse. Callaghan intervened to produce a compromise, and in 1977 the government introduced a White Paper, *The Challenge of North Sea Oil*, based on a Cabinet-commissioned study, which recommended six uses for the extra revenues: reinvigorating the inner cities, training young people and retraining older people, developing alternative energy sources, supporting the National Enterprise Board, increases in overseas aid, and a reduction in personal taxation. The White Paper also established the now-familiar *Oil Spoils* annual report into how oil revenues are distributed each year. By 1980, Britain was self-sufficient in oil, producing almost 90 million tonnes a year, and almost self-sufficient in gas.

Between 1979 and 1987 North Sea oil contributed £62 billion in revenue to Labour's coffers, and the contribution to the balance of payments was £100 billion. Without these extra revenues, it is hard to see how Labour could have tackled unemployment, invested in the social services, or tackled under-investment in the railways, roads, housing and the inner cities. Indeed, without the oil bonanza, as Denis Healey observed in *The Time of My Life,* 'Britain would have been bankrupt'.[10] North Sea oil gave Britain a huge windfall of extra revenues which undoubtedly helped Labour stay in power in the 1982 and 1987 elections; it allowed Labour governments to avoid the crises over balancing the books and runs on the pound which had effected previous Labour administrations in 1929, 1948, 1967 and 1976; and it allowed a Labour government to deliver in large part its own promises, keeping the party broadly united (apart from the 1980 Gang of Four breakaway) and retaining the public trust as evidenced in opinion polls.

Industrial Democracy

Lord Alan Bullock, a school-friend of Denis Healey, had been asked in the late 1970s to chair a Royal Commission into industrial democracy. The resulting Bullock Report recommended that workers should be represented on company boards where at least one-third of the workers had voted for it. The trade union representatives on the Commission had demanded that the workers should be represented via existing trade union structures rather than directly from the workforce. At the time, some argued that given the unrepresentative nature of the unions the scheme would not lead to industrial democracy but only increased union power, and the Bullock Report was put out to grass. Bernard Donoughue, in his political memoir *Prime Minister*, argued that: 'it would have led to undemocratic industrial democracy'.[11]

After the 1978 election, the report was dusted down and given a new spin. Learning from the German *Mitbestimmungsrecht* model of worker participation, and dismissing the unions' demands for sole representation, in 1980 the Secretary of State for Industry, Shirley Williams, introduced a White Paper, *Hand in Hand – New Partnership in Industry,* which heralded a new era of worker participation. It was a great success, and the new demands of the workforce for genuine involvement forced the trade unions into wholesale modernisation of their structures, recruitment and campaigning. The reforms can also be seen as a major contributor to the reduction in strikes and the number of days lost through industrial action. For many sectors, for example local government, railways, and mining, the early and mid-1980s saw a prolonged period of industrial calm and productivity.

Like so much in politics, the Bullock Report and the resulting Democracy in the Workplace Act (1981) heralded a major transformation in British society which few could have foreseen at the time. The changes in working practices in the private sector and the appetite for public involvement and participation unleashed new demands for democratisation in the public services and utilities to which the Labour government responded, in the period 1982–87, with the programme of what became known as 'socialisation'. For most observers socialisation stands as the primary defining characteristic of Labour in government at this time, as we shall see later in this chapter. However it is interesting to note that in the late 1970s and even as late as the early 1980s, the ideas of socialisation were ill-formed and obscure, remaining the stuff of Fabian Society seminar and pressure-group pamphlet.

International politics

On the international stage, Callaghan had three major challenges: dealing with the Soviet Union, balancing Britain's place between the US alliance and the European Community, and dealing with the aftermath of empire. Thanks to Britain's influence, the 1980s saw a thawing of the Cold War and increasing détente between NATO and the Warsaw Pact. In 1981 Callaghan appointed Welsh MP Neil Kinnock as Secretary of State for Defence, with a brief to reduce Britain's expenditure on nuclear weapons through negotiations with the Soviet Union. Kinnock proved an able negotiator, persuading the Soviets to begin reductions in their stockpiles of weapons and the Americans to remove their bases from parts of the UK, including Greenham Common.

Another small but illustrative test of Labour's international diplomacy came in 1982. It concerned a small group of islands, first settled by Lord Byron's grandfather, of which most people had never heard. British and American intelligence picked up strong signals that the Argentinian junta, led by General Galtieri, facing riots at home, planned to invade the Falkland Islands. Labour's Foreign Secretary Gerald Kaufman, like his predecessor David Owen in 1977, dispatched a nuclear submarine and small naval taskforce to join HMS *Endurance* in patrolling the Falkland Islands. The signal was clear and unambiguous, and the planned Argentinian invasion was shelved.

On the issue of South Africa, a similarly robust stance secured a positive result. Labour's 1978 manifesto stated that: 'Labour is totally opposed to the system of apartheid, and will continue to support opponents of apartheid, giving humanitarian and other aid to liberation movements of Southern Africa. We will take active steps to reduce our economic dependence on South Africa and discourage new investment in South Africa by British companies.'[12] Callaghan had discussed with Jimmy Carter and other world leaders at the Guadaloupe Summit in January 1979 a joint approach to the apartheid regime, and in the early 1980s, under some pressure from the growing Anti-Apartheid Movement, the government moved from a position of 'discouragement' of involvement in South Africa to outright sanctions (as had been earlier deployed against Rhodesia). British firms, including major banks, engineering and oil companies, were outlawed from working in South Africa from 1982 onwards, with a series of high-profile prosecutions to demonstrate the government's resolve. Britain's supply of backbone to the international efforts to end apartheid is seen by many historians as one of the major contributing factors to President Botha's release of Nelson Mandela from prison in 1984, and the dismantling of the apartheid regime which swiftly followed in the mid to late 1980s.

The Gang of Four – breaking the mould

Britain's first new political party for eighty years was launched on 1 May 1980 by the so-called Gang of Four. The four leading Labour left-wingers Tony Benn (sacked from government by Callaghan in 1978), Eric Heffer MP, miners' leader Arthur Scargill and Margaret Beckett, MP for Lincoln, declared in the 'Holland Park Manifesto' that it was time to break the mould of British politics.

The Gang of Four and their supporters rejected the consensus politics of Labour in government and called for a more robust form of socialism. The New Labour Party, or 'New Labour' as the media dubbed it, wanted unilateral nuclear disarmament, immediate British withdrawal from the EEC and NATO, the extension of state control of industry, and increased personal and business taxes. The 'Holland Park Manifesto', delivered to the media from the front drive of former minister Tony Benn's Holland Park home, stated that:

> We want more, not less, radical change in our society, but with a greater stability of direction. We want to eliminate poverty and promote greater equality. We want fair shares of the rewards of a strong economy based on public ownership, free trade unions, and full employment.
>
> We want world peace and disarmament, and equality between nations and people. We want Britain out of the EEC and NATO.
>
> With heavy hearts but calm heads, we reject the soggy centrism of to-day's so-called Labour government and demand a return to socialist values and policies.

None of the twenty-two MPs who joined Benn's breakaway 'New Labour' sought re-election in a by-election, and the rump voted with the Labour Party on most occasions between the party's launch in 1980 and the 1982 general election – where all twenty-two of them were defeated by official Labour candidates, including Tony Benn in his Bristol seat. The party soon descended into rancour; after Arthur Scargill resigned to form his own Socialist Party in 1983, 'New Labour' became no more than a Tony Benn fan club. It was wound up in 1990. Benn remains a favourite of the left-wing pressure group circuit and a prolific author of diaries and diatribes.

Labour in office 1982–87

Labour's election manifesto for the 1982 general election was described by Foreign Secretary Gerald Kaufman as the 'longest love letter in history' because of its popular appeal with the electorate. The outcome of the election saw Labour secure an increased majority, and Michael Heseltine's Conservatives slumped to their lowest share of the vote since 1945. Heseltine's barnstorming strategy of addressing huge rallies of faithful Tories in their heartlands was proved to be misguided; even the 10,000-strong Surrey rally held in King-ston-on-Thames was seen as a mistake. As the *Guardian* noted, 'For every true-blue Tory cheering Heseltine at a rally, there were twenty Labour voters watching "Uncle Jim" on television at the latest skil-fully orchestrated photo-opportunity.'

Labour's programme contained promises for a range of radical policies, developed and tested in Labour's think-tanks and journals, which connected with key groups of voters. The theme of the mani-festo was 'power to the people' and across the public services and public bodies, policies to introduce decentralisation, participation, and democratic control by local people were proposed. It promised tax cuts for the lowest paid, a 'new deal' for the unemployed, extra police, new consumer rights in the utilities, a freedom of information act, renewed efforts for peace in Northern Ireland (which led directly to the 1984 Good Friday Agreement), devolution to Scotland and Wales and extra powers for councils, the metropolitan authorities and the Greater London Council. The manifesto also promised a wind-fall tax on British financial institutions to fund a major learning and skills programme and investment in the education system. This latter policy, although it was bitterly opposed by the Conservatives, kick-started the UK computer and software industry and has been judged the major contributor to Britain's dominance in the global informa-tion technology market in the 1980s.

The most famous policy in the love-letter manifesto was Labour's 'right-to-buy' policy for council-house tenants. First discussed in the mid 1970s by Harold Wilson with Policy Unit members Bernard Donoughue and Joe Haines, and the Number 10 Private Secretary Robin Butler, right-to-buy was a scheme which gave council-house tenants the opportunity to buy their homes from the council. The capital receipts thus raised were reinvested in new homes which reflected new social needs, such as the aspiration for more affordable family homes with gardens, and inner-city flats for single people and key workers such as police, nurses and teachers.

The policy, along with high employment and the investment allowed by oil revenues, led to a renaissance in many British city centres; areas such as St Paul's in Bristol, Brixton in South London, Moss Side in Manchester and Toxteth in Liverpool became lively cosmopolitan centres for young professionals. It proved hugely successful and popular in Labour's heartlands too, and ensured continuing high turnouts in elections. Several dozen Labour MPs owed their seats in the 1980s to the right-to-buy policy.

Labour's term of office in 1982–87 was characterised by radical reforms and stable government, but further reforms were to come. At the 1986 Labour Party conference in Blackpool, flanked by his ministers and in front of cheering crowds, James Callaghan announced the 'Next Steps Forward'. The Labour conference contrasted starkly with the Tories' gathering in Bournemouth the week before which witnessed Heseltine turning on the Eurosceptics in his own party in a tub-thumping speech.

Labour in office 1987–92

Labour won a landslide victory at the 1987 general election, based on its track record and the Tories' continuing infighting. Heseltine remained as Conservative Leader despite losing a second general election. In this period in office, Labour's transformation of British society was completed, with increases in public spending and low interest rates, single-figure inflation and unemployment under a million. Callaghan's position as a world leader was reinforced with a series of international alliances and summits with Reagan, Gorbachev, and Europe's leaders.

There are plenty of disparate studies of the programme of socialisation which Labour unleashed between 1987 and 1992. What we can agree on is that socialisation, whilst drawing on older Labour values and policies, developed 'on the hoof' and was never based on a coherent blueprint or plan. Clues can be found in Labour's support for cooperative ventures, for different forms of public ownership, and in policy documents such as the 1978 manifesto, which stated that: 'council tenants will have more control in their own homes, parents and teachers will have a greater freedom to influence the running of their children's schools. Local services will be handed back to local authorities closer to the people. These are practical ways to set the people free.'[13]

But even the closest reading of Labour's runes would not have predicted the changes that were to come. It started in a modest way, and when ministers saw its success, they were emboldened to launch ever greater schemes. Socialisation was not a single scheme, but a series of forms of public ownership which fitted the purpose. It was given intellectual credibility by a network of left-wing think tanks, academics and writers, including the Fabian Society, the G. D. H. Cole Institute, and the Industrial Common Ownership Movement, whose President, John Smith MP, became a key driver of the policy in the Cabinet.

The programme started with establishment of workers' and consumers' public-interest companies in the electricity, gas and water industries, ending the state monopolies. Next came telecommunications, with the launching of regional telecommunications cooperatives based on the Hull-based and locally owned Kingston Communications. Then, in the mid 1980s, the railway industry was broken up into smaller public companies with strong consumer representation. By ending state ownership, the government allowed greater public ownership and involvement, enabled innovation and local experimentation, and permitted local enterprises to raise funds from the private sector.

The socialisation model was adopted throughout the public services, including schools, hospitals and local amenities. Local GPs' surgeries, schools and colleges, parks and libraries and even hospitals were subject to new management structures which included local people, users, and staff. The programme, despite its small-scale beginnings, transformed the structure of ownership in Britain and inspired similar programmes around the world, notably in the former USSR and Eastern Bloc.

Callaghan's defeat in 1992

It is hard to pinpoint an exact reason for Labour's defeat in 1992. Like Labour in 1951, despite a radical programme, the government seemed tired and out of ideas. Once the major planks of socialisation had been laid, ministers seemed unsure what to do next. The party had failed to renew itself in office, and there was a strong sense in the country that it was time for a change. Labour's appeal had also been eroded by a series of scandals, including a string of ministerial resignations following media revelations in 1990 and 1991. One minister was caught illegally dealing in shares; another got his secretary pregnant; a third borrowed money from a colleague and failed to declare it. The cumulative effect was a breakdown in trust between government and people.

James Callaghan himself was eighty years old, and had been Prime Minister for sixteen years. Like Churchill or Gladstone, he was respected as the grand old man of politics, but 'Uncle Jim' had lost much of his avuncular appeal. When faced at the 1992 election with a young dynamic Conservative Leader in the shape of Michael Portillo, Callaghan and the Labour Party seemed like old news. On 9 April 1992, Labour lost the general election and Michael Portillo became the first Conservative Prime Minister since 1974. Callaghan resigned as Labour Leader within weeks, and after a fiercely fought four-way contest, Gordon Brown beat Shirley Williams, Neil Kinnock and Bryan Gould to emerge as Leader of the Opposition. Kinnock easily won the election to be Brown's deputy.

Labour's golden age – an assessment

By the standards of its own previous spells in government, Labour's period in office from 1974 to 1992 stands as a success. Like the Swedish Social Democratic Party, Labour showed that it was possible for socialist parties to sustain long periods in office, and at the same time be a government of change. The lasting changes to Britain's economy and society have created a more egalitarian European country, compared to the Britain of the mid-1970s. By decisively defeating Margaret Thatcher in 1978, Britain was spared her off-beat prescriptions; her ideas for privatisation and free markets remained on the drawing board, and her career was cut short.

Under Michael Heseltine, the third leader of the Conservatives never to become Prime Minister (after Austen Chamberlain and Margaret Thatcher), a generation of Tory MPs were denied office. It would perhaps make an interesting counterfactual to consider what might have happened if Callaghan had called it wrong in August 1978 and delayed the election through the winter. Labour might have lost, and Britain might even have had its first woman Prime Minister!

Notes

1   Everything described before 6 September 1978, the date James Callaghan informed the Queen of his decision on the date for the general election, is historically accurate. Everything after 6 September 1978, when I wonder what if he had called the election for October 1978, including quotations, is invented, based on historical precedent, supposition, and in many places wishful thinking!

2   Martin Holmes, *The Labour Government 1974–79* (Macmillan, 1985) p. 125.

3   Ibid.

4   Ibid., p. 130.

5   Ibid., p. 131.

6   Brenda Maddox, *Maggie* (Hodder & Stoughton, 2003) p. 117.

7   Ibid., p. 107.

8   Labour manifesto, 1979.

9   Conservative manifesto, 1979.

10 Denis Healey, *The Time of My Life* (Norton, 1990) p. 541.

11 Bernard Donoughue, *Prime Minister* (Jonathan Cape, 1987) p. 149.
12 Labour manifesto, 1979.
13 Ibid.

Chapter 14

What if Roy Jenkins had joined the Liberal Party in 1981?

Neil Stockley

The death of Lord Jenkins of Hillhead in January 2003 saw, as is to be expected, many tributes to a major figure of Britain's post-war politics. Most were positive and generous, if not fulsome, in their praise of the man and his achievements. Yet there were some strong undercurrents, for Jenkins' death revived the debates over the Social Democratic Party and its legacy. Did it keep the Thatcher Government in office by splitting the centre-left vote? Did it provide the road map – and a badly needed scare – to put the Labour Party on the long march back to electability? Was the SDP merely a symptom of Labour's malaise in the 1980s? – a passing political fad that in the end accomplished next to nothing?

It was entirely appropriately that an assessment of Lord Jenkins' life should lead to these questions being asked. The genesis of the SDP is usually traced to his Dimbleby Lecture, 'Home Thoughts from Abroad',[1] delivered in November 1979 when he was still President of the European Commission. The speech was a forceful indictment of British politics in the post-war period. Jenkins criticised the country's economic decline under both Conservative and Labour governments, slammed the false-choice choices, see-saw politics and broken promises of the two-party system and, most importantly, called for a strengthening of the 'radical centre' in British politics.

During 1980, Jenkins held many discussions with friends inside and
outside the Labour Party about what form this 'strengthening' should
take. By the end of the year, he had teamed up with Shirley Williams, David Owen and Bill Rodgers – the 'Gang of Three' of leading
Labour politicians who were growing more and more alarmed at
their party's lurch to the extreme left.

The SDP was launched, to great media fanfare, in March 1981. The
conspirators, now the 'Gang of Four', pledged themselves to breaking
the mould of British politics. In time, twenty-eight Labour and one
Conservative MPs defected to the new party, and tens of thousands
of people, many with no history of political activity, joined. It soon
formed an alliance with the Liberal Party but, after two disappoint-
ing general election results, it was clear that the mould had not been
broken. After a bitter debate within the SDP, in 1988 the two parties
merged to form what we now know as the Liberal Democrats.

Would anything have been different if Roy Jenkins had joined
the Liberal Party upon his return from Brussels in January 1981? The
question is by no means absurd. He and the Liberal Leader David
Steel discussed it as a possibility but came to the conclusion that a
substantial number of social democrats splitting from Labour and
forming a new party would have more impact than a few defections
to the Liberals.[2]

If Jenkins had been less interested in resuming an active political
career, however, he could simply have joined the Liberal Party. He
would have fitted in rather well, for by 1980 he was already a latter-
day 'Whig', if not a committed Liberal. As Jenkins later wrote in his
memoirs:

> I had long been well disposed towards most Liberals. As Asquith's sym-
> pathetic biographer I was unlikely to be anything else ... If I came back
> quietly from Brussels to a not very political semi-retirement I thought that
> I would become a nominal Liberal, for that party was now closer to my
> outlook than was either the Labour Party or the Conservatives.[3]

With its full-frontal challenge to the two party system, the Dimbleby Lecture laid the foundation-stone of the SDP – but it can also be read as an elegant restatement of themes long pursued by David Steel and his predecessors Jo Grimond and Jeremy Thorpe. Jenkins supported a mixed economy; he believed that the private sector in a market economy would generate the most wealth and that the state should work to prevent the gap between the wealthiest and the poorest growing too large. But he was also clear that whilst it should be active in ensuring equal opportunities, the state should 'know its place' in society. He also called for a new voting system, decentralisation to the nations and regions and action to deliver a more co-operative approach between employers and employees – all core Liberal policies. Furthermore, Jenkins had worked successfully with David Steel on the latter's Abortion Bill in 1967 and the 'Yes' campaign for the 1975 EEC referendum. They had kept up close contacts during his time in Brussels. And, of course, many of Jenkins' closest friends, such as Mark Bonham Carter, were senior figures in the Liberal establishment.

Jenkins and the Gang of Three could easily have gone in different directions. First, while they agreed with Jenkins on most policy issues, their broader agendas were quite different from his crypto-Liberalism. Of course, Williams, Owen and Rodgers did not think exactly the same way, but they were all, in one way or another, still true believers in the ethos of British democratic socialism. Yes, the Gang bitterly opposed the policies of Tony Benn and his followers – but they were still egalitarians at heart. Yes, they were at one with Jenkins on the need for major industrial and political reforms – but he saw such changes primarily as a means of saving the post-war consensus that had built up around Britain's economic and social policies. His co-founders had different goals: Williams, for instance, wanted to change British society, to make it fairer and more equal, and Owen wanted to shake up the establishment and confront its failings. Their political vehicle would be a new centre-left party, without the old left and hidebound trade unions. In short, they wanted to create a new version of the Labour Party in which they had spent their whole political lives.[4]

There were also differences of strategy and outlook. Right up until Labour's Blackpool Conference in October 1980, none of the defectors had any interest in working with the Liberal Party. Indeed, few had any real knowledge or understanding of it, the one exception, David Owen, being, of course, quite hostile.[5]

Would there still have been an SDP?

Even if Jenkins had joined the Liberal Party, it is difficult to see what, if anything, would have turned out very differently. The SDP would surely still have been formed. In October 1980, Labour's Blackpool Conference called for withdrawal from the EEC, unilateral nuclear disarmament, expanded public ownership and the mandatory reselection of MPs. It was at this low-point in the political fortunes of the Labour right that Williams, Owen and Rodgers each concluded, after going through considerable anguish, that their party could not be saved. Once Labour seemed to be a lost cause, the 'Gang' and their supporters decided to leave and start afresh. It was they who took the initiative in forming the party and they who were able to take a significant number of Labour MPs, councillors and activists with them. After four years in Brussels, following a lengthy period in which he was seen as a remote, patrician figure, Jenkins simply did not have that kind of political clout. He and his allies were weighing up their options throughout 1980, but the two groups were working in parallel lines, which did not join together until the very end of the year.

Jenkins was undoubtedly a major asset to the new party, but his part in the immense enthusiasm it generated in the early months was no greater than that of Williams or Owen. The excitement over the new party was a result of many factors: the recession of 1980–81, the deep sense of frustration and disillusionment with politics, Labour's political woes and the sense that the SDP represented something new and exciting. Had he not joined, the party might have been slightly smaller and received fewer sympathetic media reports; but it would still have come into existence and got off to a very promising start.

Indeed, the essential nature of the SDP and, for that matter, the Liberal Party, would have been little changed. The SDP's leadership, policy and membership were strongly pro-Europe, supportive of NATO, against unilateral nuclear disarmament and in favour of reflation through increased public spending.[6] Jenkins was very important to joining all of this together and articulating the party's vision; at least in the early stages, he painted much of the party's philosophical landscape. But he and his closest allies did not play a leading role in developing (or changing) any of the SDP's policy positions. Similarly, it is hard to think of a policy issue over which he was at fundamentally at odds with the Liberals, or where he might have changed their position. It is unlikely that any more than a handful of backbench MPs and his more faithful allies (such as John Harris) would have gone with him – hardly enough in any case to shift the centre of gravity in the Liberal Party, even if they had wanted to.

Liberals vs. Social Democrats?

Which ever of the two parties Jenkins had belonged to, they would still have had to work closely together. In a first-past-the-post electoral system, in which the third party usually found it very difficult to win very many seats, direct competition seemed to be futile and destructive. In any case the two parties seemed to be natural bedfellows right from the beginning. Liberals and Social Democrats were at one in supporting the mixed economy, Europe, NATO, electoral reform and the welfare state.

In the early months of 1981, there seems to have been little disagreement within the SDP that some kind of cooperation would eventually be essential. Within the Liberal Party, attitudes towards the prospective new partner were somewhat more complicated and ambivalent, if not suspicious; but most senior Liberals readily saw from opinion poll evidence the political 'added value' of having an alliance. And nearly all saw the need to work with, rather than against, the new party. The question was on what terms.

In any case, the momentum towards an alliance started very quickly and here Jenkins was not always instrumental. There was a formal structure to co-ordinate parliamentary tactics in place as early as February 1981, before the SDP was officially launched. At the Königswinter Conference in April, David Steel and his aide Richard Holme met Shirley Williams and Bill Rodgers and agreed that there should be a formal electoral pact and a single 'Alliance' manifesto. From then on, the die was cast. A joint policy statement, *A Fresh Start for Britain,* followed two months later, showing the extent of the common ground between the two parties.

The importance of Jenkins' role in the SDP can also be tested by examining the party's internal machinations over how the Alliance should work. In his memoirs, Owen recounts his vision of the SDP's role within the Alliance, which was, in essence, for it to be as independent as possible from the Liberal Party. He saw the SDP as the dynamic, popular new force that would provide most of the Alliance's credibility and electoral support. No one doubted that the SDP would eventually have to come to an agreement with the Liberal Party, but Owen wanted it to develop its own brand, policies, membership, finances and organisation. If this meant taking the Liberals on at council elections and parliamentary by-elections, then so be it; he and his colleagues could then negotiate with the Liberals over seats and policies from a position of political strength.[7]

Such a strategy did not emerge. Liberals and Social Democrats did not fight each other at the ballot-box and, by the end of 1981, were embroiled in detailed negotiations over which party should fight which constituencies. The talks were difficult, protracted and at times very tense, but they were eventually concluded to the general satisfaction of both sides. A close alliance was formed and it was not dominated by the SDP.

Dr Owen claims that this had fatal consequences for the party: 'It was divisions in our own party as to whether the SDP was to be a separate party from the Liberal Party that destroyed [the SDP].'[8] There is little doubt whom he held ultimately responsible:

> I find it impossible to escape the conclusion that Roy Jenkins misled me and some of the other MPs who left the Labour Party in 1981, as well as the members of the SDP in the leadership election in 1982, about his real intentions ... While he abandoned open advocacy of a merger until 1987, he subtly and systematically undermined the SDP's independence from 1981–87. Roy used the SDP. It would have more honourable to have joined the Liberals in 1981.[9]

Needless to say, Jenkins strongly rejected these charges, arguing that he only supported a merger after the strengths and, more importantly, the weaknesses of the Alliance had become fully apparent.[10] Nevertheless, Owen's claims provide a useful framework in which to consider Jenkins' impact on the emerging power balance within the Alliance and how it could have been different had he not been in the SDP.

Owen contends that the Warrington by-election of July 1981 was the tipping point in the arguments over strategy. Jenkins fought the by-election as a 'Social Democrat with Liberal support', reducing the Labour majority from over 10,000 to 1,756. According to Owen, Jenkins' excellent showing enhanced his stature within the SDP and built a sense of legitimacy for his conception of an Alliance with an electoral pact concluded as soon as possible, and a single manifesto.[11] By the autumn the Liberal Assembly in Llandudno had voted to accept the Alliance; Williams and Jenkins shared a fringe platform with Steel and Jo Grimond, and the establishment of two joint policy commissions soon followed.

It would have taken an extraordinary sense of will, if not bloody-mindedness, for the SDP's collective leadership to decide to go it alone; all the same elements would have been in place whether or not Jenkins had fought Warrington. The various dramas over Shirley Williams are a case in point. Owen had wanted Williams to be the party's 'big-name' candidate at Warrington; his gambit was for her to take on all comers, win the by-election (which polling showed she could do) and then become leader of the SDP[12] – but it was Williams herself who spoiled his plans by deciding that she did not want to take the risk of losing. Similarly, when a by-election fell due in Croydon North-West, Williams was keen to fight it, but the SDP Steering Committee declined to ride roughshod over the Liberals when their obscure local candidate, Bill Pitt, refused to stand aside; he was duly elected.

Dr Owen blames himself for not going into bat for Williams, in part because he wanted to maintain the unity of the Gang of Four. But he also claims that there was some personal resentment on the committee following her indecision over Warrington. Jenkins' absence from the party would have altered neither Williams' decisions nor the willingness of others to take on the Liberals on her behalf.[13]

It can be seen that it would have taken a great deal more than Jenkins joining the Liberals to pit the two parties in open competition during 1981 and 1982. Even if there had there been a strong consensus within the SDP to follow Owen's strategy, however, where might it have led? An SDP candidate in Croydon North-West could have polled well and stopped the Liberal candidate from winning; similarly, the Liberals could easily have deprived Williams of her victory in Crosby in December, and caused the defeat of another Social Democrat in Glasgow Hillhead the following March. A battle between two parties who were agreed on all the main issues would have bewildered their potential supporters, eroded their credibility and lost them both support. It is more likely that one side or the other would have sued for peace after the Croydon North-West by-election, if not earlier.

Owen as SDP leader in 1983

Once he had won the Glasgow Hillhead by-election in March 1982, Jenkins defeated Owen to become, in July, the first leader of the SDP. But he did not shine in the role. A natural man of office, he did not take easily to leading a small fledgling party in opposition. He was a poor television performer, ill-suited to the demands placed by the media; more surprisingly, he found the Commons a much more difficult environment than he had during his heyday at the Despatch Box. He failed to establish a distinctive image for the SDP at the same time as the Falklands War was firmly establishing Mrs Thatcher as an authoritative and heroic national leader. With few new opportunities to attract publicity, the SDP fell into a deep trough for most of 1982.

For the 1983 general election campaign, Jenkins was the Alliance's 'Prime Minister-designate' and David Steel its 'leader'. This arrangement proved unworkable. About midway through the campaign, the Liberals attempted to replace Jenkins at the 'Ettrick Bridge summit'; it was finally agreed that Steel would, in effect, lead the Alliance bid for power. Despite a late surge in support, the election outcome was a bitter disappointment for the Alliance. It won 25.4 per cent of the popular vote – only 2.2 per cent behind Labour – but only twenty-three MPs (seventeen Liberals and six Social Democrats) were returned. Williams and Rodgers both lost their seats. The failure and eventual death of the SDP can be traced to this ignominious result.

The Alliance may have performed a little better had Jenkins joined the Liberal Party and became unavailable to take on the SDP leadership. For a variety of reasons, Shirley Williams did not want the job, so it is certain that Dr Owen would have become the SDP's first leader, possibly as early as February 1982, and led it into the 1983 election. It is safe to conclude, on the basis of his performance as Leader between 1983–87, that he would have been far more effective than Jenkins at building the SDP's profile both in the media and in the House of Commons.

He may also have provided the party with a clearer brand image. In the run-up to the 1983 election, Owen saw the party's main strategic objective as keeping a bridgehead in the Commons by retaining as many SDP MPs as possible. In his view, this meant appealing to voters from the C2 income bracket in what were really Labour seats. The key to winning their support, he believed, was to take a tough approach over foreign affairs and defence and to pursue a type of economic populism by, for example, supporting the sale of council houses to their tenants.[14] As leader in 1983, he would most likely have pursued these themes, as well as projecting a personal image of toughness and decisiveness,[15] all of which may have gone some way to improving the Alliance's campaign themes, which stressed the need for national unity and an end to confrontation politics.

In light of the Falklands conflict and with an economic recovery well under way, his emphasis on strong defence and personal prosperity might have been better pitched to the national mood than the somewhat lacklustre Alliance campaign turned out to be. And, in contrast to 1987, when the Alliance was up against Peter Mandelson's brilliant rebranding of the Labour Party, in 1983 they faced Michael Foot and Labour's most shambolic campaign in living memory.

Whether all this would have delivered a much better result for the Alliance than the one it actually got is another matter. There is little empirical evidence to suggest that, whatever his shortcomings as leader, Jenkins was a major negative for the Alliance.[16] In 1987, after four years of Owen's hard work selling the 'tough and tender' brand, the SDP and the Alliance still had the image of a moderate, classless party lacking clear policies.[17] It is unlikely that Owen would have been able to solve that problem any more quickly in 1982–83. And the issue of relations within the Alliance would still have had to be addressed; as Crewe and King have argued,[18] with the clear advantages of Owen's leadership would have come undoubted problems – principally, public tensions with David Steel and the Liberals. These are most likely to have manifested themselves in more bitter arguments over the allocation of seats to be fought by the two parties. Given Owen's forceful, abrasive style, and his essential contempt for the Liberals, it is safe to assume there would also have been a major clash over policy, most probably over defence, on which he saw the Liberals as particularly flaky.

One of the reasons for the failure of the Alliance's 1987 campaign was the 'two Davids' syndrome. The party had two leaders, Owen and Steel, and it was an open secret that in the event of the Alliance holding the balance of power in a hung Parliament, Owen might contemplate some form of cooperation with the Conservatives, whereas Steel saw himself as being on the centre-left of politics and more favourable to Labour. A Steel–Owen combination in 1983 would have brought a slightly different but no less problematic 'two-Davids' problem: who should be the putative Prime Minister? Owen could have argued that he had more MPs and governmental experience; Steel could possibly have pointed to higher opinion-poll ratings. Owen would have done better than the Jenkins–Steel combination; but so could Steel on his own. However the issue was resolved, it would have made for a difficult campaign.

Taking all the above into account, if we assume that having Owen as the SDP's leader would have given the Alliance another 2–3 per cent of the vote at the expense of Labour, and a further 1–2 per cent from the Conservatives, even so, the Alliance would not have won many more seats than it did in reality. Based on the actual voting in 1983, a further two-party swing of 2 per cent from Labour to the Alliance would have given Owen and Steel three additional seats at most, while a swing of 1 percent from the Conservatives would have yielded at most four more seats.[19] Jenkins' absence from the SDP leadership would not have helped the party any more than his presence was essential to its coming into being.

What if Jenkins had stood for the Liberals in a by-election?

Thus all suggests that if had Jenkins joined the Liberal Party, the Alliance's fortunes, and the shape of British politics in the 1980s, would hardly have changed. His arrival would have given the Liberals a higher profile and an enhanced sense of gravitas; while Steel and Williams were the most popular Alliance politicians of the early 1980s, Jenkins was arguably the most respected. There is another, more direct way, however, in which Jenkins could have changed the course of history. Rather than allowing him simply to become an elder statesman, Steel could have tried to deploy Jenkins as an electoral asset.

At the beginning of 1983, as a widely expected general election loomed, Alliance fortunes reached a new high. In February, Simon Hughes swept to victory in the Bermondsey by-election with a two-party swing of 48 per cent. The impact on the Labour Party was immense. Michael Foot's inept handling of Peter Tatchell's selection as the Labour candidate and the abysmal by-election result plunged his leadership into deep turmoil. Foot had many qualities but did not command public respect as a leader, let alone credibility as a Prime Minister. Some of Labour's Young Turks, such as Jeff Rooker, Jack Straw and Dale Campbell-Savours, began agitating for Foot to resign so that his deputy, Denis Healey, could take over.

In an effort to quell the dissent, party managers called the by-election that was due in Darlington, another Labour-held seat, for the following month. The Alliance went into the campaign in pole position but after a disastrous, SDP-led, campaign featuring a politically inexperienced candidate, finished third. This saved Foot's leadership. It is often suggested that had the Alliance won Darlington, it would have entered the election campaign closer to Labour and then come second in terms of the popular vote in 1983 – or, at the very least, taken many more seats than it did. Under this argument, the Alliance could then have challenged the Conservatives more credibly in 1987.[20]

If the Liberals had provided the Alliance candidate, and if that had been Roy Jenkins, he could well have won. Labour had many assets in Darlington, particularly the trade-union organisational base and funding that came with it, a solid candidate and a strong local party. But they were carrying the baggage of an unpopular leader, three years of internecine warfare and a pastiche of far-left policies that the party's leaders knew were incapable of being delivered. A Liberal campaign led by Jenkins could have reversed many of the Alliance's disadvantages, and the Liberal Party could have provided a skilled and experienced by-election team, with a simple campaign theme that struck a chord: 'we need Roy Jenkins back in the Commons'. On the basis of his performance at Warrington, Jenkins would have been an ideal by-election candidate.

Far from going into the 1983 general election in a nervous, apprehensive mood, the Alliance could this have been reinvigorated, possibly starting the campaign in second place in the opinion polls and posing a serious challenge to Labour for second place in the popular vote. Further defections from Labour could have been expected, both after the by-election result and during the election campaign itself. It is plausible to think that the Alliance could have gained an extra 5 per cent of the vote at Labour's expense, and 2 to 3 per cent from the Conservatives. Instead of having his reputation tarnished by the campaign, Jenkins could have been its hero.

Like the 'Owen as leader' scenario, however, 'Jenkins wins at Darlington' has very definite limitations from the Alliance's point of view. It would have delivered the Alliance at most ten seats from the Conservatives and perhaps a handful from Labour. In other words, there would have been a mild breakthrough but not on the same scale as in 1997, and certainly not enough to break the mould of British politics. The Labour Party, with its strength in the House of Commons preserved, would still have survived as the main centre-left force in British politics.

What these scenarios start to show is that the Liberal–SDP Alliance faced problems that went far deeper than any arguments about the allocation of seats or the leadership styles of Owen or Steel, or the party affiliation of Roy Jenkins. The first-past-the-post voting system rewarded the major parties and punished the Alliance, especially when its support was spread fairly evenly across the country. (See Chapter 16 for a fuller exploration of this issue.) In 1983, Labour received 27.6 per cent of the vote but won 209 seats. The Alliance had 25.9 per cent but only 24 seats. If it was to win significant numbers of seats, the Alliance had to win large numbers of seats in a few regions or, more plausibly, challenge one of the major parties, most likely Labour, for its support base. However, both the Liberals and the SDP expressly rejected 'class' politics, sometimes to the extent of campaigning on non-class, non-economic issues such as constitutional reform. When they did pursue economic issues, their message was very vague (as in the case of the Liberals) or appealed mostly to Conservatives (Dr Owen's 'social market'). They could not break into Labour's working-class or manual-worker citadels.

What if Labour had avoided disaster in 1983?

Crucially, the Labour Party did not implode either before or after 1983; indeed, it remained stubbornly resilient. There were short-term, tactical reasons, as, for example, when Denis Healey beat off Tony Benn's challenge for the deputy leadership, and many right-wing Labour MPs decided to stay put. There were longer-term reasons, including the role of the trade unions, institutional loyalty to the Labour Party and the abiding appeal of the party's ethos, myths and symbols. The strong desire by most of the party's leaders and MPs to save their careers and win power again one day undoubtedly played a part.

The stark realities of the voting system and Labour's resilience can be further seen if we consider what could have happened had Darlington been lost to Jenkins or any other Alliance politician. It is unlikely that the Labour Party would have simply stood on the road and waited to be knocked down. Foot could well have been forced to stand aside, in which case Denis Healey would have taken over and led the party into the 1983 election. He was a formidable television performer and a powerful speaker who for some years had been one of his party's most popular figures. Healey would not have toppled the Thatcher Government, but he could have saved Labour from the humiliation it received.

A Healey leadership would not, of course, have been without its problems for Labour. He would have had to have been confirmed as Leader by Labour's electoral college, which would not have been possible until the party conference in October. The similarity to the 1981 GLC election, when a moderate councillor led Labour to victory, only to be deposed by 'Red Ken' Livingstone within hours of the result being declared, would have too easy an opportunity for the Conservatives to miss.

Healey would also have faced the prospect, during the election campaign, of standing on a policy platform whose key planks he had opposed nearly all his political life, or of risking a confrontation with the party's National Executive Committee over the manifesto. This would not have been completely impossible, given the shift in Labour's balance of power by 1983. He may have been able to get commitments on defence and the EEC that he could live with, and could possibly have won the inclusion of an economic platform that at least represented the views of the Shadow Cabinet.

The main point is, however, that Healey could surely not have done any worse than Foot, under whom, it must be remembered, Labour lost a substantial amount of support over the course of the campaign. Healey would perhaps even have stayed on for a year or two as a caretaker leader, but probably no longer; he was after all, nearly seventy at the time of the 1987 election. An interim leader with so little to lose could have been willing to sow some of the seeds of Labour's eventual recovery earlier than Neil Kinnock proved able to.

Furthermore, if Healey had stemmed Labour's losses, it would have been at the expense of the Alliance as well as the Conservatives. Indeed, the scenarios set out above mostly assume that the Liberal–SDP Alliance would have done better in 1983 than it actually did. But we also need to ask what would have happened if the absence of Jenkins from the SDP had led to an inferior result? A more divided, fractious Alliance campaign, or even a late, mild Labour revival, could have had this effect. Only 20,000 voters in about a dozen constituencies stopped the Alliance winning fewer seats than the Liberals had won in 1979.

Had the Alliance collapsed in 1983, the SDP would have been all but wiped out. The merger between the two parties may well have happened three of four years earlier than it did, though not without a considerable amount of trauma. An Alliance debacle in 1983 would also probably have meant the end of David Steel's leadership; as it was, he went through a difficult period after the 1983 campaign and at one stage wanted to resign. With Paddy Ashdown only in his first term in the Commons, the most likely successor would have been Alan Beith, with David Alton and, possibly, Russell Johnston also in the frame.

A larger but still identifiably Liberal Party would have faced an uphill struggle to challenge Labour for supremacy on the centre-left, let alone to take power from the Conservatives, in 1987 and after – though it would probably not have plumbed the depths reached by the merged Social & Liberal Democrats in 1988–89. Possibly a stronger Labour Party would have beaten John Major in 1992 – as it so nearly did – ushering in a more traditional type of Labour government under John Smith; in turn, having only narrowly lost the election, the Conservative Party might not have imploded quite so spectacularly as it now has. The what ifs of history multiply unstoppably – and all resting on the decision of one man over whether or not to join the Liberal Party …

Notes

1 Reprinted in Duncan Brack and Tony Little (eds.), *Great Liberal Speeches* (Politico's, 2001), pp. 403–15.

2 David Steel, *Against Goliath* (Weidenfeld & Nicolson, 1989), pp.262–63; Roy Jenkins, *A Life At the Centre* (Macmillan, 1991), p. 514.

3 Jenkins, *A Life At the Centre,* p. 513–14.

4 See Ivor Crewe and Anthony King, *SDP: The Birth, Life and Death of the Social Democratic Party* (Oxford University Press, 1995), Chapter 7.

5 Ibid. See also Neil Stockley, 'The Limehouse Declaration and the Birth of the SDP,' *Journal of Liberal Democrat History* 30, Spring 2001, pp. 23–25, for a first-hand discussion of the defectors' motives.

6 Crewe and King, *SDP,* Chapter 16.

7 See David Owen, *Time to Declare* (Michael Joseph, 1991), Chapter 24.

8 Ibid., p.518–19.

9 Ibid.

10 Jenkins, *A Life at the Centre,* p. 535.

11 Owen, *Time to Declare*, pp.519–24.

12 Ibid., p. 520.

13 Ibid., p. 523.

14 Ibid., p. 564.

15 This is not quite the same as the 'tough and tender' themes he projected from 1983–87. These, and his adoption of the 'social market' economic approach, were only delivered after the 1983 election result, from which he concluded that the SDP would have to pursue disaffected *Conservative* voters, particularly in the C2 income bracket. Before 1983, Owen still largely adhered to the social democrats' received economic wisdoms – 'Keynesian' pump-priming of the economy, public ownership and the quest for a workable incomes policy.

16 Crewe and King, *SDP*, pp. 213 and 459.

17 Ibid., p. 518.

18 Ibid., p. 459.

19 See *The Times Guide to the House of Commons 1983*, p. 282.

20 See for example Chris Rennard, 'What Went Wrong at Darlington: Commentary' *Journal of Liberal History* 39, Summer 2003, pp. 16–17.

Chapter 15

What if Benn had beaten Healey in 1981?

Dianne Hayter[1]

D anny Mangham, the Labour Party's Chief Teller and a delegate from the National Union of Dyers, Bleachers and Textile Workers, joined the Conference platform just before 8.30 p.m. on Sunday 27 September 1981. At a signal from the Chairman, he rose to speak, a small piece of paper held firmly in both hands as if the slightest breeze would see its words flutter away. 'The final result – and the votes have been counted three times', he read, 'is as follows: Rt Hon. Anthony Wedgwood Benn: 47.219%.' A tense hush fell on the 2,000-strong audience. 'Denis Healey: 46.429%. Abstentions: 6.353%. I therefore declare Tony Benn elected deputy leader of the Labour Party.'

The cheers rang round the hall. It was no use the Chairman, Alex Kitson, even trying to speak. His own TGWU union had delivered the result for Benn and his job was now to move speedily to congratulate the victor, pausing only briefly to place his left hand on Healey's ample shoulder. He then clasped Michael Foot's wrist and held this and Benn's aloft to acknowledge the wild applause from a section of the hall. There was a blaze of photographers' lights as Brother Mangham made his way quietly out of the hall, his duty done.

Delegates were on their feet. Constituency activists were cheering, singing, waving, feet dancing, hands clapping. Two other groups sat silent. The thirty-five soft-left MPs whose abstentions had given Benn the edge over Healey now faced trouble from their local parties for their refusal to vote for Benn, though they had simultaneously failed to stop him in his tracks. And the union delegates whose crucial votes had been cast for the victor in defiance of their members' wishes also sat still. A third grouping gathered up their belongings and quietly left. These were the MPs and union leaders who had supported Healey; without a word of pre-planning, each headed for the Old Ship Hotel on Brighton's seafront.

~

Before we follow this third troupe the 200 yards along the prom, it is important to recognise that those figures are the actual votes cast and recorded that year. Not one trade union, MP or Constituency Labour Party vote has been altered. That was the result.

The single, all-important, difference between what Mr Mangham really read out and the words above stem from the interpretation of the figures. The 1981 contest was the first using the electoral college, set up that January, comprising 40 per cent for trade unions, 30 per cent for constituency parties, and 30 per cent for MPs. No prior decision had been taken about how to count abstentions. The method used on the night was to give each candidate the percentage of the votes actually cast for him, discarding the abstentions. An equally valid result, however, is obtained by allocating the votes between Benn, Healey and Abstentions. That delivers the result enumerated above.[2] No imagination is needed to conjure a Benn victory. It really was his.

~

In the bar of the Old Ship, pints were lined up as, first, the talk was of the previous dreadful eighteen months. It had been a grim time for MPs. Michael Foot had snatched the leadership from under Healey's nose; party conference had voted to undermine MPs by enforcing automatic reselection, removing their input into the manifesto and ending their sole right to elect the Parliamentary Leader (and Prime Minister when in government). Within hours of the January 1981 Wembley conference which created the electoral college, the Gang of Four had defected to become the Social Democratic Party (SDP) taking initially a dozen and then more MPs with them, to say nothing of Labour councillors, members and voters.[3] A poor result in the Warrington by-election saw the party only just hold off Roy Jenkins' challenge (with worse to follow later when the SDP and Liberals took first Croydon North-West and then, with Shirley Williams, Crosby, in high-profile by-elections). Relations within the Parliamentary Labour Party (PLP), as in local parties, were bitter. Endless fighting and turmoil had seen Labour unfit even to be an effective opposition, let alone a government.

Since April, when Benn had announced his challenge to the incumbent Healey for the deputy post (a contest which he told the BBC on 2 April would 'be unifying' for the party), Labour had been torn asunder in the relentless intramural arguments and bickering, all played out on prime-time TV. Speakers, especially former Chancellor Healey, had been shouted down at meetings, whilst the man destined to be elected deputy had failed to condemn such behaviour.[4] The atmosphere had been one of 'threats and dictation',[5] 'fear'[6] and 'personal vilification'.[7] MPs particularly felt the heat as their own reselections depended on their Benn-supporting activists. They knew the vengeance these could wreak, having seen former left icon, Ian Mikardo MP, thrown off the National Executive Committee (NEC) the previous year for daring to propose a compromise over reselection.

Over the summer, moderate MPs had sought comfort from each other, knowing that the recorded votes (introduced since the October 1980 Foot–Healey contest) would display the variance between their support for Healey and their local parties' votes for Benn.[8] Some had urged longer term courage, reminding colleagues that the electorate would also see the published votes, and that MPs 'might succumb to pressures now only to find it backfires on them when they ask the ordinary voters, who would have the last word, to return them to Westminster'.[9] All knew that, despite his popularity with the party faithful, Benn was an electoral liability. For those in marginal seats, this was equivalent to a P.45.

That Sunday evening, the post-ballot drinking continued as increasing numbers of chastened MPs, senior trade unionists, some party staff and Healey's campaign team swelled the ranks who had now progressed to the Old Ship's once glamorous ballroom. Gradually, the doyens of the moderate Labour Solidarity Campaign – MPs Roy Hattersley, Peter Shore, John Smith, Donald Dewar, George Robertson, Giles Radice, Phillip Whitehead, Ken Woolmer and John Golding – began emerging as leaders of the discussion. And these men were not quitters. All knew that a number of MPs had, before the vote, threatened to defect if Benn won. News came that Dickson Mabon, Tom McNally and Bob Mitchell had left that night. Two MPs had already been deselected[10] and many in the crush at the hotel bar made it clear that they could not stay in a PLP led by Foot and Benn. Their detestation was not just of Benn, but of what he stood for: this was not a party they recognised.

Well before the vote, there had been talk of an independent PLP, with Hattersley having been approached by some to lead this (Healey being far too loyal to Foot) and Peter Shore having failed to discount it. A hint of such talk had already surfaced in *The Guardian* and *The Sunday Times*[11] and had reached the ears of John Silkin.[12] For nearly all the party's history, it had actually been without a leader as such, the title going to the leader (and deputy) of the PLP, with these positions elected solely by the PLP. It was indeed Benn who had recently moved to create the position of leader of the Labour Party. So now, in the heat and despair of the ballroom, the proposal developed that there should be a reversal to the old titles. The PLP would elect its own leader (who would be Foot) and deputy (who would be Healey). Benn would sit on the NEC, but would have no role in the PLP. By midnight, the idea had taken shape. There was immense urgency, as the trickle of defections threatened to become a flood.

Already TV programmes were forecasting the death of the Labour Party. On *Panorama,* as the group talked, veteran historian Professor Eric Hobsbawm was turning himself into a pundit. As he said: 'Benn's total identification with the left sectarians made it evident to anyone who did not want the Labour Party to be reduced to a marginalised socialist chapel that its future required him to be defeated.'[13] The very existence of the Labour Party was now at stake, he said, predicting that, since the party had voted for Benn, it clearly had a death wish. One Tory wag, meanwhile, was threatening to table a resolution in the Commons that: 'This House has no confidence in Her Majesty's Opposition', calling on the SDP to replace Labour in that role.

Back in the ballroom, the number-crunchers (Roger Godsiff and John Spellar) who had been working since January with trade union leaders to seize back control of the NEC from the left, dissected the results from earlier that night. Not a single Shadow Cabinet member had voted for Benn. On the first ballot, he had won only 55 of the MPs' votes to Healey's 125, and on the second, 71 to 137.[14] Thirty-five Tribunites, tribally unable to tick the Healey box, had nevertheless not been able to bring themselves to vote for the man whom the unions and activists had just delivered as their deputy leader.

As the myriad of conversations slowly focused into a single one, the moderates hung on the words of their emerging and much-needed leaders, willing a spokesperson to appear. He came, not from the ranks of the Shadow Cabinet but in the form of Healey's trusted lieutenant, George Robertson (showing the iron will and strategic determination he would later need as Secretary-General of NATO). 'This is what we do', he began. A door opened, in crept two unexpected MPs – Martin O'Neill and Jeff Rooker – fresh from a meeting of fellow-abstainers. They signalled to Robertson to continue, and with their blessing. His message was simple: we accept Wembley, we accept a deputy leader of the Labour Party, but we elect our own deputy leader of the PLP. We put it to the PLP and get a majority there. As Secretary of the moderate Manifesto Group of MPs, Robertson knew he could deliver that vote. 'The only two tasks – at least I had thought there were two', he said, looking pointedly at O'Neill and Rooker; 'Our only task is to persuade Foot that, under PLP Standing Orders, it is the deputy leader of the PLP, not of the party, who is in the Shadow Cabinet.' He looked again at the two abstaining MPs, each knowing that Kinnock could deliver Foot. They smiled in acknowledgement, nodded and left.

Unbeknown to the Old Ship's guests, Kinnock had come within a ballpoint of voting for Healey. He had been desperate to stop Benn winning, as he knew the damage such a result would wreak. He was not alone. Many of the old or soft left hated Benn, though such was the distrust between right and left that the former had never guessed it. Yet the signs had been there. While the right hated the endless attacks on the last Labour government (of which Benn had been a prominent member,[15] whom the loyal moderates had kept in power by trooping through the lobbies late at night for a government with no majority[16] and destabilised by a four-fold oil-price rise), the left resented Benn's lack of support for their causes (such as CND) at the time, and his failure to resign over any of the issues for which he now castigated the government in which he had served. In the summer, veteran left stalwart Janey Buchan MEP had published an open letter remonstrating with Benn for purporting to be the conscience of the left and for aligning himself with those claiming that: 'those who are not for us [that is, supporting Benn] are against us'. This was, she claimed, an attitude which led to the 'corruption of Stalinism and eventually the gulags'.[17] Benn's failure to rebut the tactics and 'meanness of spirit' of his supporters distanced her and much of the old left from his cause. Janey's husband, Norman Buchan MP, pointedly withheld his vote from Benn in the crucial contest.[18]

That night the thirty-five abstainers faced a dark choice. They were already being vilified by Benn's supporters, especially Margaret

Beckett, in a vitriolic public attack. They had been warned. Prior to the vote, the Rank and File Mobilising Committee had written: 'Any member of the electoral college is perfectly entitled to abstain. Everyone of the left accepted this right. Accepting, however, is different from understanding. By all means abstain, but don't expect to be understood.'[19] It was a warning of the difficulties they would face in their own reselections. Now, having taken their decision, the abstainers had opened themselves to retribution and also split themselves off from former close comrades, such as Robin Cook, Jack Straw and Frank Dobson, who had voted for Benn.[20]

They stood on the threshold. They knew the moderates were correct about the electoral fortunes of the party under Benn. Already support was slipping away. 'Two and a half years after the victory of Mrs Thatcher's Conservatives, Labour had lost another one in five of its voters and no longer had majority support in *any* group of the working class, even the unskilled and unemployed.'[21] The thirty-five feared that Benn would soon challenge Foot for the leadership. They sensed that his uncompromising views on defence would further turn off solid working-class votes.[22] But they also knew that the moderates were bent on expelling Militant from within the party's ranks, a decision which would be resisted by Benn to the last, and on which some of them had yet to make the shift which they would later find possible.

There were some on the left who were already there. Hobsbawm, for whom Kinnock was to show great admiration, described the infiltration: 'A mixed coalition of lefts within the Labour Party and "entryist" revolutionaries … had joined … increasingly coming together behind the project of winning control of the party under the banner of the increasingly radical ex-minister Tony Benn … their strategy relied on the ability of small groups of militants among a largely inactive membership to capture Labour Party branches and, reinforced by the politically decisive "block vote" of left-led unions at party conferences, to impose a more radical leadership and policy on the party.'[23] However, for most of the left, dealing with Militant was not yet on their political agenda.

There was, however, one patch of common ground between the right and the soft left. This was their knowledge of what the SDP would do. Until that night, the defecting MPs had determinedly resisted resigning to fight by-elections (and were cold-shouldering Bruce Douglas-Mann, who had left Labour determined to fight his seat under new colours[24]). Every Labour MP now knew that the gloves would be off. By Tuesday the SDP were likely to be challenging Labour to thirty by-elections – perhaps fifty if more Labour MPs decided their future no longer resided in the party of their youth. If the Tories decided not to field candidates, the PLP could lose over half of these.

In one part of the room, as the MPs agreed a holding line for the press ('We note Tony Benn has been elected by the Electoral College as Deputy Leader of the Labour Party'), the big beasts of the union world (Terry Duffy, Frank Chapple, Tom Jackson, Roy Grantham, Bill Sirs, Bryan Stanley, Sid Weighell, Derek Gladwin and David Basnett – only the TGWU was missing) planned their next move. These men knew two things. First, that their members depended upon the return of a Labour government for their jobs and well-being, and that the likelihood of that eventuality had all but disappeared that night. And second, that while their own positions within their unions were safe (as they had cast their unions' votes in accordance with their members' wishes), the decision of the giant TGWU to throw its 1.25 million votes (8 per cent of the total electoral college) behind Benn, in defiance of their consultation, which had given seven out of eleven regions for Healey, offered powerful ammunition to Mrs Thatcher in her wish to introduce legislation on individual balloting within trade unions, an area of democracy jealously guarded as the preserve of the unions' own rulebooks. 'Do you think?' mused one, 'she might even make *us* stand for re-election?' Even those elected by postal ballot found that idea chilling. Their wise heads knew that the TGWU vote jeopardised more than just General Secretary Moss Evans' own position with his members, who were likely to be highly irate with the delegation's cavalier disregard of their views.

Robertson, himself a former trade-union organiser, now set about with union staffers Godsiff and Spellar to draw up a list of tasks to be achieved before a mass breakfast at 7 a.m., when the gathering had agreed to reconvene.

John Smith, together with a young associate from the bar, Anthony Blair, was to visit Kinnock, PLP Standing Orders in hand.[25] These rules clearly stated that, in opposition, the Parliamentary Committee (the Shadow Cabinet) consists of the four officers of the PLP (leader and deputy leader of the PLP, together with the Chief Whip and Chairman of the PLP) together with other elected members. So it would be quite constitutional for Benn to be excluded – becoming what today looks a little like the 'Chair of the Labour Party', an NEC and party, but not Parliamentary, position. With Kinnock in tow, they intended to substitute Peter Shore – an old family friend and ally of Foot – for young Blair in their delegation and move on to see the Leader of the Labour Party.

The trade unionists would fan out round their colleagues and hit the phones to the TUC General Secretary and other allies, emphasising that this step was not a negation of the constitutional Electoral College. Basnett, Chapple and Grantham were tasked with the key objective: selling the strategy to Healey, whilst Gladwin set out for former Prime Minister Callaghan to ensure that he was on side.

Whitehead would find psephologist Peter Kellner for advice on what a mass by-election strategy by the SDP might achieve, and to gain ammunition as to what a Benn victory meant to voters. It was not simply that Benn was so much less popular than Healey, but that he had been chosen by the very unions whom the electorate still distrusted so soon after the 1978–79 'Winter of Discontent', reinforcing the view of a party dominated by left-wing trade unions.

Radice and Golding were deputed to get every moderate MP to approach their abstaining colleagues and impress on them the cost of blinking at this moment, whilst Dewar, Cunningham and Woolmer would seek out potential defectors to assure them the fight would be carried by the whole of the centre as well as the right of the PLP, and that they no longer had to face this alone. They knew from their work since February that the NEC balance would change on Tuesday,[26] and that they would now also be able to count on other soft-left NEC members such as abstainer Joan Lestor, whom Hattersley and Betty Boothroyd were despatched to find.

No one would be resting that night, so there was little fear of disturbing people's sleep. The main players arranged to meet at 5 a.m., prepared to brief the press at 6 a.m.

This was an age before pagers or mobile phones, yet everyone could be located. One strength of the party traditions is that every politician and union delegation stays in the same hotel each year, with the senior members lodged at the Grand Hotel. What conversations or arm-twisting took place that night is not recorded, but at 6 o'clock the journalists gathered in the dining-room of the Old Ship. Martin Linton of the *Guardian*[27] recalls:

> I had a 5 p.m. deadline, so knew I could verify any story. The radio people, like John Cole, had to go on live and were being counter-briefed by Jack Straw, David Blunkett, Michael Meacher and Robin Cook from Benn's team. They had wind of the right's strategy and were threatening legal action, though veteran Labour adviser Derry Irvine had not been optimistic about its success. It felt like a whirlwind. As a party member (and councillor) of many years standing, here was my party tearing itself asunder, the PLP – founded in 1906 – claiming independent status from the members and machinery that put MPs in office. But I lived in Battersea, where our majority had fallen and where our focus groups (the first in the country)

already showed a further haemorrhaging of support. I knew in my bones that we couldn't win the south for Labour without the middle ground. Yet my local party had voted 52:10 for Benn and believed he would carry us to a great victory.

As a journalist, I knew I was watching one of the UK's biggest political stories unfold before me. I had been reporting on this for some time so everything had prepared me, yet Tuesday's lead story, and the interpretation we would give it in the editorial, was the main comment party members would read. So I felt an enormous responsibility. Many of my *Guardian* colleagues had already opted for the SDP and this would be my one chance of bringing the paper over to a Labour Mark II instead. It was a scary prospect. The atmosphere in the room was as frenetic as the SDP launch witnessed only six months before. Every one of us knew that who walked through the door onto the top table – where ten seats were assembled – would determine the outcome of this venture. Without Kinnock it would be doomed.

Kinnock and Foot were old friends and allies, and both had moved away from Benn's clasp. Foot had challenged Benn in June to run against him, rather than against Healey, and had used his speech at the TUC to defend MPs, their role and the record of the last Labour government, while damning those who now sought to rewrite its record. He had even attacked Benn in print[28] and given everyone to understand he supported Healey.[29] Yet at the crucial moment he had withheld his vote from Healey, denying him re-election. Foot, the great parliamentarian, had now to decide whether to heed MPs or the conference whose darling he had become.

It was well after 6 a.m. when the doors swung open. Led by Peter Shore, eight others followed. Joan Lestor was one, her head held high and her face determined. It was a brave walk, through journalists unused to that hour of the day, demanding answers to shouted questions, jostling for a first quote.

Robertson took the chair and nodded to Shore to commence. It was a clever move, this anti-Common-Market, quiet but determined and much-respected politician taking the floor. 'The majority of the PLP', he said, 'have not voted for Tony Benn to help lead us in Parliament. We recognise that the party in the country wants him in their counsels and on the NEC. We do not deny him that. But we have called for a Special PLP where we will seek nominations for the deputy leader of the PLP. We will then work under whoever is elected to this position.'

The questions began: 'Isn't that against the rules?' 'What does Michael Foot say?' 'Who will you elect?' 'Won't you all get deselected?' 'Roy Jenkins has challenged you to resign your seats: will you do so?' A tenth person joined the table and stood to respond:

> Well, with my majority I could easily resign and win. What will that prove? Our task now is unity – to reunite the party. That requires the consent of all its parts. And MPs are one part of that. It is in Westminster that a democratic socialist party delivers programmes for its people. Unity is what Michael will work for and we will agree a strategy to achieve that.

Kinnock's manner, even more than his words, was testimony to his determination. The time to choose sides had come. He managed to make it look like an easy decision.

By 7 a.m. the news had spread. The abstainers had divided but most followed the 'our own Deputy' line and work continued with potential defectors as the battle had yet to be won. The trade unions, voting that day for the NEC, secured gains in the women's and trade union sections. However, the moderates lost the Healey vote on the NEC (with Audrey Wise taking Benn's vacated constituency seat), denying them the necessary majority to deal with Militant. They did, though, have enough votes to bounce a compromise 'no expulsions and no deselection' resolution through the Committee, safeguarding MPs' own positions. The soft left were devastated, the real losers in the piece. As the *Statesman* had predicted in the summer, Benn's challenge had led to the break-up of the British left.[30]

The rule amendments passed in the subsequent year's conference re-established a Leader of the Parliamentary Labour Party who would be the Leader of the Labour Party (chosen by the electoral college), and a Deputy Leader of the PLP (elected by MPs). The unions were forced by their members to consult before casting votes, whilst constituencies moved to one-member-one-vote (OMOV) ballots. Just as the TGWU had cast its vote contrary to its members' views, it was clear that the constituency activists also did not represent rank and file party members. In the twelve constituencies where balloting had taken place, all went for Healey, by about 2:1. The EETPU announced it would fund any future such ballots in constituencies, hastening the day for an OMOV rule change in the party.

In recognition that it was 'Kinnock the brave' who had made the leap, he topped the Shadow Cabinet poll in November and – despite losing his NEC seat for his pains – led the non-Bennite left in the party. Militant, however, could not be touched as party matters remained the preserve of the NEC. They extended their grasp from Liverpool to Sheffield, Manchester and London, where it was Mrs Thatcher who reduced their power by taking funds and decision-making out of the hands of local authorities.

The SDP, so sure they would inherit the party's electorate with Benn's victory, had not counted on Kinnock's bravery, nor his determination to see the party back in power – though others had recognised this in him.[31] Nevertheless, '[t]he future of the party was not certain until after the disastrous election of 1983, when Michael Foot ... was succeeded by Neil Kinnock [who] ... saved the Labour Party from the sectarians. After 1985, when he secured the expulsion of the Trotskyite "Militant Tendency" from the party, its future was safe.'[32]

In October 1981, there was still much work to be done but the unions, having supported the independent streak in the PLP, then set about recapturing the NEC to provide Kinnock with the majority he would need to move the party forward. Looking back now, Martin Linton recalls:

> It was a night in my life I can never forget. Like a trapeze artist swinging on an unsteady rope, the party would jump to one side or the other. The decision taken – though it would need fifteen more years to see its results – returned Labour to a party of government. Giving in to the Benn victory might have finished it for all time.

Notes

1 All references are accurate.

2 George Cunningham, *Was Tony Benn the True Winner Against Healey?* (unpublished, 1983). Because the abstentions were almost exclusively amongst the MPs, it meant that the remaining MPs – who were predominately pro-Healey – effectively each had another 1/35 of a vote. This gave the incumbent the vital 'eyebrow' margin which ensured his victory. Spreading the 35 votes across the whole electoral college by counting abstentions, as in this scenario, would withhold that advantage from Healey and tip the result to Benn.

3 The Campaign for Labour Party Democracy somewhat bizarrely described 'The Electoral College decision [as] a victory for the Party as a whole' (CLPD circular, 25 March 1981 – the week of the founding of the SDP). This celebration of events further dispirited the non-Bennite members of the PLP.

4 For example, at a PLP meeting, Laurie Pavitt MP, an old left-winger, spoke about being attacked bitterly and personally, and asked Benn simply to use his influence to get the people concerned to amend their method. Benn declined to act and said it was all about 'issues' not personalities. (Interview with PLP Secretary, 25 January 2002.)

5 *Observer*, 24 May 1981.

6 Lord (Ken) Woolmer interview, June 2003.

7 Roy Mason MP in *The Observer*, 28 June 1981.

8 83 per cent of constituency parties backed Benn; only 28 per cent of MPs.

9 John Grant MP, 26 September 1981.

10 Eric Ogden and John Sever.

11 Colin Brown, front page, *The Guardian,* 28 August 1981, and David Lipsey in *The Sunday Times,* 30 August 1981.

12 'There was talk of a third political grouping, a "New Labour Party" or a "Parliamentary Labour Party" … There was talk of the Fabian Society being the nucleus of this new

party: it had offices in Westminster, a secretariat, mailing lists.' John Silkin, *Changing Bat-tlefields* (Hamish Hamilton, 1987), pp. 38–39.

13 Eric Hobsbawm, *Interesting Times: A Twentieth-Century Life* (Allen Lane, 2002), p. 272.

14 *Report of 1981 Labour Party Conference*, pp. 340–44.

15 He served in every Labour Cabinet from 1964–79.

16 The Chief Whip, Michael Cocks MP, had complained in 1979 that he had lost eight MPs in the last year of that government – the majority killed by cardiovascular disease, an ailment exacerbated by stress and strain.

17 *Labour Weekly*, 7 August 1981.

18 *Report of 1981 Labour Party Conference*, p. 340.

19 *Mobilise for Labour Policies*, September 1981.

20 Ibid., pp. 340–44.

21 Hobsbawm, *Interesting Times,* p. 267.

22 Though few were to guess that the Falklands War would shortly throw this into stark reality, when Foot was able to support 'our boys', while Benn called for the return of the fleet (*The Sun*, April 1982).

23 Hobsbawm, *Interesting Times,* pp. 266–67.

24 George Cunningham, May 2003. In the event, Douglas–Mann did resign but lost the by-election to the Tories at the height of the Falklands War.

25 For only once in his twenty-year career with the party, PLP Secretary Alan Haworth had taken himself off to Egypt, so little could he bear to hear the results.

26 Five seats changed hands, from left to right.

27 Now MP for Battersea.

28 *Guardian*, 10 September 1981.

29 One MP, Peter Archer, used this in his letter of justification of 3 September to his local party members as to why he would, unlike them, support the current deputy leader.

30 *The New Statesman*, 12 June 1981.

31 Such as the party's national agent, David Hughes (interview, 16 June 2003), and the trade unionists who already favoured him as successor to Foot over Hattersley.

32 Hobsbawm, ibid, p.268.

Chapter 16

What if the SDP–Liberal Alliance had finished second in the 1983 general election?

Robert Waller

On 9 June 1983 the Conservatives won the general election easily, although they polled just 42.4 per cent of the vote. The opposition was almost evenly split, with Labour achieving a mere 27.6 per cent and the Social Democrat–Liberal Alliance, in its first national contest, hot on their heels with 25.4 per cent. Suppose they had closed that gap of just over two per cent, pulled ahead of the ailing Labour Party, and finished second in terms of votes? How might subsequent history have been different? Would Labour have bounced back eventually, as we now know it did, or would the humiliation of ceasing to be even the second party have resulted in a spiralling decline? Conversely, would the spectacular early impact of the Alliance have been maintained? Far from seeing yet another third-party disappointment, as the Alliance flattered only to deceive, metamorphosing painfully, after two more name changes, into the Liberal Democrats, still beyond the fringes of power, might a new party of government have emerged?

I shall reflect on this counterfactual possibility addressed in this chapter in two distinct ways. First, we shall see that given the workings of Britain's first-past-the-post electoral system, it was actually well nigh impossible for the Alliance to have finished second in terms of both votes and seats. Even if they had won the support of substantially more voters than Labour, they would still have been second in the numbers of MPs returned. This may well have led to future developments not being significantly different from the actual, unfair though that will seem to some.

Second, though, I shall leave the cold eye of academic analysis aside, and allow constructive imagination to plot a path more akin to informed fantasy – one which will lead to the early twenty-first century, indeed with Tony Blair occupying 10 Downing Street, but with very different prospects in a much altered situation. This is of course by definition utterly contestable, and is meant more to amuse than enlighten. In the spirit of all such exercises in 'virtual history', though, it may stimulate debate, in this case as to the correct analysis of the dramatic developments in the British politics of the last quarter of a century.

~

Labour's abysmal performance in June 1983 was their lowest share of the vote in a general election since 1918, when the party was less than twenty years old and had never formed a government. The causes of this disaster included memories of the failings of their 1974–79 administration, ending after the 'winter of discontent' with James Callaghan's defeat on a motion of no confidence. This had been followed by internecine strife between left and right over the constitutional arrangements and balance of power within the party, substantial infiltration at constituency level by extremist elements such as the Militant Tendency, the defection of nearly thirty Labour MPs and other prominent figures to form in 1981 a break-away party, the SDP, and the leadership of the veteran left-winger Michael Foot. Neither the party's leadership nor its policies carried conviction among the bulk of voters, and its ratings in the opinion polls on issues, competence, and, of course, unity, plummeted. Its 1983 manifesto was famously described as 'the longest suicide note in history', drifting ideologically and impractically far from the centre ground.

Meanwhile, the SDP had formally allied with the long-standing centrist Liberals, who could add proven local campaigning and organising ability and enthusiasm to the weighty and experienced leadership of the Gang of Four. After a series of dramatic by-election successes between 1981 and 1983, the new Alliance appeared a genuinely new competitive option to those not wishing to support the radical brand of government which was being developed by Mrs Thatcher – and there were many of those for, despite the Falklands factor, and the Prime Minister's subsequent aura of invincibility at the polls, it should be recalled that in 1983 the Conservatives were to secure their lowest share of the vote in victory since 1922.

The 1983 general election thus represented the first apparent three-way contest for government, and the first in which there was a genuine doubt about who would finish second, since 1923. However, although Labour and the Alliance breasted the tape almost side by side in numbers of votes gained (8.46 million and 7.78 million respectively), 209 Labour MPs were returned, compared with only 17 Liberals and 6 for the SDP. *The Sunday Times* described the result produced by the first-past-the-post electoral system as 'a new order of unfairness'.

What if the Alliance had polled another 350,000 votes, or just over 1 per cent, more, at the expense of Labour? Undoubtedly they would have claimed second place morally. But the electoral arithmetic shows that with an even share secured in this manner the Alliance would have gained only four seats, to make a total of twenty-seven. Labour would still have returned 199 MPs, actually losing nine of the ten to the Conservatives.

What if …

Table 1: '1983 General Election' – C 42.4%, Alliance 26.6%, Labour 26.4%

Conservative	403	+9 from Labour, –3 to Alliance
Alliance	27	+3 from C, +1 from Lab
Labour	199	–9 to C, –1 to Alliance

Let us now suppose that Labour's slump into third place had been entirely due to voters choosing the Conservatives instead. In this case the Alliance would have finished second in votes, but would have had at best only one more seat than they actually did.

Table 2: '1983 General Election' – C 44.7%, Alliance 25.4%, Labour 25.3%

Conservative	420
Alliance	24
Labour	185

If Labour had done still worse, but only to the Tories' benefit, the number of Alliance seats would have progressively declined even as their relative advantage in second place over Labour grew. For example:

Table 3: '1983 General Election' – C 50.0%, Alliance 25.4%, Labour 20%

Conservative	492
Alliance	18
Labour	119

Clearly this route of analysis does not lead to a transformation in the likely path of history.

We must instead speculate on a situation in which the Liberal–SDP Alliance finished second as a result of an increase in its own vote. There are two problems here as well, though. If such an advance had come substantially as a result of an even more catastrophic implosion of the Labour vote than there actually was, this would have gained few extra constituencies. This is because there were (and indeed still are) rather few Labour seats which are vulnerable to a 'centre' party challenge. Even if there had been a further hypothetical swing of 5 per cent from Labour to Alliance in 1983, they would only have won five more Labour seats. Their best prospects by far of making more of an impact in the House of Commons were to take seats from the Conservatives.

However, the second and even more serious problem then would have arisen. Even if (in a fairly extreme speculation) Labour were to have lost another 5 per cent compared with the genuine 1983 result, and the Conservatives were also to have lost 5 per cent, and the Alliance were to have gained 10 per cent, the following surprising result would have been obtained on a uniform swing model:

Table 4: '1983 General Election' – C 37.4%, Alliance 35.4%, Labour 22.6%

Conservative	346	−51 to Alliance
Alliance	99	+51 from C, +25 from Lab
Labour	184	−25 to Alliance

What on earth is going on here? That second problem concerns the distribution of the various parties' votes. The Alliance found that its support was very evenly spread, both socially and geographically. In the real 1983 election, 546 of the 632 Alliance candidates obtained a share within 10 per cent of their national average. Crudely put, in the above model they would have got about 35 per cent in the vast majority of seats, not enough under first past the post to beat whichever rival was stronger in that area. Conversely, Labour could hold on to almost all the seats they did get, because they had already been restricted to their strongholds in such areas as the inner cities, the coalfields, and industrial Wales and Scotland.

A bizarre phenomenon should be emerging by now. *It was impossible for the Liberal–SDP Alliance to have finished second in terms of both votes and seats in the 1983 general election*. They would have had to finish first in terms of votes to come second in constituency terms – or even first, if they did well enough.

This evidence fuels complaints against the inequitable consequences of our current Westminster electoral system. It might be pointed out that should the Alliance (or the Liberal Democrats today) reach a critical breakthrough point of around 40 per cent they too would come to benefit from the workings of the mathematics. If they were to obtain around that share evenly across the country they would win most of the seats rather than narrowly losing them, and the system would operate heavily in their favour. However, there is no doubting that in the circumstances of 1983 the Alliance would have had to do considerably better than it did to reap a substantial reward in terms of the number of constituencies won, while Labour would have been insulated from a meltdown by the pattern of distribution of their vote. This factor undoubtedly should be taken into account when considering the question of 'what if' the SDP–Liberal Alliance had finished second in that year.

Nevertheless, we may still undertake a 'thought experiment' diverging from reality. Finishing second in terms of votes, even if not in seats, may well have had a significant psychological and ultimately practical impact on the subsequent course of history. Let us then take what must be an increasingly speculative diversion down that path.

~

In our hypothetical general election of June 1983 the Alliance finished second in terms of the national vote across the 650 UK constituencies. The spectacular slump in Labour support, exacerbated by opinion polls showing the collapse of their vote even compared with 1979, stimulated massive media and public interest: in reality, the election day BBC–Gallup poll showed that an additional 25 per cent of people had seriously considered voting for them, but had believed that they had no chance of winning. A substantial and rapid advance during the election might have overcome this credibility gap or 'wasted vote' theory, resulting in a bandwagon effect. Under these assumptions, on our imaginary 9 June the Conservative share also declined to 37 per cent (let us take Table 4 above as our counterfactual starting point). Mrs Thatcher's Government's highly partisan approach and patchy economic record had not yet convinced a major section of the predominantly centrist electorate. This meant that the Alliance picked up 50 extra seats, reaching a total of almost 100, easily the highest number for a third party since the 1920s.

This shock result had profound consequences. Far from losing seats in 1983 following the defections of twenty-seven MPs in 1981–82, the newly founded Alliance had more than doubled its numbers in the Commons. Many more former Labour members had retained their seats for the SDP Alliance, including James Wellbeloved (Erith and Crayford), Tom Ellis (Clwyd SW), George Cunningham (Islington South and Finsbury) and most importantly Shirley Williams, the by-election victor in Crosby. The sole Conservative defector, Christopher Brocklebank-Fowler, had also been returned at Norfolk NW. There had been gains too from the Tories, for the SDP as well as the Liberals: the new town of Stevenage (Mrs Williams's former seat), Edinburgh South and Edinburgh Pentlands, Bath and the ancient university seats of Cambridge and Oxford West and Abingdon.

Encouraged by this, and by the bitter recriminations within the shattered Labour Party, there was a further flood of defections in the months following that fateful June. Among them, scarcely noticed at the time, was the thirty-year-old newly elected member for Sedgefield in County Durham, a very bright and ambitious lawyer called Tony Blair. It was a logical inference to draw from the cataclysm of 9 June that he would have no future within the Labour Party. Many long-standing and previously loyal activists had also left after the election, leaving the party to fall even more under the influence of Marxist activists, who interpreted the result as an overwhelming demonstration that Labour's approach had not been sufficiently left-wing.

Perhaps most critical of all was the decision of some of the leading unions (such as the GMWU and the EETPU) to disaffiliate from the Labour Party, although initially they did not decide to transfer their financial and political participation and influence to the Alliance. With the election, under the new constitutional rules, of the Liverpudlian Chairman of the party, Eric Heffer, rather than Neil Kinnock, to the party leadership on Michael Foot's retirement in 1984, Labour became committed to pursuing an even more pure socialist path in its search for the recovery of the mass working-class vote.

Over the next three years the tide continued to flow with the Alliance, boosted by its new media support from the *Daily Mirror* and the ambivalent position of the *Sun*, which could hardly ignore its continuing by-election success in both Labour and Conservative vacancies, for example at Chesterfield in March 1984, when Tony Benn failed to return to his beloved House of Commons, and at the Conservative seat of Enfield Southgate in December of that year, when the thirty-one-year-old Conservative candidate Michael Portillo found that he could not take the seat's loyalty for granted. Although still third in numbers of seats, the Alliance seemed an unstoppable fresh new force. Labour continued to haemorrhage support at the base and at the centre. The Thatcher Government's battle with Arthur Scargill's miners during the year-long strike in the coal industry presented an unattractively confrontational image.

In the general election of 1987, the Alliance leader Roy Jenkins, who had presented a much more statesmanlike and moderate impression in both the Commons and on national TV than Thatcher and Heffer, held off the challenge of George Galloway (touted as a future leader of the new Socialist Labour Party) in Glasgow Hillhead. Returned with Jenkins was a much larger parliamentary Alliance Party – the official merger between the Liberals and SDP having been approved four months before the election in order to encourage an image of unity. It had been opposed only by Dr David Owen and a number of long-standing Liberal activists, mainly in the north of England. Dr Owen left to form and lead a breakaway party, the Real SDP, but held only his own seat at Plymouth Devonport, thereafter appearing a somewhat isolated figure on the back benches until his later decision to accept a senior position in NATO. In the 1987 election, the Alliance strengthened its grip on second place and, indeed, with a substantial rise in tactical voting (boosted, for example, by the former punk singer Johnny Rotten) it was now second in terms of seats as well, as the disproportionate effects of the first-past-the-post system were reduced. Mrs Thatcher's overall majority fell to just twenty-one seats.

The Conservatives were severely rattled, and with continuing by-election defeats, including that of the former child prodigy William Hague at Richmond (Yorkshire) in February 1989 by the united Alliance candidate, Mrs Thatcher's slender majority was whittled away until by late 1990 she was effectively dependent upon Ulster Unionist votes. In these circumstances it came as little surprise (except apparently to the Prime Minister herself) when she was challenged for the party leadership by the former Defence Secretary Michael Heseltine; after the second round of voting after her withdrawal, John Major became Prime Minister. His position was weak from the start.

Major proved a likeable and more moderate leader, but he was not able to win an unprecedented fourth consecutive term for his party at the 1992 election (delayed for the full five years due to his lack of an overall majority). Signs of a highly damaging rift over Europe were already appearing, and with Labour only just beginning to move back from the far left following Heffer's replacement as leader, after their second successive disaster in 1987, by the Tribunite Robin Cook (who ironically had been a campaign manager for Neil Kinnock), the Alliance's uniquely united pro-European stance seemed particularly attractive. The veteran former Home Secretary and Chancellor of the Exchequer, Roy Jenkins, had handed the leadership of the Alliance over to Shirley Williams, ten years younger in age, after the 1987 election. She now became Britain's second female Prime Minister, though promised to retire within one term in office; she would turn sixty-five in July 1995. Although Mrs Williams's standards of promptness were somewhat disconcerting to the 10 Downing Street staff, she was perceived as a popular, humane and uncombative leader – and only retired two years later than promised, in 1997.

Mrs Williams was much assisted in her five years as Prime Minister by the continuing weakness of Labour. Mr Cook's attempts to pull his party back towards the centre were intelligently formulated and precisely argued, but he seemed to suffer both from his strongly pro-European convictions and from interpersonal difficulties with other senior figures from the democratic socialist tradition who had stayed with the party through its Militant-influenced years, even for some reason his fellow Scot, Gordon Brown. Meanwhile the Conservatives had troubles of their own.

John Major had resigned with dignity and a sense of humour after the 1992 election, reflecting that he would now have more years than he expected to follow his beloved Surrey county cricket team (he was later to become a highly successful President of Surrey, the MCC, and the International Cricket Conference). What followed was far from dignified, however, as the pro- and anti-European factions within his party embarked on one of the most protracted and bitter factional struggles seen in the history of British politics. As William Hague, having lost to the Alliance at Richmond in 1989 and only recently returned at the general election (having been selected to replace the retiring Cecil Parkinson at Hertsmere), had declared that his inexperience and youth precluded him from standing for the leadership – he was just thirty-one – the main contenders were the Europhiles Kenneth Clarke and Michael Heseltine, and the Euro-sceptic Norman Tebbit; this was not the most well-mannered battle. Douglas Hurd also stood, but received the votes of few MPs. In the last round of voting Clarke prevailed, mainly as he was seen as the most electorally robust candidate; however, such was the continuing rift over Europe that many felt that as official leader of the opposition he had less in common with his sceptical backbenchers than with the Prime Minister. This was to have lasting consequences for the British political system three years later, after Europe had moved firmly to centre stage.

The issue which brought it into the spotlight was the Exchange Rate Mechanism (ERM). Having entered this controversial arrangement in October 1990 under the Tories, the commitment of the new Alliance government to the principles of being good Europeans meant that they did not allow sterling to leave the ERM even in the crisis of autumn 1992, when a less ideologically driven administration might have.

Staying in the ERM in September 1992 forced devaluation of the pound sterling by 7 per cent initially, and by a further 5 per cent in November. There could be no big interest rate cuts in 1993, thus giving no direct stimulus to consumption and investment. There followed a period of long and deep falling house prices, arrears, and defaults leading to repossessions, with an associated loss of stability in the mortgage lending industry. The loss of housing equity was to have a severe knock-on effect later in the decade when consumption failed to grow as hoped. Unemployment remained higher for longer than it would have if the UK had dropped out of the ERM in 1992, as domestic and export demand were still so sluggish. Fiscal policy came under pressure too; with the economy in deep recession from 1992–94, the 'automatic stabilisers' increased the deficit further. Higher direct taxes bore especially heavily on London and the South East. Sterling did not bounce back after 1996, with very negative results for the 'new economy' chiefly based on services; while at the same time the long-term manufacturing decline in the Midlands and North continued, due both to international competition and the renewed militancy of some of the key unions still in the hands of the far left. Some commentators blamed much of the grim economic history of the 1990s on the Williams Government's so-called 'black September', with its fateful determination to devalue in line with the ERM commitment.

The disastrous persistence with ERM membership and its economic effects led to a drastic drop in the popularity both of the Williams Government and of the riven Tory party. Labour, adopting a more Eurosceptic line driven by the still predominantly socialist activist core, and under a new leader Gordon Brown, who had replaced Robin Cook partly due to the latter's stance on Europe, now showed substantial signs of recovery, especially with the reaffiliation of the TGWU under its Euro-pragmatic General Secretary, Bill Morris.

Faced with this threat, Mrs Williams and Mr Clarke adopted the historic decision to back the introduction of proportional representation (under the Additional Member System) for Westminster elections, which finally passed the Commons in 1995. For some reason this had not figured prominently in the earlier policy promulgations of the Alliance government, once it had been elected with an overall majority on 40 per cent of the vote in 1992. The unspoken assumption that this might lead to a possible future coalition between the Alliance and the Europhile wing of the Conservatives after a realignment within the British party system was to be borne out in the surprise 'Alliance-alliance' after the 1997 general election.

By this time the United Kingdom had a new Prime Minister. Although the successive leading figures in the former Liberal Party, David Steel and Paddy Ashdown, had loyally served as deputy leaders and in high Cabinet Office (as Home Secretary and Foreign Secretary respectively) it was expected that it was a 'Liberal' turn to be leader of the Alliance Party on Mrs Williams's retirement at the beginning of 1997 (she had originally said that she intended to take up her position at Harvard University in 1995, but was running a little late, an academic as well as personal prerogative). Indeed, it was rumoured that Mr Ashdown had been promised the succession to Mrs Williams at a lunch at the famed Priory House Restaurant at Stoke-sub-Hamdon in his Yeovil constituency. However, any such agreement, if made, was not kept. Instead there was a swift election among the entire membership in which Mr Ashdown was defeated by Tony Blair, some said by a slick media and rather personal campaign organised by the skilful Communications Director Peter Mandelson. Mr Blair's support by the main newspapers and apparently by the BBC TV and radio channels, which had often been accused of pro-European bias, also helped.

Although the Alliance share of the vote dropped by over 10 per cent to 29 per cent, this was actually sufficient to keep Mr Blair in office after the 1997 election, held on a gloriously sunny May day, due to his announcement the following day of a coalition with the Conservative Party (who had obtained just 25 per cent after their campaign had been racked by further deep divisions over Europe, among other matters relating to the future direction of the party). Kenneth Clarke was appointed Chancellor of the Exchequer, but no Eurosceptic achieved office of any kind. Labour had recovered to 32 per cent of the vote, but observers noted that the percentage for minor parties, encouraged by the PR voting system, had risen sharply to 14 per cent, including 6 per cent for Sir James Goldsmith's Referendum Party and a rise in the Green vote.

Under these exciting new democratically legitimated circumstances, brought about by the new electoral arrangements, Tony Blair faced a new Leader of the Opposition, Gordon Brown. Kenneth Clarke usually sat on his left at question time, when Mr Blair made his visits to the Commons, and the Home Secretary David Blunkett to his right.

Few others appeared to be entirely happy, though. The Eurosceptic Conservatives, excluded from government but sitting on the other side of the House from their accustomed position, argued that Mr Clarke would never have been leader if the method of electing the party leader had been expanded from MPs alone to the entire membership. Labour could see little way of obtaining power even if it should become the largest party in the popular vote, as long as the coalition should hang together – no single party had obtained over 50 per cent of the vote in living memory, not even in 1945. PR greatly reduced the 'wasted vote' reasons against voting for minor parties, and also against party splits. Finally, the former Liberal element of the Alliance became increasingly restless with the apparent rightward shift under Tony Blair, and the coalition with the Conservatives, with whom their annual local government electoral battles still lay. Only their continued allegiance to the European project, inspiringly and ardently led by Mr Blair, maintained their loyalty to the Alliance, and the wider coalition.

It was this ardour (and, cynics argued, the lack of fear of an electorate which was a feature of PR systems) which led Mr Blair and Mr Clarke to lead Britain into the Euro, after the second referendum was passed by 50.9 per cent of the vote (accompanied by strong complaints about the wording of the question), as a member of the first tranche of countries in 1998 – which was said by other Europeans to have been achieved a year or so earlier than it might have been without Britain's staunch support of the EU cause throughout the nineties.

Having been a member of the ERM, Britain could still enter economic and monetary union (EMU) at the earliest possible date. Like other countries, it was allowed to join this predominantly political arrangement without satisfying the full debt/GDP criterion. Entering at an unfavourable exchange rate, and inheriting the higher unemployment, depressed housing market and weaker government finances which followed from the decision to remain in the ERM in autumn 1992 (which had led to the failure to recover in the mid-1990s), there was now added the crippling fiscal rules of the EMU

Stability and Growth Pact, forcing a tightening of economic policy at a time when otherwise it might have been thought inappropriate in the national interest.

The disastrous economic and political effects of this decision were only beginning to become apparent when Mr Blair sought his second full term of office in September 2001, having decided to delay the elections because of the ill-handled foot and mouth epidemic (although the same Parliamentary constitutional changes as had brought Westminster electoral reform had fixed the term of Parliament at four years – as in those other crises during both world wars, elections could still be postponed by sovereign Act of Parliament). The Alliance section of the coalition dropped again, to 24 per cent. Mr Clarke's section of the Conservative Party also managed 24 per cent. Mr Brown's Labour Party increased to 33 per cent. Many Eurosceptic Conservatives joined the UK Independence Party, which also picked up the late Sir James Goldsmith's Referendum votes; but other voters took a different kind of nationalist line.

Particularly in the highly segregated former mill towns of northern England, such as Burnley, Oldham, and Bradford, the BNP, led by an articulate Cambridge graduate and trying (without complete success) to rebut allegations of neo-Fascism, also did well locally, despite its incompetent and sometimes brutish campaign, and although it came nowhere near winning a constituency directly, they obtained MPs for both the North West and Yorkshire regions of England on the top-up system under the Additional Member form of PR (first tried in the Scottish Parliament and National Assembly for Wales established under the devolution-minded Williams government in the early 1990s).

After the 2001 general election there was a lengthy and opaque period of negotiation among politicians, which reminded some observers of the unseemly bargaining in New Zealand after PR had been introduced in 1996. The Blair–Clarke regime did not quite have an absolute majority in the Lower House, and after three months their survival was only ensured when the Sinn Fein leader Gerry Adams announced that in future his seven MPs would attend and vote if the government was in danger. The oath of loyalty to the Queen was suspended in their case; commentators were not quite clear what else might have been agreed to secure this historic compromise. The Reverend Ian Paisley, leader of the largest unionist party, the DUP, proclaimed that Mr Blair had secured his eternal damnation by descending through the very gates of Hell to sup with Beelzebub.

More earthly retribution was soon to follow, however. As Tony Blair's second term staggered through economic crises, about which little could be done given the central economic control from Frankfurt (a point witheringly and repeatedly made by the Leader of the Opposition, Mr Brown) it was ill-fit to pay for its active involvement in US President Jeb Bush's military adventures in Iraq, Syria and Iran – proclaimed the Millennial Crusades by the religious right in America, both Christian and Jewish, and seen in a similar light by much of world Islamic opinion.

It was at the commencement of the second of these wars, in late 2003, that the Alliance finally split. The left of the party, consisting largely of former Liberals, but ironically led by Charles Kennedy, who had originally been returned to Parliament in 1983 as an SDP member, declared that they could no longer stomach the warmongering, and repudiated the government. On the other hand the Conservatives were substantially reunited by the nationalist surge, although they had to change their leader after Mr Clarke resigned to pursue his interests on the board of a major tobacco company, saying he would not even be partially responsible for innocent and unnecessary deaths. Some doubted the electoral appeal of his replacement, the youthful if balding 42-year-old William Hague, but it was felt that in time he might 'grow into' the job, one which may well take him into 10 Downing Street. Mr Blair now found himself at the head of a coalition three-quarters made up of Conservatives, although he dismissed parallels with David Lloyd George between 1918–22 and Ramsay MacDonald from 1931–35. The latter stages of his career, he told the *Guardian,* had been fruitfully guided by conviction rather than intellect.

As the 2001 Parliament proceeded into its second half, over twenty years had passed since that dramatic 1983 general election when the young and inspiring Alliance had surged past a flailing Labour Party. Observers had witnessed both a realignment and a dealignment within British politics: realignment, involving a major shift in loyalties and support between parties; and dealignment, implying a reduction in the strength of loyalty to the party system as a whole. Nine parties were now elected from English constituencies and regions (under the PR system) in addition to those in the ever-more distinctive other countries within the United Kingdom. The destruction of the two-party system which had been so decisively signalled in 1983 had been followed by a stable three-party pattern of competition for government. The introduction of PR (AMS) had not reversed the decline of turnout; indeed, only 54 per cent of the electorate had voted in 2001, and many voters professed that elections now decided nothing. These dissatisfied customers said that the general election result always ended in a hung parliament and negotiations among politicians in 'smoke-filled rooms' (although this was unlikely after the total tobacco ban – except snuff – in the Palace of Westminster in 1999). Coalitions were also as likely to be remade in the middle of the fixed-term parliaments.

In the seventh year of his premiership the SDP Alliance leader Tony Blair faced an uncertain future, for himself and his country. The whole of the Eurozone was slipping into negative growth, and the single interest rate seemed to suit few of the multifarious nations of the European Union, now seeking to expand further and considering another name change to the USE. He could do little about the economy or economic policy, though – too many of the key decisions were made elsewhere. Meanwhile the continuing instability across the whole of the Middle East and the apparently ever-increasing and everlasting commitment of his American allies was not only causing splits in Parliament but fuelling discontent in Britain itself, with increasing extra-parliamentary violence involving the far left anti-capitalists, the far right nationalist-racists, and young Muslims. Parliament itself did seem less an effective vehicle for democracy, despite the constitutional changes which had been introduced. Mr Blair did not seem able even to count on the members of the all-appointed Senate, even though so many of its members owed their positions to him. Meanwhile, in the Lower House, glaring at him from the opposition despatch box, he faced the weekly assaults of a man who had entered Parliament in the same fateful year as himself, 1983, but had (it was said narrowly) made a different calculation: the man who so eagerly desired his job, opposition leader Gordon Brown.

Chapter 17

What if Arthur Scargill had balloted the NUM in 1984?

David Mills

Arthur Scargill's refusal to hold a national strike ballot of the National Union of Mineworkers (NUM) in 1984 is considered by many to have been a strategic error of monumental proportions. By not holding a ballot, he handed his opponents within the National Coal Board (NCB) and the Conservative government the moral high ground and left the strike fatally weakened from the outset. The strike set the stage for a transformation of the British economy and provided Margaret Thatcher with the springboard from which she won her historic third successive general election victory.

It was also the last occasion on which a major trade union mounted a political challenge to the government of the day. The failure of that challenge cleared the way for the 'modernisation' of the Labour Party to begin in earnest. Labour cemented its position as the second major party at the 1987 election, while the SDP–Liberal Alliance embarked on a messy merger from which its successor, the Liberal Democrats, took several years to recover.

Had Scargill held a ballot, however, history could have been very different.

The importance of the ballot

It is now widely accepted that the Conservative government had prepared itself for a confrontation with the miners at some point in the 1983 Parliament, and had taken the precaution of increasing coal stocks to unprecedented levels to safeguard against a loss of production in a national strike. But the *casus belli* came in March 1984, four months into the NUM's national overtime ban, when the NCB informed the union that it intended to be able to close pits for 'purely economic' reasons, rather than on grounds of safety or exhaustion. As a first step towards the reduction of over-capacity in the industry, 4 million tonnes of production would be eliminated, accounting for roughly 20 mines and 20,000 jobs.

Rather than holding a ballot to sanction the strike, as Rule 43 of the NUM Rule Book stipulated, Arthur Scargill chose to proceed on the basis of Rule 41, under which union's National Executive could grant individual approval to strikes, opening up the prospect of a 'rolling strike' without a national ballot. This had never been used before in the NUM's history to sanction a nationwide strike. Scargill had already called ballots for a national strike over pit closures in 1982 and 1983, and had lost them both, by a 60:40 margin. He was wary of holding another ballot for the simple reason that he did not think that he would win one.

The NUM Secretary and Scargill lieutenant Peter Heathfield justified the use of Rule 41 by saying: 'I hope we are sincere and honest enough to recognise that a ballot should not be used and exercised as a veto to prevent people in other areas defending their jobs.'[1] This reflected a fear that the areas which did not feel under threat from the NCB's plans to close uneconomic pits – notably Nottinghamshire, the second biggest coalfield in Britain – would, along with miners who did not want to strike in other areas, outnumber those more militant members who did favour industrial action.

Yet contemporary opinion poll evidence suggests that Scargill may well have won a ballot had he held one in April 1984. In March 1984, a MORI poll for Weekend World found 62 per cent of NUM members in favour of a strike. By mid-April, a MORI poll for the *Sunday Times* showed 68 per cent in favour of strike action, 26 per cent against, with 6 per cent uncommitted. Assuming that the uncommitted had not voted, this would have produced a 72 per cent vote in favour of a ballot, well above the 55 per cent hurdle required by the NUM's Rule Book.[2]

The impact of a ballot

A nationwide pithead vote in favour of industrial action held, say, in April 1984 could have removed a number of significant problems which the NUM faced, and provided the miners with a number of powerful weapons with which to successfully prosecute the strike. Taken together, these could have significantly altered the course of the strike, to the point where the Coal Board and the government would have had to sue for peace.

First, had a strike ballot been held and won, the strike would have been more solid. While there would probably still have been some miners in areas like Nottinghamshire who would have voted to continue working, the fact that a ballot had been held and won would have done a lot to dissuade these miners from continuing to work. Writing after the strike, the NCB Chairman Ian MacGregor said that 'Nottinghamshire and its 31,000 miners were key to the strike', adding: 'If we could keep this vast and prosperous coalfield going, then I was convinced, however long it took, that we could succeed.'[3] Its twenty-five pits accounted for a quarter of the NCB's total output and were crucial to keeping the central belt of Midlands power stations going throughout the strike. Perhaps equally importantly, Nottinghamshire provided an example to miners throughout the rest of the country who were less inclined to follow their President's orders.

In the absence of the discipline which a strike ballot could have provided, the NUM leadership fell back on the sort of mass picketing which had closed the Saltley Coke Depot in Birmingham in 1972, the defining event of Arthur Scargill's career hitherto. These tactics were undoubtedly successful in some areas, at least in the short term. But not only did instances of violent mass picketing lose the miners support among the general public and the wider Labour movement, they also stiffened the resolve of anti-strike miners in areas such as Nottinghamshire not to be intimidated.

There is no guarantee that a strike which was buttressed from the beginning by a vote in favour of industrial action would have brought a series of other unions out in effective secondary action. After all, there were laws against secondary action on the statute book (though in the event, the government preferred not to use them, in case their use triggered precisely the sort of secondary action they were designed to prevent). And it is likely that other trade-union leaders used the lack of a ballot to justify their lack of industrial support for a man and a union they feared. Yet a ballot could have helped the NUM to attract more support from other trade unions. Even without a ballot, other unions with left-wing leaderships, such as ASLEF, the TGWU and the NUS were willing to provide considerable support to the NUM, both financially and industrially.

Had a ballot been held and won, perhaps the crucial role would have played by the National Association of Colliery Overmen, Deputies and Shotfirers (NACODS), the union which represented most of the mine safety managers. In the event, even in the absence of a strike ballot, in September 1984, NACODS' left-wing leadership almost brought the dispute to an end by threatening their own strike. In her memoirs, Thatcher describes how she feared that the NACODs leadership would use the 82.5 per cent vote in favour of strike action from their members in order to force an end to the main miners' strike on the NUM's terms.[4] The knowledge that they were coming out in support of a more solid, democratically sanctioned strike could have ensured that the smaller union came to the aid of the NUM, and helped to ensure a settlement favourable to Scargill.

The impact on the Conservative Party

Crucially, the lack of a strike ballot gave the Conservative Government the moral high ground in the dispute. While Scargill may have presented his decision not to hold a ballot as a defiant refusal to kow-tow to the NUM's class enemies in the Conservative Party and the media, it was interpreted by the Thatcher administration, perhaps correctly, as a sign of a lack of confidence in his own members. Had the NUM voted in favour of strike action, and not been faced by the problems which the lack of a ballot presented, it is reasonable to assume that these voices would have been heard more clearly. Faced with a democratically sanctioned strike, deprived of the coal provided by the Nottinghamshire coalfields, and faced with a united trade-union movement, the voices of those in the Cabinet who did not share Thatcher's relish for a knock-down, drag-out fight with the Conservative Party's old enemy might have prevailed.

Even without the ballot, there were elements within the NCB and the government who favoured settling the dispute early on terms which Scargill could at least have presented as an honour-able draw (had not such a concept been utterly anathema to him). While coal stocks were high throughout 1984, a near-total shut-down which a successful ballot could have helped to ensure, accom-panied by sympathetic action by NACODS and other unions, could have forced the government to settle long before the last tonne of coal was burned in the power stations. Any deal would have centred on a settlement which saw the NCB drop their demand to be able to close pits on purely economic grounds. This principle was sacro-sanct throughout all of the negotiations between the NUM and the NCB, and MacGregor's insistence on retaining it was the reason why

Scargill rejected the settlement – the so-called 'honourable draw' – which many of his critics in the Labour movement feel he should have accepted in October 1984.

The wider economic significance of the strike lay in the fact that the NCB's case represented 'the right of managers to manage', which was to become a mantra of Thatcherite businessmen by the end of the decade. By facing down a strike which aimed to prevent economic decisions being taken in the nationalised industries, Thatcher signalled that she was intent on changing the British economic environment, laying the economic foundations for the rest of her premiership. By demonstrating that she would fight for the principle of managers to manage against assertive trade unionism, she made possible the great denationalisations of the 1980s, which in turn eased the problems in the public sector accounts in the mid-eighties. The sales of 51 per cent of British Telecom and all of British Gas, British Airways and Rolls-Royce which took place between November 1984 and May 1987 brought in £21 billion alone (at 2000 prices).[5] While it is easy to overstate the importance of the proceeds of privatisation, there is no doubt that they contributed to the economic buoyancy which helped to secure the Conservatives their 1987 election victory, not to mention the political sense of purpose which these sales generated.[6]

Losing a strike fought upon such a fundamental economic principle would have been devastating for the Thatcher administration. But it would also have dealt a fatal blow to the Thatcher myth and very possibly to her premiership. Finding prominent Conservatives who would admit after the strike had been won that they would have considered giving in to Scargill is like trying to find Tories who will admit that they should have acquiesced in the Argentine invasion of the Falklands. Yet even in the situation which prevailed, *sans* ballot, Alan Clark points the finger at Tom King, Michael Heseltine and Willie Whitelaw (not to mention Energy Secretary Peter Walker) as possible supporters of a compromise, with Jim Prior and Francis Pym waiting on the backbenches.[7]

Two decades on, and with the image of mid-1980s Thatcher as an unstoppable force of nature fixed in our minds, it seems unthinkable that Conservative MPs would have deposed her, the leader of a party with a Commons majority of 144. Yet six years later, with her majority still in three figures, those same MPs defenestrated her. Had Thatcher been unwilling to back down in the face of power cuts and industrial paralysis, she could well have been the victim of a coup (or a counter-revolution, as her supporters would have seen it) within her own party.

The demands to face down the trade unions would not have disappeared. Even if Thatcher had resigned, there would still have been 'Thatcherites' in the Cabinet of her successor (Geoffrey Howe? Michael Heseltine?). Pamphlets would have been written, fringe meetings addressed and speeches made by those who believed that, sooner or later, the Conservative Party had to take on and beat the trade unions. Maybe the retreat would have been temporary, and armed with a new mandate they would have returned to the battle. But for the time being, the voices of those who wanted to take a hard line with the trade unions would have been drowned out by those who preferred a respite, however brief.

With a three-figure majority in the Commons, the new Conservative Prime Minister would have been able to do what John Major did in 1990, and let the Parliament run its full course before calling an election. However, with the unfinished business of trade union reform still be accomplished (and perhaps feeling a Major-like desire to win a mandate for himself), the next election could have come as early as spring 1986. The Conservative Party would still have enjoyed the support of those who wanted to see the power of the unions curbed, along with other sections of the electorate who had supported it in 1983. But it is difficult to see how a defeat by Scargill and the loss of

Thatcher could have had anything other than a depressing impact on the morale of activists and on the party's fortunes as a whole.

The impact on the Labour Party

If the defeat of Arthur Scargill made Margaret Thatcher, it also had a profound effect on Neil Kinnock and the party he led.

When the dispute began, Kinnock was appalled that Scargill had gone ahead without a ballot. Yet not wishing to give Scargill the excuse that lack of backing from the Labour leader had caused his defeat, Kinnock equivocated on the issue, a course of action which he now says he regrets.[8] Had Scargill held a ballot, it is reasonable to assume that Kinnock would, at the very least, have given the dispute the same degree of support he gave to the ballotless strike. The son of a miner himself, Kinnock would no doubt have been delighted if the miners avoided the privations which the year-long strike, defeat and pit closures imposed upon them. Yet had the strike ended in a victory for Scargill, Kinnock would have been placed in a difficult position. As his biographer points out, if Thatcher been defeated by Scargill, the victory would have been his, and not Kinnock's or the Labour Party's.[9] If Scargill had won after holding a strike ballot, the same would surely have been true.

When the strike began, Kinnock was just embarking on the long process of overhauling Labour's organisation and reviewing its policies. When it ended, in the defeat which Kinnock realised at the start was inevitable without a ballot, he used it as an object lesson to his party on the need to embrace 'modernisation'.

After a Scargill victory, his position as leader would probably have been secure. Faced by a resurgent left, it seems unlikely that the right of the Labour Party, led by deputy leader Roy Hattersley, would have challenged Kinnock. For its part, the left lacked a convincing figurehead, apart from Tony Benn, whose defeat in the deputy leadership election marked the high water mark of his influence in the party.

Kinnock would have also been safe from a direct political challenge from Scargill himself. It is very unlikely that Scargill would have made a bid for a leading role in the party since, as Paul Routledge notes in his biography of the NUM leader, after his defeat as a Communist candidate in a council election in 1960, Scargill had always shown a marked reluctance to stand for election in any other organisation other than his NUM citadel.[10]

Had Scargill won the strike, Kinnock would undoubtedly still have tried to modernise Labour. However, the left, in the trade unions and the constituencies, would have used the miners' victory as a rallying point. The leading historian of the relationship between the trade unions and the Labour Party during that period, Lewis Minkin, notes that defeat in the miners' strike was an important factor in the formation of new policy alignments between key trade unions and the Labour leadership between 1985 and 1987.[11] If Scargill had prevailed, then at the very least, the party's shift away from a policy of withdrawal from the EEC might have been thwarted, while other attempts to resile from the 1983 manifesto in the areas of the withdrawal of trade-union immunities would surely have been shelved.

Labour's presentational successes of the mid to late 1980s could also have been affected. In these circumstances, it is hard to see Neil Kinnock making the same electrifying speech to the party's conference at Bournemouth in 1985. While it is best remembered for its attacks on Derek Hatton and Militant Tendency, the speech was, in effect, Kinnock's challenge to all of his opponents on the left, telling them that there was no alternative to his process of modernisation. It effectively relaunched his leadership. With a more assertive left bolstered by a Scargill victory, such a relaunch would have been even more problematic than it turned out to be.

Overall, it seems likely that, in the event of a Scargill victory in the miners' strike, Kinnock would have made even less progress in his reform of the party's policy and presentation than he actually did. Under such circumstances, it seems reasonable to assume that a Labour Party which seemed just as in thrall to the trade unions as it did in 1983, and just as split as it was in 1983, would have performed little better than it had at the 1983 general election.

The role of the SDP

The 'joker in the pack' in determining what would have happened had Arthur Scargill held a ballot and won the strike is the Social Democratic Party, and particularly its leader David Owen.

As leader of the SDP, Owen was convinced that Scargill should be beaten. During the course of the strike, he visited Ian Macgregor on a number of occasions,[12] expressed his support to Margaret Thatcher during a private meeting after the memorial service for Yvonne Fletcher,[13] and helped to arrange financial support for the breakaway Union of Democratic Mineworkers.[14] Some of this opposition to Scargill sprang from Owen's opposition to a strike without a democratic ballot. Yet Owen had left Labour over the issue of the power of trade unions in the party, and even if a ballot had been held, any resolution of the dispute which saw Scargill and the unions strengthen their position within the country would have been anathema to him.

One of the ironies of the period was that the end which Owen fervently desired – Scargill's defeat – ended up helping the modernisation of the Labour Party which ultimately ended any hope of the SDP breaking through and establishing itself as a long-term serious rival to Labour. Owen says now that when he heard Kinnock's speech to the Labour conference in Bournemouth in 1985, he knew that, sooner or later, the game was up for his party.

In the aftermath of a victory by Scargill, the question of whether Kinnock would have been able or minded to press ahead so single-mindedly with modernisation of the Labour Party is moot, to say the least. In the absence of a united Labour Party espousing the broadly social democratic policies which the 1987 Labour manifesto contained (Kinnock would, of course, call them 'democratic socialist'), the SDP might have been able to occupy the political space which Kinnock's modernisation was to deny them. Of course, the Alliance would still have faced substantial obstacles in a 1986 general election. In large areas of the country, neither the Liberals nor the SDP posed a credible threat to the two main parties. The 'dual leadership' of Steel and Owen would still have attracted criticism, and opponents and the media would still have exploited policy differences between the two parties and leaders, notably on defence.

But at that time, the Alliance was enjoying its most sustained spell of popularity since the period just after the SDP's launch in 1981. Between the second quarter of 1985 and the second quarter of 1986, the Alliance's opinion poll ratings hovered around the 28 per cent mark, never falling below 27 per cent and rising as high as 31 per cent.[15] It is possible that those former Labour voters who had voted for the Alliance in 1983 and who drifted back in 1987, impressed by Kinnock's stand against the left, might have stayed put. This could have helped the Alliance to hang on to seats and gain more in areas where they and the Tories were close. Furthermore, Owen's personal identification as an opponent of trade union power could also have helped to attracted support from Conservatives keen to keep left-wing Labour candidates out, while his personal reputation for decisiveness, even fierceness, could have attracted floating voters who had admired the same qualities in Mrs Thatcher.

It is also likely that Labour would have been deprived of the 'Kinnock factor' which helped it to whittle away Alliance support during the 1987 election campaign. Having begun the campaign two points behind the Alliance, Labour ended it with an 8 per cent higher share of the popular vote. In a situation where the relaunch of Kinnock had not been possible, this process might have been diminished, or even reversed.[16]

The general election of 1986

In this scenario the 1986 election looks less like the re-run of the 1983 election which the 1987 contest turned out to be, and more like the general election of February 1974. Edward Heath's question to the electorate after his own battles with the NUM – 'who governs?' – would have been posed once more.

Asked to choose between a dispirited Conservative Party, mourning the loss of its leader and cursing the NUM, and a divided Labour Party whose modernisation had been stalled by a revivified left, the electorate could have looked rather more closely at the Alliance, and the SDP in particular. Led by a serious politician with experience of Cabinet government, a confident performer in the Commons and in the media, the Alliance, and the SDP, would have been well placed to benefited from a situation where both major parties seemed to be stymied by the challenge posed by militant trade unionism. The result could have been something like this:

1986 election result

Party	Seats
Conservatives	315
Labour	242
SDP	38
Liberals	35
Others	20

Such a result would have opened up the prospect of a hung Parliament, in which both the Alliance as a whole and the Alliance parties separately would have held the balance of power – or rather, the choice of whether to support a Conservative minority government.

With Thatcher out of the picture (if not out of the Commons), it is possible to envisage the Alliance supporting a minority Conservative administration, whether in full coalition or not. Several of Mrs Thatcher's Cabinet had been supporters of electoral reform during the 1970s, and the offer of a Speaker's Conference on the issue, backed by a promise to legislate its conclusions, could have been sufficient to win Alliance support, at least in the short term.

During the 1987 election, David Steel and David Owen insisted that they would negotiate as an Alliance and would enter into coalitions as an Alliance. Yet, the different attitudes of Steel (and his party) and Owen towards possible coalition with the Conservatives hint at an even more dramatic outcome, one outlined by *Guardian* columnist Hugo Young in July 1986:

> Maybe Dr Owen wants to be, above all, free. If a hung parliament is returned, he would like to be unencumbered by the Liberals … [I]n a certain configuration of seats, he would want to keep open the Tory option: do a deal with a new Conservative leadership as the last hope of precluding what would be, for Owen personally, the ruin of his political life – the installation of Neil Kinnock in Downing Street.[17]

The logic of Owen's aversion to merger after the 1987 election was that, one day, the SDP might be in a position to support a different party to its Alliance partner. A general election held in the wake of a Scargill victory over Thatcher could just have provided the opening for this to take place. As Crewe and King note, Owen was markedly more critical of Labour than the Conservatives. Throughout the 1983 Parliament, his speeches were peppered with comments like 'We have yet to finish the job of demolishing the Labour Party', and 'Mr Kinnock's Labour Party is so buckled and bent by the hard left that it can neither walk nor think straight.'[18]

At the same time, Owen was making clear that he saw the possibility of cooperation with the Conservative Party as much more likely (and preferable) to a deal with Labour. Crewe and King cite an interview in the *Independent* from April 1987, in which Owen said:

> The rebels in the Conservative Party – pretty mild rebels, the wets – are at least basically arguing for the things we want. There's common ground. The

rebels in the Labour Party are arguing for things we find a total anathema, so that's the difficulty we have.[19]

Even 'unencumbered by the Liberals', he would have faced bitter opposition from colleagues in the SDP had he sought to support a government run by such Conservatives. Bill Rodgers' insistence in his Tawney Society lecture in May 1985 that the SDP was 'unequivocally on the centre-left'[20] gives a taste of the criticism that an accommodation with the Conservatives would have prompted. But the key elements of his strategy as SDP leader – to attack Labour and to aim to hold the balance of power – would have been vindicated.

The mould of British politics would have been broken. And it would have been broken by the miners.

Notes

1   Peter Wilsher, Donald Macintye, and Michael Jones, *Strike: Thatcher, Scargill and the Miners* (Deutsch, 1985), p. 81.

2   Ibid., p. 78.

3   Ian MacGregor with Rodney Tyler, *The Enemies Within* (Fontana, 1986), pp. 195–96.

4   Margaret Thatcher, *The Downing Street Years* (HarperCollins, 1993) pp. 366–75.

5   John Kay, 'Privatisation in the United Kingdom 1979–1999' (www.johnkay.com, 2001), p. 7.

6   Ibid., p. 10.

7   Alan Clark, *The Tories: Conservatives and the Nation State 1922–1997* (Phoenix, 1998), pp. 477–78.

8   Interview for Brook Lapping TV Production, cit. in Brenda Maddox, *Maggie: The First Lady* (Hodder & Stoughton, 2003), pp. 159–60.

9   Martin Westlake, *Kinnock: The Biography* (Little, Brown, 2001), p. 292.

10 Paul Routledge, *Scargill: The Unauthorised Biography* (HarperCollins, 1993), p. 38.

11 Lewis Minkin, *The Contentious Alliance: Trade Unions and the Labour Party* (Edinburgh University Press, 1991), p. 420.

12 MacGregor, *The Enemies Within*, p. 318.

13 The WPC gunned down from the Libyan Embassy; David Owen, *Time To Declare* (Penguin, 1992), p. 614.

14 Ibid., p. 613.

15 Poll data cited by Ivor Crewe and Anthony King, *SDP: The Birth, Life and Death of the Social Democratic Party* (OUP, 1995), Table 16.13, p. 522.

16 Poll data, cited by Crewe and King, *SDP*, Table 19.1, p. 523.

17 Hugo Young, *Guardian*, 24 July 1986, cited in Crewe and King, *SDP*, p. 358.

18 Crewe and King, *SDP*, p. 364.

19 *Independent*, April 2 1987, cited in Crewe and King, *SDP*, p. 364.

20 Lecture by William Rodgers MP, 'My Party – Wet or Dry?', Tawney Society Lecture, 16 May 1985, cited in Crewe and King, *SDP*, p. 335.

Chapter 18

What if Mrs Thatcher had had to resign over Westland?

Sir Bernard Ingham

Nigel Lawson, in his tome, *The View from No. 11*,[1] claims that Margaret Thatcher could not possibly have survived if Leon Brittan had spilled the beans about his leaking of the Solicitor-General's letter to Michael Heseltine, the event which brought the denouement of the Westland affair. Instead, 'he meekly accepted the role of scapegoat'.

I wonder what Lord Lawson, not to mention Brittan (now also a peer of the realm), knows that I don't, since I was at the epicentre of that ridiculous earthquake which rocked the British Government in 1986. The more I look back on the hysteria it engendered, the more it exemplifies Macaulay's aphorism, 'We know no spectacle so ridiculous as the British public in one of its periodical fits of morality'.

The basic facts behind this seizure are simple. Westland, a modest £300m helicopter company in Yeovil, fell on difficult times. Heseltine, Defence Secretary, suddenly discovered a passionate determination to integrate it into Europe without having the necessary vehicle – an interested partner – to achieve his ambition. The Government's position, led by Thatcher, was to allow Westland to find its own salvation. It did just that by linking up with the American company, Sikorsky.

Heseltine, driven by some curious fervour, eventually resigned before Westland went American without actually making his position crystal clear. He just walked out of a Cabinet meeting over Thatcher's handling of the affair; he had latterly accused her of denying him a proper Cabinet hearing. Immediately after he had departed No. 10, officials flew into its press office to ask me what he had said to the press on his way out. Had he said he had resigned? Not unnaturally, I retorted that it would have helped if they had tipped us off that he was leaving. So I had to dispatch my press officers into Whitehall to track down journalists who might have been outside and soon confirmed, via Chris Moncrieff, Political Editor of the Press Association, that the Defence Secretary no longer regarded himself as a member of the Government.

Over the closing months of 1985, before his New Year resignation, Heseltine pulled every trick in his extensive repertoire of political and presentational manoeuvres. The one that caused terminal trouble was the appearance of his letter to Lloyds Merchant Bank in *The Times* suggesting that Westland might lose work in Europe if it linked up with the American company Sikorsky. Thatcher was concerned about 'material inaccuracies' in this letter and the Solicitor-General, Sir Patrick Mayhew, who it turns out had been employed by Heseltine to advise on his letter, was asked officially to point these out to him. No wonder Mayhew is reported to have said later that it was like being the family solicitor to both the Montagues and the Capulets.

The Department of Trade and Industry leaked the substance of Mayhew's letter to the Press Association ostensibly – or so they told me – to forestall the issue before a press conference which was due at 4 p.m. on 6 January 1986. This takes me back to Lawson's suggestion that Thatcher was part of a conspiracy to leak the letter. All I can say to that is that, if there was a conspiracy, I was not part of it. That, you may well think, would have been a curious omission on the part of the conspirators, especially as the DTI, in the form of its Director of

Information, rang me up to say that she had Industry Secretary Brittan's authority to leak the letter and asked me to perform the actual leaking. I recall my ample eyebrows shooting heavenwards in surprise when the idea of leaking the letter was put to me and rejecting point blank the specific request for me to do the dirty deed. 'No', I said, 'I must keep the Prime Minister above that sort of thing.'

My one regret is that I did not advise the DTI to forget about the idea, too, even though I made it very clear that I was extremely unhappy about it. On that basis Brittan claimed at least tacit approval by No. 10. There followed a humdinger of a political and media hullabulloo, an investigation by the Cabinet Secretary, Sir Robert (now Lord) Armstrong, and Thatcher saying, as she prepared a crucial Commons speech on the affair – more, I thought, with gallows humour than foreboding – that she might be out of a job by 6 o'clock that evening.

As it turned out, Neil Kinnock, Labour leader, blew any chance he might have had of getting rid of 'that bloody woman', as she was called, with a hopelessly bad speech. Thatcher was off the hook long before 6 p.m. The episode claimed a second cabinet minister – Brittan – who went not just because of his bad judgement but because he was also a hopeless presenter, certainly on TV. I am sorry to say – and here I agree with Lord Lawson – that he also departed in more than a whiff of anti-Semitism. And that generally was it – apart from its launching a thousand inquests – until Heseltine rose fatally to challenge Thatcher's leadership of the Tories in November 1990.

So, against that brief sketch of Westlandgate, as it was inevitably called, let us first consider what it was really about. Thatcher says that Heseltine claimed at various times that it was about Britain's future as a technologically advanced country, the role of government in industry, Britain's relationship with Europe and the US and the proprieties of constitutional government. She also claims it was about his personality, his own 'overwhelming belief in himself'.

For me, it was a painful demonstration of the tensions which can arise in a government when a senior Cabinet minister goes off the rails and treats collective responsibility with contempt. It also put on daily display the nauseating hypocrisy of the British media, whose shock and horror over a leak carried about as much conviction as Dracula fainting at the sight of blood. Their constitutional piety had to be seen to be believed. It contrasts sharply with their acceptance little more than ten years later of – nay, connivance in – the Blair Government's policy of systematically 'trailing' policy developments, even when that leaking is selective and to the commercial disadvantage of those denied the information.

I have always seen Westlandgate as a desperate and not entirely successful attempt to besmirch Thatcher because she was so straight, even unworldly. Her propriety in an increasingly dirty world was undoubtedly a challenge to the numerous 'knockers' in politics and the media. What cannot be denied is that the affair was a symptom of the underlying turmoil within the Tory party over Europe which has dogged it for close on twenty years, and which has contributed so far to Conservative MPs stabbing three of their leaders in the back. It demonstrated the fractious nature of politically the most successful post-war government and lends credence to my argument that we should not wonder why Thatcher fell, after eleven and a half years, but why she lasted that long. The manner of her fall four years later, and the shock it caused, still rankles with the increasingly aged rank and file of her party.

How much better or worse would it have been had she bitten the dust over Westland? Before we examine that question it is necessary for purposes of background to examine what we mean by 'a leak', since this makes the affair appear even more ludicrous.

In government, a leak is defined as 'an unauthorised disclosure of information'. Under the British system, only ministers can authorise disclosure. On that basis, the disclosure of the substance of Mayhew's letter by the DTI was perfectly above board. That Brittan authorised the leak has never been disputed. It also has to be said that the idea that law officers' advice is never revealed is disingenuous. Their advice is implicit in the announcement of most governmental decisions. It even became explicit when Blair's Attorney-General published his justification for war with Iraq; though that, of course, was in another age, if only seventeen years on.

However, there is also another necessary convention, indeed, courtesy, to be observed – or it had to be in 1986 – if the charge of leaking is to be avoided. That requires the minister who is minded to authorise disclosure to clear it with those other ministers involved or affected. Brittan cleared it with neither Mayhew nor Heseltine. So it was, if you like, a half-leak or, at worst, a leak for want of courtesy.

It should be remembered that Heseltine seldom cleared his various public initiatives with his colleagues, some of whom – not least Thatcher – were occasionally lost in admiration at his resourcefulness. Since Heseltine was in no position to come over all indignant about a leak, let alone a half-leak, therefore, we are entitled to ask whether all the fuss and pother stemmed from the *amour-propre* of the law officers, or more specifically that of the late Sir Michael Havers QC, the Attorney-General. Certainly, he got on his high horse about the whole thing, notwithstanding his remarkably indiscreet performances about Westlandgate at the bar of the Garrick Club, according to journalists who were able to give me first-hand accounts of his matinees.

Frankly, the whole business came to stink in my nostrils. It was by any standards as tawdry as it was inconsequential, and the only purpose served in writing about it again is to reduce it to the absurd spasm of a decaying democracy which it undoubtedly was.

~

So, let us play consequences. I shall not content myself with the one set by my examiners at Politico's. Instead, I shall rehearse a number of consequences in order better to illuminate the specific one I am asked to address.

First – and this is really intriguing – what if Heseltine had not caught the Westland bug which propelled him to stake all on Europeanising it, and found nothing in the company crucial to Britain's strategic defence interests? He had for a time fascinated Thatcher, who was nonetheless wary of him, with his managerial methods. There is also no doubt that he was in his element seeing off the Campaign for Nuclear Disarmament challenge in 1983 as Britain supported the European deployment of cruise missiles. I worked with him closely on that enterprise and was privileged to see a real campaigning politician at work.

But the Ministry of Defence exposed Heseltine's limitations as a strategic thinker and policy-maker and it was clear from the speed with which Thatcher replaced him on his resignation – it was a matter of mere minutes – that he had outstayed his welcome at the MoD. She may well still have concluded that it was better to have him inside than outside the tent, assuming he would have accepted demotion, but it would have been clear that he had reached his ceiling and it would be downhill all the way from then, at least while she remained Prime Minister. In fact, he rose again to be Deputy Prime Minister under John Major – which demonstrates that as long as he was in active politics, Heseltine was always going to be a big beast.

Consequently – since we are playing consequences – Heseltine would always have been in with a real chance to succeed Thatcher had he kept his nose clean. That he failed to do so when he eventually mounted his challenge in 1990 – but only after the real Brutus, Sir Geoffrey Howe, had left him with no alternative, given the nature of Howe's resignation speech – may well be an example of the sort of justice that parties can somehow contrive to dispense when confronted with would-be assassins. My conclusion is that Heseltine blew it over Westland in 1986. After that eccentricity, he could never be sure of the crown. Thatcher's downfall in 1990 was thus a Pyrrhic victory for him. It also plunged their party into a turmoil from which, to repeat, it has still not completely recovered. Heseltine has much to answer for.

His Westland behaviour also cost us the possibly exhilarating experience of a Heseltine Government. I use the word 'possibly' advisedly. No one knows the real timber of a politician until he acquires ultimate responsibility. But it is pretty clear from Heseltine's nature that we would have heard echoes of Harold Wilson and anticipated Tony Blair. Wilson was an early taste of Blair's obsession with presentation and, of course, he was interventionist; Blair's style of government has been dominated by intervention for presentation's sake. He will promise anything today, if current circumstances are deemed by spin doctors to demand it, and try to finesse it away tomorrow.

Heseltine was always the hottest presenter in Torytown and he was an avowed interventionist. Indeed, he gloried in it. As he proudly declared at his party conference in 1992, 'If I have to intervene to help British companies, like the French government helps French companies, or the German government helps German companies, or the Japanese government helps Japanese companies, then I tell you I'll intervene before breakfast, before lunch, before tea and before dinner. And I'll get up the next morning and I'll start all over again.' As if Thatcher had never intervened on behalf of British companies! But it all depends on what you mean by intervention. Heseltine's intervention would have been different, if not necessarily more effective. I fear a Heseltine Government would have earned the phrase 'all spin and no substance' long before Blair's came to merit it.

Heseltine denied us the opportunity to find out whether it would have been so by his Westland brainstorm and Willie Whitelaw's failure to contain him. It is often said that Thatcher was never the same again after Whitelaw, her Deputy Prime Minister, suffered his stroke in December 1987. But the fact remains that Whitelaw, with whom I enjoyed working for several years when he was the minister in charge of presentation, signally failed to put Heseltine in his box before he could do any damage. Perhaps Westland demonstrated that Whitelaw had passed the zenith of his powers as chief clearer of the undergrowth in the Thatcher Governments.

What if he had managed to contain Heseltine on this occasion, and Brittan had continued as Industry Secretary? It should be remembered that Brittan had fairly recently been demoted from the Home Office largely because of his presentational incapacity. Indeed, Thatcher found herself with three men occupying the top front-line jobs – Howe, Lawson and Brittan – none of whom was God's gift to communication; Douglas Hurd (now Lord Hurd) was moved from Northern Ireland to Home Office to improve matters. I shudder when I recall the tales of antipathy among rank-and-file Conservatives at the sight of Brittan on TV.

It was clear that because of this, despite his brain power, he was on the wane as a leading political player. Westland also demonstrated that he was no match for Heseltine in a scrap. A blighted career lay in front of him even if he had been spared Heseltine's single-minded campaigning unless – and this is where he might successfully have changed tracks as a QC – he had become a law officer. He undoubtedly had the brain of a potential Lord Chancellor, if that now conveys the compliment intended after our experience of Lord Irvine of Lairg in that post as a Blair crony (he was Blair's boss in their former chambers). Yet, on the whole, I conclude that Westland was the making of Brittan. He largely disappeared from British sight to become – ironically, given his stance over the helicopter company – one of the more intelligent members of the European Commission.

Brittan's potential as a law officer brings me to another consequence. What if Attorney-General Havers had not stoked the fires over Westland? He got so worked up about it that he even threatened to put the police into No. 10 to investigate the leak. If only he had and Thatcher had been able to welcome Scotland Yard's brightest and best through the famous black door. I would have preferred that to the investigation by the Cabinet Secretary. By its very nature it was easy for the 'knockers' to dismiss Armstrong's investigation as a white-wash when he came up with a 'misunderstanding' between the DTI and No. 10.

I have never been clear what the misunderstanding was, unless it was that the DTI misinterpreted my own – and other – pressure, including on the morning of the leak, to be more robust in their defence of the government's line that Westland should be allowed to seek its own salvation. As far as I am concerned, that pressure fell so far short of advocating leaking the Solicitor-General's letter that I rejected the idea, as I have indicated, when it came out of the blue to me. Armstrong conducted a thorough inquiry. I provided him with written evidence as well as being interviewed by him. So far as I know, nobody was reprimanded. I certainly wasn't. Havers' police-men could not have done better to please the 'knockers'.

Havers undoubtedly stirred it, however, though perhaps only mar-ginally, given the bloodlust which the British media develops on these occasions. Brittan's resignation gave them the next best thing to a Thatcher resignation. But what if an official had resigned to take the rap? There would not have been much point in Colette Bowe, Brittan's press secretary, putting her head on the block. After all, she had her Secretary of State's permission to disclose the contents of Mayhew's letter. And, while I had refused to leak for her, as she asked, I had not in the end advised her not to do so either. But the most I could have done would have been to advise. Unlike Alastair Camp-bell, Blair's Director of Communications, I had no authority over any colleague outside No. 10 because of the deliberate dispersal of power from the founding of the Government Information Service immedi-ately after World War II. It was not, however, in the nature of Margaret Thatcher to sacrifice her staff for her own convenience. Nor do you contemplate resignation if you continue to enjoy your boss's confidence. In any case, however, I never deluded myself that if any No. 10 official had put the metaphorical revolver to terminal use, it would have satisfied the media's lust for blood; it would have had them baying ever more loudly for the Prime Minister's.

So, what if Thatcher had sacked Heseltine? She certainly had reason to do so, for he was never a team player. Moreover, she had the opportunity to do so weeks before the leak. What is more – and this is another irony – my advice persuaded her against doing so. I can disclose this because, believe it or not – and by now you can believe anything – someone else unknown leaked the details to the *Observer*.

One evening before Christmas 1985, Brittan came over to No. 10 demanding that Heseltine be fired. Thatcher took the demand seriously. She summoned Whitelaw, the Chief Whip, John Wakeham (now Lord Wakeham), the Cabinet Secretary and her private secretaries to a conference in her study overlooking St James's Park. I was across at the Commons briefing journalists. As soon as I returned I was directed to the meeting, whereupon I was presented with an Armstrong draft of a letter it was proposed to send to Heseltine warning him about his behaviour. 'You can't send that', I said. 'It's just a yellow card. We all know what he will do. He'll ignore it. And what will you do then? If he calls your bluff you will be in a much weaker position.'

'So we shall have to sack him', replied Thatcher. To which I responded as follows: 'Well, by all means do so. But I can tell you I have just come from talking to journalists and there is no doubt who has their sympathy. It's Heseltine. He's winning the argument. Sack him and you will make him a martyr to the European cause. Is that what you want?'

So nothing was done, and Brittan retired not best pleased with me. Nor, as it turns out, did that advice make for a comfortable life in the immediate future for those concerned. But was it sound advice?

What if Thatcher had sacked Heseltine at that juncture? There would have been no Westlandgate, which would have been a blessing. Westland would have gone American and Brittan would have remained in the government though, as I have explained, without a bright future unless he had moved into the law officers' sidings.

On the other hand, Heseltine would have become, if not a martyr to the European cause, an even bigger lion in the Conservative jungle. He could have presented it as having been fired by an autocratic Prime Minister who, either out of her personal animus or because of her Euroscepticism or her uninterventionist ways – perhaps he might have said all three – had denied him a proper hearing in Cabinet. He would never have been short of listeners had he chosen to stalk the land rather than bide his time – a strategy which would probably have served him better, assuming he was capable of it.

The Times described his eventual departure a few weeks later as 'a very good resignation'. I conclude it would have been an even better sacking. He would have been cut off in his prime on a wave of sympathy. The government was not in good odour, having apparently lost some momentum, and 1986 was to become an *annus horribilis* of the Thatcher years, along with 1980 ('you turn if you want to, the lady's not for turning') and 1990. But most important of all, Heseltine would not have been tainted with the same doubts about his judgement, control, opportunism and calculated ambition that clouds so many resignations. He would have been better placed to win the Tory leadership as and when Thatcher either ran her course or became vulnerable. In 1990 John Major, Thatcher's protégé, was handed the short straw because he wasn't Heseltine.

This, then, is the appropriate juncture to turn to the original question: what if Thatcher had had to resign over Westland? I do not believe that it was ever realistically on the cards. But if, by some quirk of injustice, it had occurred, we would then most likely have discovered whether a Heseltine Government would have been as exhilarating an experience as it would have been different. He would have only recently resigned. She would have gone under a cloud. His position might not have been as strong as if he had been fired; but he would have been seen as the leading alternative, offering an alternative Tory approach.

And, let's face it, 1985 had not been a great year for Thatcher. True, the miners had been defeated. But unemployment persisted above three million, MPs were beginning to worry about whether they could win the next election on existing economic policies, and Francis Pym, sacked after his stint as Foreign Secretary during the Falklands campaign, had raised the standard of rebellion in the form of the Centre Forward movement which, as it turned out, scored no goals.

If I am right that Whitelaw was well past his peak, who else might have sought to thwart Heseltine's ambition? Pym? Possibly, but his movement was a damp squib and he lacked the killer instinct. Howe? Maybe, but surely too boring. Lawson? Doubtful, since he seemed not to have the ultimate ambition. Hurd? He failed against Major in 1990 and there is no reason to suppose he would have been more attractive with far less experience under his belt in 1986. Tebbit? Possibly, to keep the Thatcher flag flying but could this acerbic dry have prevailed over the golden boy with the golden mane? Major? No. His foot was still on the lowest rung of the ministerial ladder in the Department of Health and Social Security. It is difficult to believe that Heseltine would not have succeeded and almost immediately begun to unwind Thatcherism.

But what of the Opposition? Thatcher's demise would have been a feather in the cap of Kinnock; he would have won plaudits for helping to bring her down instead of letting her off the hook. That would have transformed morale in the Labour Party. It would have presented Heseltine or any Tory leader with a formidable challenge in 1987 or 1988, especially as the differences between the parties would have narrowed. I doubt whether Kinnock would have won the election.

But, either way, you can be sure of two things: we would have been back on the return journey to the failed 'tax, spend and intervene' consensus of the post-war years and hell-bent on becoming a full member of what is now called the European Union.

The failure to force Thatcher's resignation preserved the conditions for the eventual revival of the British economy and a decade and more of prosperity. It ensured that we retained what was left of our sovereignty and held up the relentless march towards a United States of Europe. It also created the conditions in which someone had to reform the Labour Party. That fell to Blair who, after six years, has yet to persuade us that it has made any real difference to Britain, other than to put it ever more in the insufferable grip of the politically correct.

Notes

1   Nigel Lawson, *The View from No. 11: Memoirs of a Tory Radical* (Bantam Press, 1992).

Chapter 19

What if John Smith had lived?

Mark Stuart

At 8.05 a.m. on Thursday 12 May 1994, John Smith died during an early morning bath in his Barbican flat. He had suffered a second, massive heart attack, following his first six years earlier. Smith's death, aged only fifty-five, robbed the Labour Party and the country of a great Prime Minister.

The outpouring of public grief in the week after his death was both genuine and highly unusual from a British electorate that rarely holds its politicians in high esteem. This chapter argues that had Smith lived, he would have won a landslide victory at the 1997 general election, though probably not one as sizeable as Tony Blair achieved.[1] It also challenges the idea that Smith was not a moderniser, and points out that he did have a policy agenda recognisably his own.

Perhaps the most fascinating period had Smith lived would have been 1994–97, when the key planks of Labour's economic policies would have been discussed and formulated. It will be argued that disagreements would have emerged between Smith and Gordon Brown, his Shadow Chancellor, over certain aspects of economic policy. Lastly, this chapter argues that had Smith become Prime Minister, his style of governing and running the Labour Party would have differed radically from Tony Blair.

~

The premise of a comfortable Smith landslide at the 1997 general election is based on three main arguments. First, Smith would have won because the Conservatives had lost their polling lead over Labour on economic competence. Even though they had held a lead on this issue since 1964, they lost it following Black Wednesday, 16 September 1992, when Britain fell out of the Exchange Rate Mechanism (ERM), and never got it back. Roy Hattersley agrees that: 'John Major lost the 1997 election during the high summer of 1992.'[2] Bob Worcester and Roger Mortimore support Hattersley's thesis, arguing that 'the way the Tories self-destructed after 1992, Labour would probably have won under Neil Kinnock; certainly, the election was already won and lost for the Tories before John Smith died.'[3]

Second, the Tories were hopelessly divided over Europe. Having spent ten months arguing publicly night after night over the parliamentary ratification of the European Communities (Amendment) Bill (more commonly known as the Maastricht Bill) as early as 1993 the Conservatives were perceived by the voters as a divided and virtually unleadable party.

In his unrivalled study of New Labour, Steven Fielding claims that Brown and Blair were right to engage in further modernisation of the Labour Party because the economy might have recovered to benefit the Tories and because 'few could have predicted Conservative divisions over Europe would have intensified as the election approached'.[4] Heath, Jowell and Curtice agree that with the benefit of hindsight the Conservatives were 'set on a self-destructive path with their civil war over Europe, and that Smith's approach would almost certainly have delivered victory in 1997', but that in 1994 'one might have expected the Conservative instinct for self-preservation to have been stronger' because previous incumbent governments had recovered to win general elections from similar mid-term slumps in popularity.[5]

Both sets of arguments fall down because Conservative divisions were *already* apparent by the time of Smith's death. In the immediate aftermath of Maastricht in July 1993, George Robertson, Labour's spokesperson on European Affairs, was able to argue with some justification: 'With every week that passed, with every one of the 260 hours of debate [on the Maastricht Bill], with each of the defeats, surrenders and retreats inflicted upon it, the authority and credibility of the Government drained away.'[6] Even Tristan Garel-Jones, the Tories' own Minister of State at the Foreign Office, later admitted that his party 'bled to death' for over a year trying to ratify the Maastricht Treaty.[7] Therefore, the Tory divisions over Europe could not be healed in time for the 1997 general election, and these divisions were already apparent to the electorate by 1993. Smith, who always held to the view that governments lost elections, rather than oppositions winning them, correctly sensed in his bones that Rome was on the verge of collapse from within.

Third, Smith would not have won by as much as Blair because of 'the Blair effect'. New Labour's leader was able to tap into the aspirations of disillusioned middle-class voters south of the Watford Gap in a way that Smith could not do, at least to the same extent. All the polls from the second half of 1994 show an enormous leap in the Labour lead over the Conservatives after Blair became Labour leader. Almost immediately, Blair gained a leadership satisfaction rating of 58 per cent, some nine points higher than Smith had achieved in the final poll taken before his death.[8] And after only one year, a Gallup poll showed that Blair was the most popular Opposition leader since records began, with 68 per cent of respondents claiming he was doing a good job, compared with Smith's peak of 53 per cent.[9] Smith's views on comprehensive education and his consistent belief that the better-off should pay more in tax would have put off some, though not all, of these floating voters.

Not everyone agrees that Smith would have won in 1997. Charles Clarke, formerly Neil Kinnock's Chief of Staff and now Secretary of State for Education and Skills claims that Smith lacked the exceptional leadership qualities needed to win:

> John was the classic consensual person, who could have become Prime
> Minister if he'd inherited the job from the previous Labour Prime Minister,
> *à la* Callaghan. He never had the leadership quality that was required to
> *grasp* leadership.[10]

Philip Gould, Blair's polling guru, also believes that 'despite reasonable poll leads, Labour was not on course to win next time around'.[11]
Only six months after Smith's death, on 11 November 1994, Gould
wrote a paper claiming that 'Blair and Prescott connect in a way John
Smith never did. He was trusted but did not really impact on people in the way that the current leadership does.'[12] Gould's evidence
was based on focus groups, which showed that Labour's negative
image among voters, in the wake of the party's defeat in 1992 – as a
party dominated by the unions, 'holding people back', and restricting
consumer choice – 'had not substantially altered by the summer of
1994'. Smith had 'helped Labour, and he certainly healed Labour',
but Gould's focus groups demonstrated that Smith 'did not transform
perceptions of Labour'.[13]

Election experts aplenty have also cast doubt on the assumption
that Smith would have won in 1997. As early as 1994, Ivor Crewe and
Anthony King added a note of caution by pointing out that in the
mid-1980s and early 1990s Kinnock had enjoyed similar opinion poll
leads over the Conservatives, only to go down to defeat in general
elections.[14] Much later, detailed analysis of the local and European
election results by the Heath, Jowell and Curtice troika showed that
Labour's victories in 1994 were mainly due to disgruntled Tory supporters staying at home, and that any switchers were from Conservative to Liberal Democrat, rather than substantial numbers of Tories
going straight across from Conservative to Labour.[15] In other words,
the electoral impact of the ERM devaluation and the Tory divisions
over Europe was to make Tory voters stay at home or to switch to the
Liberal Democrats. Indeed, Paddy Ashdown's party polled strongly
during Smith's leadership,[16] suggesting that although the Tories

would have lost in 1997, Labour would have struggled to win an out-right majority. However, such an analysis underestimates the extent to which the bulk of the electorate desperately wanted to get rid of the Tories in 1997, and the clearest and most certain way of doing that was – and still would have been under Smith – to vote Labour.

Another important effect of a comfortable Smith victory in 1997, but not one on the scale of Blair, is that the Tories would have suffered a nasty defeat, but not a catastrophic one. Perhaps just over 200 Conservatives would have been spared, leaving the party with a chance of winning the 2001 election. It is at least plausible to argue that a Smith victory in 1997 would not have destroyed the Tories for a generation in the way that Blair's landslide did. In such circumstances Michael Portillo might have clung on to his Enfield Southgate constituency, and it is probable that in such circumstances he would have emerged as Tory leader. Remember, the only Tory electorate for the 1997 Tory leadership contest was the parliamentary party. (William Hague introduced the party membership element in Tory leadership contests during his period as leader, 1997–2001.). A Portillo-led Conservative party might have embarked on a very necessary modernisation of its policies and image at a much earlier stage.

What Smith would have done

It is necessary to get away from the idea that Smith was not a mod-erniser, or that he believed in 'one more heave', merely waiting for the Conservatives to collapse from within. Such an analysis is just a creation of Peter Mandelson, who was left totally out of the loop under Smith's leadership, and resorted to briefing unhelpful sto-ries to the press. Smith realised that if it was ever to be re-elected, Labour had to change further – the real debate concerned the pace of reform. Although Smith liked both Tony Blair and Gordon Brown, and realised how talented they were, he often thought that they tried to run before they had learned to walk. Smith preferred to reform the

Labour Party at a pace with which the vast majority of its members would feel comfortable, and this he succeeded in doing. Although he had to risk his leadership to introduce the one–member–one–vote (OMOV) reforms in September 1993, the aftermath of their introduction resulted in no bitter backlash against Smith either from the unions or the wider Labour movement.

In February 1994, Smith described the debate about getting rid of Clause Four as 'academic'.[17] He was right, since Labour had never implemented its famous Clause Four, Section Four – worker control of industry – when in government. Privately, Smith felt that it would be damaging to party unity if he took on the issues of OMOV and Clause Four at the same time.[18] In November 1959, John Smith's hero, Hugh Gaitskell, had discovered to his cost the huge symbolic importance of the clause to the Labour movement. Nevertheless, before his death, Smith faced calls from Jack Straw (in May 1993)[19] and Neil Kinnock (February 1994)[20] to completely rewrite Clause Four. Roy Hattersley reveals that Smith considered sacking Jack Straw:

> Jack had told John beforehand, John had told him not to go ahead, but he went ahead and did it anyway and I had to intervene to point out that the young man didn't mean any harm.[21]

Had Smith lived, he would have put his own imprint on Clause Four, but he would not have completely rewritten it. One of Smith's last ideas before he died was to issue a statement outlining his own Christian socialist beliefs, based on his famous R. H. Tawney lecture.[22] The statement would have been issued in June 1995, and put to the party conference for October of that year. It would have been laid alongside Clause Four, rather than seeking to replace it. David Ward, Smith's main policy adviser, has since confirmed that this would have happened.[23]

In any case, while the eventual change to Clause Four was merely a piece of symbolism, the OMOV reforms fundamentally altered the distribution of power within the Labour Party – away from trade unions and towards individual party members, especially in the area of candidate selection. Smith's OMOV reforms may be seen as opening the floodgates, making it far easier for the Labour movement to accept the reform of Clause Four. Thus, Smith deserves his place in Labour history as a moderniser, albeit a cautious one.

One of the problems that Smith had was that because OMOV dominated his first year as leader, other policy developments either had to be held back for later in the Parliament, or were aired but largely ignored in the media. For example, in that first year, Smith spent a great deal of time referring to his fairly radical agenda of constitutional reform.[24] His whole approach to devolution to Scotland, Wales and the regions was enthusiastic, and had Smith lived, there would have been no attempt to control the process of devolution from the centre, as occurred under Tony Blair. Indeed, it is extremely rich for Blair to have championed a pure form of OMOV when Smith was leader, and then to have resorted in government to old-fashioned Labour stitch-ups to prevent Rhodri Morgan and Ken Livingstone from being selected as Labour candidates in Wales and London, and to weed out left-wing Labour candidates for the Scottish Parliament. Mavericks like Dennis Canavan and Ken Livingstone would have operated happily within the Smith fold, rather than being cast out into the wilderness.[25] However, in the area of constitutional reform, Blair deserves credit for enthusiastically pursuing the Northern Ireland peace process, something that Smith, given his well-known Unionist sympathies, would probably not have done to the same extent.

One of Smith's most significant policy innovations as leader was the establishment of the Social Justice Commission under the chairmanship of Gordon Borrie[26] in 1992. The aim of the Commission was to take a fresh look at the workings of the welfare state fifty years on from Beveridge, or as the Commission's blurb put it, 'to promote social justice[27] by developing a long-term strategy to cope with the three major revolutions – economic, social and political – that had altered Britain's society'.[28] Borrie's role was to arbitrate between academics invited on to the Commission, already wedded to certain left-wing spending commitments, and Labour Party figures on the Commission, such as Patricia Hewitt, his deputy, operating out of the Institute for Public Policy Research (IPPR), whose views were also well known.

The Commission was free to explore what it wanted, but Smith made it clear that he would not be bound by any of its findings. The intriguing question remains as to how Smith would have reacted to the Social Justice Commission's final report – set out in *Social Justice: Strategies of National Renewal* – published in October 1994 five months after his death.

After two interim reports were published in July 1993, Smith expressed enthusiasm for them, and insisted that members of the Shadow Cabinet should read them. Both *The Justice Gap* and *Social Justice in a Changing World* were very slim documents, merely outlining broad principles rather than going into great detail. However, by the autumn of 1993, Smith became concerned that the devil might lie in the detail of the final report, and that the Commission had started to publish policy papers in advance of the final report. Expressing general principles was fine (as outlined by the two earlier pamphlets), but Smith feared the political dangers that lay in appearing to commit the party to specific (and potentially costly) policies.[29]

Just as the Labour leader was offended by social injustice at home, Smith wanted to close the gap between the rich industrialised North and the poorer countries in the South by updating some of the ideas first expressed in the Brandt Commission report.[30] He aimed to outline a series of reforms to international institutions in the form of a *Penguin* paperback. One of his most radical ideas was to call for the Group of Seven (G7) (now known as the G8 following the addition of Russia) industrialised countries to become a permanent core of an economic equivalent of the United Nations Security Council, expanding its membership to include some of the larger Asia–Pacific and Latin American countries. Smith also advocated merging two of the Bretton Woods institutions established in 1944 – the International Monetary Fund (IMF) and the World Bank – under the wing of this new Economic Council. After Smith died, David Ward was informed that Tony Blair did not want to run with these ideas.[31]

On 4 November 1993, Smith gave the Robert Kennedy Memorial Lecture in the Oxford Union on the future of the United Nations, in which he called for an increase in the permanent membership of the UN Security Council, probably to include Germany and Japan by virtue of their impressive post-war economic record and their major financial commitment to the UN, and possibly India, Brazil and Nigeria, all of whom had strong claims as major powers in the developing world.[32] Such radical ideas are not normally associated with Smith, but they reveal that he did have a set of ideas and policies that would have been brought forward in the run-up to the 1997 election.

It is also plausible that Smith would have attempted to join the single currency very early on in the first term of a Labour government. Almost everything points to it: Smith's original belief in European entry, in defiance of the Labour whips in 1971, his faith in the Exchange Rate Mechanism (ERM), and the extent to which he drew many of his economic ideas from continental Europe. David Ward claims that Smith intended to commit a Labour government to hold a referendum on the single European currency before John Major did.[33] Lord Desai disagrees: John was a strong European and a conviction politician. Had John lived, we would have been in the euro without a referendum.

In his biography of Peter Mandelson, Donald Macintyre at least entertains the possibility, albeit among other scenarios, that a successful Smith Government might have entered the single currency in his first parliament.[34] However, Smith's enthusiasm for the euro would have been tempered by his pragmatism, and his natural caution. Overall, Smith probably hoped to join the euro, and would have given the issue his very strong leadership, but at the same time he would have made a hard-headed assessment based on the economic and political circumstances at the time.

In a wider sense, the whole direction of Labour's economic policy under Smith is perhaps the most fascinating aspect of the 'what ifs' because certain New Labour policies might not have been introduced had Smith lived, while other 'Old Labour' policies might have remained.

Smith (or Brown's) economic policy, 1994–97

The three main historical debates concerning the development of Labour's economic policy after 1994 as they relate to John Smith are: the extent to which Gordon Brown, the Shadow Chancellor since 1992, was in control of economic policy (or whether John Smith, the former Shadow Chancellor, was in charge); the degree to which there might have been disagreement (or indeed agreement) between the two men on how to proceed on key aspects of Labour's stance; and therefore how economic policy might have differed had John Smith lived.

Perhaps, just as Blair has behaved as an extra Foreign Secretary during his premiership, so, if Smith had lived he would have taken on the role of an extra Shadow Chancellor. Roy Hattersley believes that it would have been in Smith's temperament to have interfered on Brown's patch; not only had John been Shadow Chancellor immediately before (indeed for a five-year period, from 1987 to 1992), but also he had been Brown's boss as Shadow Chief Secretary to the Treasury, from 1987 to 1989, and would have been used to pulling rank with Gordon on economic matters – although that is not to suggest that Gordon would have not persuaded John to accept some of his ideas.[35] Alternatively, by an early stage in his Shadow Chancellorship, Brown had imposed his authority by more or less ditching the entire content of Smith's 1992 Shadow Budget. Smith had also appointed Brown as chairman of the Economic Policy Commission (EPC), a joint committee comprising Shadow Cabinet and NEC members, responsible for the direction of Labour's economic policy.[36]

In reality, probably neither politician was fully in charge, and there would have been a need to have reached agreement on three important matters of economic policy: whether to stick to the Tory levels of government spending for the first two years of a Labour government; whether to increase the top rate of income tax from 40 to 50 per cent; and whether to make the Bank of England independent.

Seyd and Whiteley take the view that had Smith lived, he would not have agreed to stick to the Conservative spending commitments in Labour's first two years in office, as Blair and Brown subsequently did.[37] That contention of course assumes that Smith would have exercised sufficient leverage over Brown to overrule him. Murray Elder, Smith's Chief of Staff, believes that had Smith lived that there would have been 'very considerable tensions' between John and Gordon over whether to commit the Labour Party to freezing public spending at Tory levels for the first two years of government. Gordon took the view that the 1987–92 Policy Review formula of only increasing spending 'when resources allow' (beyond the specific commitments on pensions and child benefit) – which became known as 'Beckett's law', after Margaret Beckett's, Shadow Chief Secretary to the Treasury, 1989–92, strong defence of the policy – would always leave Labour vulnerable to Tory attack. Labour needed to be 'much fiercer'. John was much more of the view that incoming ministers in a new Labour government would need a bit of money to spend after eighteen years. Had Smith lived, Gordon would have fought that view 'tooth and nail … there would have been a fierce battle'.[38]

However, Lord Desai believes that had John Smith lived, there would have been no need to stick to the Tory spending limits: 'He [Smith] may have believed in progressive taxation in a Croslandite sense, but he was a fiscally prudent person – fiscal prudence was John's other name.' And because the electorate had so much confidence in Smith, Desai argues that Labour would have won the election with a more redistributive package than Brown and Blair eventually came up with. There would have been no need for the deal between Tony and Gordon to stick to the Tory spending plans, or the abandonment of a 50 per cent income tax band. Instead, without the prudent Smith at his side, Brown had to establish his *own* reputation for prudence.[39]

Seyd and Whiteley argue that Smith would not have ruled out raising income tax rates for the lifetime of a parliament, as New Labour did.[40] Certainly, the commitment not to raise the basic rate of income tax was and is one of the Ten Commandments of New Labour (or rather, one of its five policy pledges listed on its famous pledge card of 1997). As Shadow Chancellor, Smith had committed the Labour Party to increasing the top rate of tax from 40 per cent to 50 per cent.[41] Even though many people (not including the author) blamed Smith's Shadow Budget for losing Labour the 1992 election, he was unrepentant, and continued to believe on grounds of morality and fairness that the better-off should pay substantially more in tax under Labour. While he accepted that his Shadow Budget had to go, that did not mean abandoning the commitment to introduce a 50 per cent tax band. Although Brown would not admit it now, he supported the principle of a 50 per cent tax band, but disagreed with Smith over when to announce it. After Smith died, Tony Blair vetoed the idea of a 50 per cent band, and Brown lost his chance to introduce it. However, to be fair to Brown, once the voters were persuaded of Labour's economic competence, he has introduced mildly redistributive tax policies as Chancellor, but he has done so without too many people noticing.

One of the difficulties of predicting what a politician would have done had they lived is that the world moves on relatively quickly after their death, and this is especially true in terms of economics. In the 1980s, globalisation caused Labour to abandon Keynesian economics in favour of supply-side reforms. By the mid-1990s, Gordon Brown began to see the merits of an independent Bank of England. Lord Desai was not initially in favour of Bank of England independence, but he also concedes that 'the climate changed rapidly around 1997', adding that: 'John's principles were at a deeper level. He was not an instrumentalist. In 1994, he would have been opposed, but who knows what his position would have been by 1997?'[42]

The fact remains that Gordon Brown would have faced an uphill task persuading Smith of the virtues of independence, because the latter had a long track record of supporting a politically accountable way of running monetary policy.[43] On 9 January 1990, Smith had declared in a newspaper interview: 'Don't think that having been elected to Parliament and given responsibility for running the economy by the Prime Minister I would hand over a large chunk of my responsibilities to the Bank of England.'[44] Nor did Smith support (in the run-up to the Maastricht Treaty) the idea of an independent European Central Bank, preferring the French model of a politically accountable bank by strengthening the role of the Council of Economic and Finance Ministers (ECOFIN).[45]

However, by the time of his death, Smith had developed his own policy ideas in this area. In the autumn of 1993, the Labour Party agreed in a policy document that the Bank of England should become more open and more representative by replacing the Bank's existing court with a new Monetary Policy Board which would have included 'regional representatives and members drawn from industry large and small and from the trade unions to ensure here as elsewhere that the views of all industry and workforce are heard'.[46] The Board would have been responsible for monetary developments and would have produced a regular report (which would have been made public), but to the elected Chancellor rather than the unelected Governor of the Bank of England.

With the benefit of hindsight, Gordon Brown's policy of independence for the Bank of England has proved to be a great success. He had studied the troubled financial history of previous Labour governments: what better way to establish confidence (although Brown would not admit this reasoning) than through handing over the most important lever over economic policy – interest rates – to an independent group of bankers? From the evidence available, it seems that Smith was not persuadable in 1994 that an independent Bank of England was a good idea. Had he lived, however, Brown might have persuaded him to change his mind by 1997.

A different style of government

Perhaps the most striking difference between a Blair and a Smith premiership would have been seen in the style of government. Unlike Tony Blair (and indeed Neil Kinnock), Smith was entirely at home in the House of Commons. Indeed, Smith loved the Commons, enjoying spending an inordinate amount of time chatting with backbench Labour MPs in the tearooms, or more often than not, enjoying 'a dram and a tale' in the Members' Smoking Room. Under a Smith Government, the whole running of the country would have been transmitted from the dispatch box of the Commons Chamber (where Smith excelled) rather than the Press Office at Number Ten. Smith would have at least tried to maintain the House of Commons as the epicentre of political debate rather than relegating it to the periphery.[47]

Just as importantly, Smith viewed the management of the Parliamentary Labour Party (PLP) in the same way as Harold Wilson and James Callaghan: as a delicate balance between left and right. Although Smith hailed from the right, he was perhaps best loved on the left, not just because he had worked with Tony Benn at Energy (1974–76) and Michael Foot (at the Privy Council Office handling devolution legislation, 1976–78), but also because he was prepared to listen to what the left had to say, even if he disagreed with it. Under Blair, the left has been ostracised and, more generally, the Prime Minister does not feel comfortable spending any length of time mingling with his own backbenchers. Rather, groups of Labour MPs are summoned to see Blair, who seems to have forgotten one of the most important facets of party leadership in the House of Commons – a willingness just to sit there and listen to the gripes of backbenchers.

Unlike Blair and Kinnock, Smith was comfortable about the person he was. Smith was neither cocky nor arrogant; rather, he had an attractive self-assurance that allowed him to communicate directly with the general public, rather than through an army of spin doctors. So, under Smith, there would have been less insecurity at the heart of government than has occurred under Blair. There would also have been less of an entourage of lackeys around the leader, and less reliance on focus groups. It is worth remembering, nay rejoicing, that both Peter Mandelson and Philip Gould were ostracised under Smith's leadership. On a rare occasion, Smith was dragged to a focus group in Essex, and sat there mechanically popping peanuts into his mouth, listening to the horrific views of forty women. Smith disliked intensely tailoring his political message too closely to the language that the pollsters believed was effective with the electorate, and he was not easily packaged.

Members of Smith's team expressed concern throughout his short leadership that he was adopting too low a profile in the media. However, Smith lacked Blair's overwhelming desire to be on the front page of the newspapers every day. He would have been an old-fashioned, approachable, down-to-earth Prime Minister, sure of his values and of his long-term goals, competent without being flashy, and the country would have respected him for that.

Conclusion

Party politics would also have been more normal had Smith lived because, instead of stealing so much of the Conservative agenda as Blair did, Labour under Smith would have been more recognisably Labour: closer to the unions (who trusted him), more progressive on taxation, less reluctant to engage in reform of the public services. Such a state of affairs would at least have left the Tories with some of the language with which they had traditionally attacked Labour: as a party controlled by the union barons and public-sector interests and intent on taxing the middle classes to the hilt. Instead, the Tories have been totally flummoxed by Blair's decision to steal their own clothes, and to appeal to the *Daily Mail* tendency, parking himself firmly where the floating voters are situated. Since 1997, the Tory party has acted as a think tank for Labour: every time the Tories come up with a policy idea that horrifies traditional Labour supporters, Blair adopts it, pushing the Tories further to the right. The only solution for the Tory party is to repel the Blairite boarders rather than sailing off into the distant blue yonder.

So perhaps Blair's greatest achievement has been to annihilate the Tories for a generation, something that Smith would not have achieved. The only problem is that large swathes of his own party are not sure whether that achievement involves turning the Labour Party into the Tory party. Frank Dobson often said of Smith that if he was a stick of rock and you broke him in half, the writing on the inside would say 'Labour'. Everybody knew that Smith had a burning desire to tackle inequality and injustice, values that had been imparted to him on his father's knee in the Highlands. Smith saw the Labour Party as the best means of achieving social justice, and had been a member since the age of sixteen. Blair's strategy is entirely understandable, because it is geared towards continual re-election, but political parties are not organisms that can adapt constantly to the whims of the voters. Rather, they have roots and souls, represented in the Labour Party by the unions, the membership and the ordinary backbenchers, a majority of whom now believe that New Labour is no longer recognisably Labour.

Labour lost its soul on 12 May 1994, and if the 'what ifs' of history are not to remain just that, it badly needs to rediscover it – both by reinvigorating the memory of John Smith's brand of socialism, and by rediscovering a more consensual style of running the party.

Notes

1 For academic support for this assertion, see Patrick Seyd and Paul Whiteley, *New Labour's Grassroots: The Transformation of Labour Party Membership* (Palgrave Macmillan, 2002), p. 7.
2 Roy Hattersley, *Fifty Years On: A Prejudiced History of Britain Since the War* (Little, Brown, 1997), p. 376.
3 Robert M. Worcester and Roger Mortimore, *Explaining Labour's Landslide* (Politico's, 1999), p. 88.
4 Steven Fielding, *The Labour Party: Continuity and Change in the Making of 'New' Labour* (Palgrave Macmillan, 2002), p. 99.
5 Anthony Heath, Roger Jowell and John Curtice, *The Rise of New Labour: Party Policies and Voter Choices* (Oxford University Press, 2001), p. 102.
6 George Robertson, 'Maastricht Madness', *Tribune,* 30 July 1993.
7 Interview with Rt Hon. Tristan Garel-Jones, 19 November 1996.
8 Leonard P. Stark, *Choosing a Leader: Party Leadership Contests in Britain from Macmillan to Blair* (Macmillan, 1996), p. 159.
9 *Daily Telegraph*, 9 June 1995.
10 Gould, *The Unfinished Revolution: How the Modernisers Saved the Labour Party* (Little, Brown, 1997), p. 145.
11 Ibid., p. 178.
12 Ibid., p. 223.
13 Philip Gould, 'Why Labour won' in Ivor Crewe, Brian Gosschalk and John Bartle (eds.), *Political Communications: Why Labour Won the General Election of 1997* (Frank Cass, 1998), pp. 5–6.
14 Ivor Crewe and Anthony King, 'Did Major win? Did Kinnock lose? Leadership effects in the 1992 election', in Anthony Heath, Roger Jowell and John Curtice (eds.), *Labour's Last Chance? The 1992 Election and Beyond* (Dartmouth Publishing, 1994), p. 144.
15 Heath et al., *The Rise of New Labour* pp. 102–03.

16 For example in October and November 1993, the Liberal Democrats polled between 23 and 26 per cent, compared to a 1992 general election performance of 18 per cent.

17 *Today,* BBC Radio 4, 24 February 1994.

18 Tudor Jones, *Remaking the Labour Party: From Gaitskell to Blair* (Routledge, 1996), p. 134; John Rentoul, *Tony Blair* (Little, Brown, 1995), p. 413.

19 Jack Straw, *Policy and Ideology* (Blackburn Labour Party, 1993).

20 Neil Kinnock, *Tomorrow's Socialism,* BBC 2, 5 February 1994.

21 Interview with Lord Hattersley, 3 March 2003.

22 John Smith, 'Reclaiming the Ground', R.H. Tawney Memorial Lecture, 20 March 1993.

23 Colin Brown, *Fighting Talk: The Biography of John Prescott* (Simon & Schuster, 1997), p. 259; Rentoul, *Tony Blair,* pp. 413–14. Smith's intended statement of aims echoed Gaitskell's 'New Testament' aims of February 1960, except that Gaitskell had been forced to come up with his version as a result of the conference defeat on the rewriting of Clause Four that he had suffered three months earlier. The NEC accepted Gaitskell's statement of aims on 16 March 1960. Philip M. Williams, *Hugh Gaitskell* (Oxford University Press, 1982, revised paperback edn), pp. 330–32.

24 See for example, John Smith, 'Reforming Our Democracy. Speech to Strathclyde University', in Brian Brivati (ed.), *Guiding Light: The Collected Speeches of John Smith* (Politico's, 2000), pp. 176–88. Smith's boldness on constitutional reform did not, however, extend to supporting the introduction of proportional representation at Westminster, although he supported holding a referendum on the issue.

25 Although, under a Smith-led government, more power would have been granted to the London Assembly as opposed to the London Mayor.

26 Director General of the Office of Fair Trading (OFT) since 1976.

27 The Commission went to a great deal of effort to define 'social justice', coming up with something incorporating a hierarchy of four ideas: that all citizens were of equal value to society; that citizens were entitled to have their basic needs met; that each person should have the right to develop their life chances to the fullest of their abilities; and that society should attempt to reduce, and if possible, eradicate, unjust inequalities. Commission on Social Justice, *Social Justice: Strategies for National Renewal* (Vintage, 1994), pp. 17–18.

28 Commission on Social Justice, *Strategies for National Renewal,* pp. 61–90.

29 Private information.

30 Independent Commission on International Development Issues, *North-South: A Programme for Survival* (Pan, 1981) (Brandt Report).

31 Interview with David Ward, 7 June 2003.

32 John Smith, 'Reinventing the United Nations', The Robert F. Kennedy Memorial Lecture, 4 November 1993 in Brivati, *Guiding Light,* pp. 240–52.

33 Rentoul, *Tony Blair,* p. 438. Chris Smith agrees; interview with Rt Hon Chris Smith, MP, 11 February 2003.

34 Donald Macintyre, *Mandelson: The Biography* (HarperCollins, 1999), p. 252.

35 Interview with Lord Hattersley, 3 March 2003.

36 Andy McSmith, *Faces of Labour: The Inside Story* (Verso, 1996), p. 326.

37 Seyd and Whiteley, *New Labour's Grassroots,* pp. 7–8.

38 Interview with Lord Elder of Kirkcaldy, 12 February 2003.

39 Interview with Lord Desai, 10 June 2003.

40 Seyd and Whiteley, *New Labour's Grassroots,* pp. 7–8.

41 What is often forgotten is that in Labour's Policy Review process before 1992, Smith fought hard for a 50 per cent band against those members of the Shadow Cabinet who wanted a 60 per cent band.

42 Desai was never as concerned as Smith about political accountability with regard to a European Central Bank, but rather about the need for fiscal and monetary co-ordination between European finance ministers. Interview with Lord Desai, 10 June 2003.

43 Roy Hattersley agrees that John Smith would not have been keen on the idea of an independent Bank of England, though Hattersley is now a convert. Interview with Lord Hattersley, 3 March 2003.

44 Sarah Hogg interview with John Smith, 'Commanding the economic heights: John Smith's peaks of ambition', *Daily Telegraph,* 9 January 1990.

45 See, for example, John Smith, Speech to Keidanren Japan–EC Committee, Tokyo, 11 April 1991.

46 Statement to Conference, *Labour's economic approach. A new agenda for democracy. Prosperity through co-operation* (Labour Party: Walworth Road, London, 1993), pp. 19–20.

47 This is not to deny that the gradual decline of Parliament would have continued under Smith – but not to the extent that it has under Blair.

Chapter 20

What if Paddy Ashdown had joined the Blair Cabinet in 1997?

Stuart Thomson[1]

Roy Jenkins was the architect of much of the New Labour project, having been a close adviser to Tony Blair both before and after he became Prime Minister. His death brought together in mourning many of his former colleagues from the Labour Party, the Liberal Democrats and the Social Democratic Party he had helped to form.

Two of those gathered at his memorial service in Westminster Abbey on 27 March 2003 had more than just his passing to consider. Blair and his cabinet colleague Paddy Ashdown, the leader of the Liberal Democrats, had six years jointly in government to reflect upon, and now had to deal with the loss of the man who had acted as a 'bridge' between the two of them before entering government.[2] Leaving the service, Ashdown, in particular, was in reflective mood; turning to Blair he said: 'Not for one minute do I regret coming into government with you, Tony – but I wish I could have avoided splitting my party.'

The early stages

Paddy Ashdown became the leader of the Social and Liberal Democrats on 28 July 1988. His background in the Royal Marines[3] was followed by a period with the Foreign Office with a posting in Geneva.

He then returned to the UK to spend time in industry, with Westland Helicopters in the Yeovil area, followed by a job as a youth worker with Dorset County Council. Ashdown became the MP for Yeovil in 1983 and rose quickly to the position of Liberal spokesperson on Trade and Industry. He also served as a spokesperson on Education and Science and on Northern Ireland.[4]

From early on, Ashdown saw the reform of the constitution as a main plank of his platform. Writing in 1989, he stated that: 'What we need next is a new political settlement, a new deal for all our citizens which sets out the terms of a better contract between members of a society and their government.'[5]

Ashdown spent the early years of his leadership trying to rebuild the credibility of the Liberal Democrats, as they now called themselves. The Conservative Party still dominated politics, but the Labour Party under Neil Kinnock had begun to rebuild some credibility of its own. Ashdown took over a party which was demoralised and lacking support. The low point came in 1989, when the party came fourth behind the Greens in the Euro-elections. At this time it was not unusual for the Lib Dems to be attracting only 3 per cent support in the opinion polls. At the 1992 general election, Ashdown managed to consolidate the position of the party a little more, but it was to be during the years following this election that he was to come to the fore, helped by two events – the collapse of the Conservative Party and the election of Tony Blair to the leadership of the Labour Party.

The collapse of the Conservatives in the years following 1992 was spectacular by any measure. Mired in allegations of sleaze, with a leader – John Major – who was seen as weak and unable to lead his party, and having increased taxes when they had claimed that they would not, the party was on a downward spiral. However, it was the breakdown of its image as a party that could be trusted to run the economy, following the ignominious withdrawal from the Exchange Rate Mechanism (ERM), which set the tone for the Conservatives' downfall.

Alongside the Conservative Party's collapse, New Labour was being born. Tony Blair became leader of the Labour Party in 1994 and soon set about making it more appealing to the electorate. Blair changed the way the party made policy, removed unpopular policies and even gained the agreement of the party to alter the wording of Clause Four, that part of Labour's constitution which committed it to socialism. Another part of the Blair programme was to widen inclusion in British politics – old divisions should be abandoned and, in particular, Labour and the Liberal Democrats should work together more closely, ending their historical divisions. Blair talked openly of socialism and liberalism coming together and of creating 'a radical century ... Division among radicals almost one hundred years ago resulted in a twentieth century dominated by the Conservatives.'[6]

Ashdown was, of course, also changing perceptions about his own party. In his Chard speech after the 1992 election,[7] he began the process of moving closer to Labour – a process which was effectively completed when the policy of equidistance, which placed the Lib Dems no closer to Labour than to the Conservatives, was abandoned in 1995. The introduction to the party's 1997 general election manifesto heavily criticised the legacy of the Conservative government but did not even mention Labour.

Government

The issue of cooperation between Labour and the Lib Dems had been raised on a number of occasions in the run-up to the 1997 general election and both leaders had left the possibility open. Most commentators had assumed that this was to open the way for the Lib Dems to be invited into government if Blair did not achieve a large overall majority. The parties agreed on many policies, and their election manifestos emphasised similar priorities – health, welfare, low inflation, low interest rates, public transport.

When Ashdown and three of his colleagues were invited to serve in government, however, despite the fact that Labour had achieved a massive majority, nearly everyone in the country was staggered. The Lib Dems' forty-six seats, their highest number since 1929, did not appear to justify their inclusion in a government which had a huge majority of its own.

It remains a matter of some conjecture as to why Blair finally took the decision, and many have looked to a variety of explanations.

The opinion polls had shown consistently that Labour would win the election, but the size of any potential majority was far from clear. Blair was cautious and did not envisage a large majority. For this reason he effectively promised to include the Lib Dems in his cabinet, and when his 179-seat majority was delivered, he still felt obliged to fulfil his side of the bargain, as did a number of his inner circle of advisers, Robin Cook in particular, as a prime instigator of the idea. Blair was also concerned that if he broke his promise and if it should ever become public, not only would the media have a field day but it would destroy the trust that he hoped people would develop in his premiership. He considered the issue of trust to be a vital one; learning from the mistakes of the previous Conservative administration, he felt it essential that it be retained, even if it meant taking decisions which would be unpopular within the party. In 1997 Labour had not been in power for nearly twenty years, and needed to prove itself capable of governing. A failure to deliver on a promise that early on in his government could have undermined his attempts and ended the party's chances of any further electoral success.

Blair was not forced into the decision by his advisers. He also saw the benefit of providing real proof of his willingness to create 'a radical century'. He had been given the once-in-a-generation opportunity to banish the Conservative Party from serious electoral politics, and the only way to do this, he believed, was to create a progressive movement of the whole of the left – Labour and the Liberal Democrats.

The Conservative Party was so unpopular – the level of tactical voting against them in the election had been unprecedented in British politics – that many in the country welcomed the prospect of relegating them to the history books. The 'anti-Conservative' nature of the move was stressed heavily to Labour Party members and they were effectively told that 'it's now or never'.

The memberships of the two parties themselves, however, were not totally convinced. During the years before the election, discussions had been ongoing between Blair, Ashdown and their close personal advisers to set out the various options, from full coalition through to informal alliance. Indeed, some early groundwork had been put in, over constitutional reform, by Robin Cook on Labour's side and Robert Maclennan for the Lib Dems.

The reaction of the two parties has been widely discussed. Antagonisms, especially at local level, were never far from the surface. At local elections the battles between Labour and the Lib Dems were some of the most unpleasant and vitriolic. But the unpopularity of the Conservatives provided an opportunity for the anti-Tory agreement at national level. Both leaders were careful not to describe the agreement as a coalition; instead, they were 'working together in government' through a policy of 'cooperation'. This would enable campaigning to continue, especially at a local level, and would not mean that the parties would have to agree on all matters. The chance was taken, as it was felt that by making the agreement a success, party members and activists would be more likely to sign up to it. Lib Dem MPs were more enthusiastic than their Labour colleagues, realising that the opportunity was an unexpected bonus providing them with a opportunity to make a real impact on policy. The majority of Labour MPs, however, did not agree with 'cooperation', especially given the size of their majority.

The move also enabled Blair to ensure that he could see off the more extreme left in his own party. While this awkward squad would not be problem for a Prime Minister with a three-figure majority, it would undoubtedly be more vocal in future Parliaments as the party's majority dwindled, as it invariably would. Yet the level of public approval, the general swell of anti-Conservative feeling, and Blair's own popularity left them powerless to offer any alternative. The Campaign Group of MPs, those representing the left of the party, realised that they were being sidelined by the agreement.

In the Cabinet, 'cooperation' offered Blair the benefit of balancing the personality battle on his own terms. Blair had become convinced that within several years Gordon Brown would look to replace him as Prime Minister; by bringing Ashdown on board, he ensured that the axis of power would lie very firmly with Blair himself and a Blair–Ashdown–Cook triumvirate.

The ability to deliver on 'cooperation' also demonstrated Blair's personal strength to the country and to his party, providing a clear demonstration that he was really a conviction politician. He saw the agreement as a fundamental element of the new politics he was trying to introduce in Britain. It was also believed that he was attempting to recreate the spirit of the great Labour government of 1945, which had used Liberal ideas from Keynes and Beveridge to great effect. In many ways, Blair was trying to show that, in a modern setting, he could be as radical as his 1945 predecessors – 'cooperation' was a flagship policy staking out his territory.

Inviting Ashdown and his colleagues into government was a complete surprise to many but appeared to show a real shift in how politics was conducted in the UK. Given Ashdown's popularity for the preceding few years, the public were enthusiastic. 'Cooperation' showed clear water from the Conservative century.

Cabinet

Ashdown's enthusiasm for the agreement was obvious to everyone from day one. He had succeeded in making the Liberal Democrats a powerful voice in British politics for the first time in nearly a century. But having Ashdown alone in the Cabinet would not be acceptable to his party; alongside him came Menzies Campbell and in junior, non-Cabinet, positions, Charles Kennedy and Simon Hughes. It had been thought that Alan Beith, another senior Lib Dem, would be among those Ashdown took with him into government. Beith, however, was not enthusiastic about the terms of 'cooperation', and turned the opportunity down; Kennedy was chosen instead.

Ashdown was made Foreign Secretary, Campbell was given Defence, whilst Kennedy was given a Parliamentary Under-Secretary position dealing with environmental matters and Hughes a similar position in the Home Office. Ashdown and his colleagues had initially wanted to have control of complete ministries, as they believed that their power would be enhanced; this was also usually the basis of agreements entered into among coalition partners in continental Europe. This, however, could never be accepted by Blair, especially given the size of his majority – the decision was controversial enough internally. Rather than pushing too hard for this, Ashdown instead chose to fight for the inclusion of key policies such as proportional representation, on which he was successful.

Some members of the new cabinet, such as Gordon Brown and John Prescott, remained sceptical but did not express outright opposition to 'cooperation'. Other, more supportive, figures such as Robin Cook, were given senior positions, in his case Home Secretary. Blair used the opportunity of bringing in the Lib Dems to let go of some of his less favoured colleagues who had served in the shadow cabinet, including David Clark and Gavin Strang.

There were many in the leadership of the Labour Party, however, who were not keen on 'cooperation' and certainly did not want the Lib Dems in government with them, especially given the size of the Labour majority. One in particular, Jack Straw, had been an outright opponent for some time, an attitude forged by years of battles in Blackburn. As

soon as Blair made known his intention to invite Ashdown and his colleagues into the cabinet, Straw launched an open attack on his leader's
position, making it impossible for him to be given a position in the
new Cabinet. Straw would use his position on the back benches to try
to 'hold the leadership to account' and to call on them not to lose sight
of what the real Labour Party wanted to achieve.[8]

From the Lib Dem perspective it was important that they gained
some concrete policy agreements from their larger partners. Their
influence on policy across the board was obviously an important
consideration, but more important was agreement on major constitutional programmes and, most importantly for the party, the introduction of electoral reform, though only after a referendum.

The trade unions were not happy with 'cooperation' but gave Blair
the benefit of the doubt, just being glad that the Conservatives had
been ejected from office. The experience that the unions had of the
Lib Dems was often at activist level, where there was some tension.
At national level, however, many union leaders had more time for the
Liberal Democrats and the policies they advocated, especially those
concerned with public services and additional spending. What the
unions were less keen on was the idea that somehow the birth of the
Labour Party, which represented the interests of the workers, was a
historical accident and that Britain would have been better off if the
left, in the widest sense, had stayed united.

The trade union movement remained important enough in the
Labour Party that before any public announcements were made,
the leaders of several of the larger unions had been 'sounded out'
about the possibility of 'cooperation'. In effect, this meeting between
Blair, John Edmonds (leader of the GMB), Bill Morris (leader of the
TGWU), Ken Jackson (leader of the AEEU) and Roger Lyons (leader
of the MSF) was more a case of Blair telling them what he was about
to do. He was, however, careful to stress that enhanced trade union
recognition rights were not being sacrificed.

Performance of the government

The first term of the Lab–Lib Dem government implemented many policies which would ensure that the political system of Britain would be altered forever. It was seen as one of the great reforming governments of the century. Devolution was introduced in Scotland and Wales, after the referendums promised in the Labour manifesto. The Lib Dems did not believe that these were necessary and, also in contrast to Labour, that more and greater powers should be devolved. They managed to exert enough pressure to ensure that Labour backed down from their initial idea of a referendum in Scotland posing two questions: whether devolution should be introduced, and whether the new Scottish Parliament should have tax-varying powers. In the end the choice was simply for or against devolution. Both the Scottish and Welsh referendums were successful and led to Lab–Lib Dem coalition governments in each of their respective Parliaments.[9]

The Lib Dems did not get every constitutional reform that they wanted – a Bill of Rights was not introduced. However, on balance, huge constitutional changes were made. Even the working practices of the House of Commons were altered. A two-stage process was put in place whereby the House of Lords would be replaced with a new chamber, 80 per cent of which would be made up of representatives elected by the regions and nations of the UK. Despite much wailing from more conservative elements of the country and some of the right-wing press, particularly the *Daily Mail* and *The Times*, who complained of the end of an era and the rise of the professional politician, the reforms went ahead.

The most important constitutional change, which had been a fundamental condition of the Lib Dems entering government, was the introduction of electoral reform for Westminster. Given the level of mistrust of proportional representation in his own party, however, Blair was simply not in a position to agree to the Lib Dem demand outright. A compromise was struck whereby a committee would deliver its verdict on the best form of PR for the country and the public would be given a vote in a referendum, on a simple yes/no response to the option on offer. This was difficult for Ashdown to decline, as his programme was largely based on giving people more democratic power – what better way of making this a reality than by the greater use of referendums? Also introduced were regional assemblies, local mayors and PR in local and regional elections and those for the new parliaments in Scotland and Wales.

The committee that considered the issue was established a mere six months after the government came to power. There appeared to be no great urgency, given the Parliamentary timescales involved – a decision on the type of PR in the first term and a referendum in the second – but everyone involved wanted to see action. The committee was chaired by the close friend of both Blair and Ashdown, Roy Jenkins, and its final recommendation was for a 'alternative vote-plus' ('AV plus') system – essentially, first-past-the-post with wings.

For the most part, the two parties agreed on the key issues of policy, which helped to paper over some of the cracks. There was a considerable degree of consensus between the parties before they entered government in areas such as economic policy, spending and welfare. The parties differed little on macroeconomic policy, and on day five of the new government, independence was given to the Bank of England, showing just how high a priority low inflation was for both parties. Gordon Brown's budgets proved to be popular with the supporters of both parties – increased spending on health and education, new lower tax rates, a windfall tax. Both parties were committed to the public services, especially health and education, and these priority areas received much attention during the first term of the government. The Lib Dems had insisted on a policy of universal nursery education for all three- and four-year-olds before entering into cooperation,[10] and this was easily accepted by Blair. The Lib Dems also pushed for more spending on health care, especially in the early years of the government, but given the power of the Treasury and the relative weakness of the Lib Dems it was inevitable that they would lose this particular battle.

However, some issues brought stresses to the fore. Labour raised the possibility of the introduction of tuition fees for higher education, forcing students to pay for some of the fees they incurred whilst studying. It was relatively easy for the Conservative Party to talk about opposition to the idea, as it was middle-class parents and children who would bear the brunt of the fees. The Lib Dem ministers were placed in a much more difficult position – openly to criticise Labour would blow a hole in 'cooperation', while saying nothing would be very unpopular within their party. Ashdown and his colleagues chose the path of fighting the proposals hard in the cabinet and briefing against colleagues in the Department for Education who were floating the ideas publicly. Before the proposal became official government policy, a compromise was reached whereby a cap was placed on the amount which could be charged, and an exemption was created for those from poorer backgrounds. This was the best the Lib Dems could hope for, as Labour was fundamentally against higher direct personal taxation, at least in their first term, including the graduate 'repayment plan' which the Lib Dems had been floating.[11]

On environmental policy the Lib Dems were given a freer rein, especially as Charles Kennedy had a role to play in this portfolio. The government's environmental credentials became one of its centrepieces, bringing favourable comparisons with the record of some of the Scandinavian countries who had long been admired for the prominent role they gave to environmental matters. However, this was not liked by all in government. Labour had spent much time rebuilding bridges with the business community and many of the environmental measures brought open criticism from business groups such as the Confederation of British Industry. Gordon Brown, in particular, was widely seen to be unhappy with the level of environmental taxation he was forced to introduce in his budgets. A carbon levy, a plastic bag tax, and charges on companies to cover the costs of recycling were all brought in – though Brown did his best to offset this lower corporation tax and VAT relief for smaller companies. This did not stop the criticism from the business community. Similarly, higher recycling targets were set for local authorities, but many chose to pass the associated costs on to Council Tax payers, which caused both parties problems during local elections, losing them seats to the Conservatives. The Lib Dems, however, were able to use environmental arguments, supported by their environmental credentials, to stiffen the government's resolve in opposing the fuel protesters of September 2000.

The other great issue of disagreement was the Labour Party's line on law and order, and home affairs more generally. In the approach to the 1997 election Labour had stressed that it was 'tough on crime and tough on the causes of crime'. To keep the electorate happy it believed that it was best to focus on being 'tough on crime' but, from the perspective of the Lib Dems, the emphasis should have been on the other part of the equation, being 'tough on the causes of crime'.

Simon Hughes' junior position in the Home Office was very much an attempt to show that there was a clear Lib Dem influence in this area, but disquiet was still expressed by many in his party as their leaders signed up to tougher entry requirements for asylum-seekers, the end to an automatic right to trial by jury in some cases, the shrinking of the Legal Aid budget and a 'three strikes and you're out' approach to criminals (three convictions and then a mandatory five-year sentence). They could, though, point to policies such as a mandatory age for the retirement of judges, a more joined-up approach to the youth justice system, an overhaul of the Crown Prosecution Service and an increase in the number of police officers. For his part, Hughes was largely kept away from the media in case he did not follow the agreed policy line. Among many in the Labour Party, particularly those close to Blair, Hughes was not trusted and only kept a position in government to keep a wing of the Lib Dems happy with 'cooperation'.

The privatisation of the air traffic control system had been dismissed by the Labour Party when in Opposition but was reconsidered by some when the party entered government, mainly as a way of raising finance. The Lib Dems were fundamentally opposed, appearing to be closer to Labour Party members on this issue then its own leadership was. The policy was conveniently sidelined before too much damage was inflicted.

The Conservative Party

Along with the rest of the country, the Conservative Party had initially been stunned into inactivity by Labour's move. The Conservatives were very unclear about what their approach should be to the new government – and, with splits still rife over the issue of Europe and the introduction of the euro, the party was worried about the impact that electoral reform would bring with it. The prospect of the launch of a new Eurosceptic party, taking members and MPs from the Conservative Party, was a serious possibility. However, it soon became clear to the Conservatives that if the Lib Dems did not get their tactics right they would face the danger simply of being submerged by Labour, leaving, in effect, a new two-party system – a straight fight between the left (Labour plus Lib Dems) and the Tories.

The new Conservative leader, William Hague, chosen to succeed John Major for his Thatcherite credentials, set out to present a clear right-wing programme. Instead of having to fight on two fronts – against Labour and the Lib Dems – the party now had only to fight the government. The Conservative Party positioned themselves as the 'One True Opposition'. Yet, as with any new Opposition, especially after having spent so long in government themselves, the Conservatives found it difficult to establish new policies to accompany their new slogan. The political space may have been on offer but the party did not move very quickly to fill it. If it had been able to bring forward new policies then they might have been able to take advantage of some of the government's disagreements with business in areas such as environmental taxation or recycling – but they missed their chance.

The 2001 general election

What was most noticeable about the 2001 general election was how the Conservative Party managed to make some gains without achieving any real breakthrough. Despite constitutional change, the turnout was low and the level of interest in the campaign was minimal. The Lib Dems argued forcefully that this was because PR had not yet been introduced. The next election, due by 2006 at the latest, would of course be fought under a different system, assuming that Parliament introduced the legislation.

In their guise as a real alternative to the government, the Conservatives managed to regain a number of seats from the Lib Dems. Several seats which had unexpectedly gone to Labour in 1997 also returned to the Tory fold. There was less anti-Tory tactical voting then there in 1997, from which the Lib Dems in particular had benefited. Academic research suggested that Labour and Lib Dem activists had not got involved in the same way as in 1997 and that this had cost both parties votes – crucial in those seats where the majorities were small.

Some believed that the Labour leadership might use the outcome of the 2001 election as an opportunity to end the policy of 'cooperation' but Blair feared that all this would show was that the electorate had been fooled in the first term – the same type of argument he had used for not increasing income tax. Activists had shown their mistrust, but this did not alter Blair's course and 'cooperation' endured.

Hague remained in charge of the Conservative Party, as most of the party's MPs realised that it would have been impossible to expect to remove Labour's majority in just one term; some could also see success in the promised referendum on the euro. Hague also benefited internally from those who wished to keep their leadership options open in the event of a split caused by the introduction of PR.

Personalities

The government was dominated by several big personalities – Blair, Ashdown, Brown and, to a lesser extent, Cook. Blair and Ashdown had enjoyed a close personal relationship for many years before Blair invited the Lib Dems into government in 1997. The two had met secretly to consider the possible forms that cooperation could take and under what circumstances it would be appropriate. This close personal understanding was to prove essential in government.

Their personal relationship was boosted by the inclusion of Cook, a long-time advocate of both closer links and electoral reform. This duo or, if required, trio, could be brought to bear on Brown. Although Chancellor of the Exchequer, with all the power, prestige and influence that this brought, Brown was always seen to be in a position of weakness. His allies, including John Prescott, did not carry Ashdown's weight – though if needed, he could always rely on support from the Labour backbenches.

The press became obsessed with the power plays at the heart of government; stories even circulated that if Blair were ever to step down, then Ashdown would be made Prime Minister, in a deal finalised as part of the 'cooperation' arrangement. All concerned were quick to distance themselves from such stories, especially given the Lib Dems' lower electoral standing after 2001. The rumours, however, refused to go away, and in effect placed Brown against Ashdown; Brown saw himself as the natural successor to Blair, one who would put the Labour Party first and make decisions unhindered by any 'cooperation'.

All four of the main players had teams of advisers they could rely upon in policy and communications. Blair largely used the group he had built in opposition, as did Ashdown, who especially called on the talents of Richard Holme. Whilst the Labour Party in opposition had benefited from an effective media relations operation, the cash-strapped Lib Dems were less experienced; yet on entering government, they swiftly learned the effectiveness of good media relations. Briefing trusted political journalists became one of the key weapons in the Lib Dems' armoury in dealing with the majority Labour Party, assisting them in getting their way in policy matters.

Two figures in Blair's team were particularly important – Peter Mandelson and Roger Liddle. Both had pushed hard for 'cooperation' and Mandelson, in particular, understood the media well. Liddle had moved between Labour, the old SDP, the Lib Dems and then back to Labour, and while this meant that all parties were slightly suspicious of him, he understood their workings – a useful asset. Both men proved their value in terms of both policy ideas and presentation, though Mandelson's own ambitions, combined with a lack of a political judgement, called his insider status into question on several occasions.

Alastair Campbell had proved a key figure for Blair in opposition in building his communications machine, but with the Lib Dems claiming to concentrate more on policy, there was a fear of Labour being seen to concentrate too much on presentation. Campbell's influence on Blair remained, but he carried less weight in government and became a more shadowy figure behind the scenes.

All this did little to assist in the image of pluralistic politics and reinforced the picture of a government engaged in infighting. The media became a key battleground and a first step in winning ground on policy, especially important in the era of 'cooperation'.

If a choice had to made about who was the most influential person behind the scenes in the government, though, it would have to be Roy Jenkins. He remained the lynchpin for both Blair and Ashdown until his passing in January 2003.

Split

Alongside economic policy, one of the main areas in which the parties were in wide agreement was foreign policy. Ashdown was a popular choice as Foreign Secretary, especially given his military background; the public, as they had done in many previous opinion polls, saw Ashdown as a strong leader and he consistently polled well.

The government took a strong line on many foreign and related issues. In particular, Kosovo, to which Ashdown brought a strong personal interest and expertise, came to symbolise the foreign policy approach of the government. Working closely with the United Nations and other international bodies, Britain was at the forefront of advocating early and sizeable intervention. Whilst some of the UK's European partners were slow to react, Ashdown, strongly supported by Blair, committed British troops to a UN force. Britain was deemed to be 'in charge' of the situation. The government's policy was clearly one of interventionism.

The government also was well aware of the importance of clear symbols of intent, and debt relief, a ban on land mines, and sanctions against those countries which abused human rights were all quickly implemented after 1997; the press dubbed the approach an 'ethical' foreign policy. Although the term was never used by the government itself, it did seem to be genuinely attempting to introduce a more ethical dimension, for instance through measures to prevent arms exports to countries with records of human rights abuses, and through military intervention in instances of particularly flagrant abuse.[12]

Britain's European partners welcomed the new, more positive, relationship they were able to enjoy with the government; it made a welcome change from the previous Conservative administration. With a clear commitment to joining the euro, Britain put itself at the heart of decision-making in Europe. Work soon commenced on a new constitution for Europe, which raised the possibility of a joint foreign and defence policy alongside common tax rates. With the government clearly advocating a European approach and with the Conservative Party split over the issue, it was claimed that Europe had finally been accepted by the population of Britain.

Following the 2001 election, the government had to deliver on its promise of giving the public referendums on two issues: entry to the single European currency, and the introduction of PR for elections to Westminster. It was agreed that both would be held on the same day. The government, fronted by Blair and Ashdown, strongly supported a 'yes' vote in both referendums.

Brown's resignation from the government over the euro issue was spectacular, to say the least. While he was known not to be enthusiastic about the prospect of entry, few thought it a resigning issue, especially as a small majority of the public appeared to favour the euro, and it seemed more likely to be the culmination of continuously being sidelined by the Blair–Ashdown axis in government. His resignation speech was held up by experts as one of the all-time classics, rating alongside Geoffrey Howe's. Brown criticised Blair and Ashdown for a style of government which placed too much emphasis on politics and not enough on the economic reality of the situation.

Brown's record as Chancellor, and his gravitas, gave the 'no' camp a real boost in the final weeks of the campaign. The Conservative Party, who had tagged the referendum day as 'Save Britain Day', used the resignation as proof that they had been right all along. Not only was the party against entry to the euro but they also believed that PR would see the end of stable one-party government in Britain.

When the final votes came though, Britain had voted *against* entry into the euro but *for* PR. It appeared that the electorate had supported electoral reform because 'cooperation' between Labour and the Lib Dems – political parties working successfully together – was widely viewed as a success. Brown's very public resignation from the government, however, had effectively ended the debate on the euro. The somewhat confusing results appeared to show that a new, more discerning, electorate had emerged, one which could vary their vote depending on the issue. Maybe the new way of doing politics really had engaged the public.

With Brown gone, and a failed vote to enter the euro, the credibility of the government was undermined. Blair was on the brink of resignation. He was only saved by the government's policy towards Iraq.

Iraq

The situation in Iraq had been developing for some time.[13] The British and American governments had been working through the UN to implement an inspections programme to ensure that Iraq did not possess any weapons of mass destruction. Behind this, however, the government was keen to see the Iraqi leader, Saddam Hussein, replaced. His appalling human rights record and brutal internal repression had made him a focus of the government's drive to put human rights near the top of its foreign policy considerations, and was always the government's primary argument against the Iraqi regime. Many plaudits had been won for the government's policy of cancelling debt for countries who signed up to a human rights agreement; their approach to Iraq was the flipside of the policy.

In line with the 'ethical foreign policy' established since 1997, the government took a very hands-on approach. Iraq's failure to comply with their demands appeared to force the hand of the UN Security Council, but despite the efforts of the UK, and rather less of the US, who were not so worried about having a UN mandate – the Security Council would not pass a resolution endorsing military action.

This left Blair and Ashdown in a difficult position. They had both repeatedly advocated a role for the United Nations, the representative of the international coalition; indeed, its agreement was required under international law before action could be taken. Against the lack of a resolution, however, had to be balanced the government's desire to counter the threat posed by Iraqi weapons and, most importantly, to see an end to the continued human rights abuses for which it had continually criticised the regime. For Ashdown the decision was an especially difficult one – he had always been a firm advocate of the power of international institutions such as the UN – but his personal commitment to helping the people of Iraq escape a life under the shadow of a tyrant won through. Given Ashdown's earlier unequivocal commitment to the Gulf War, when he had worked closely with then Prime Minister John Major and the leader of the Labour Party Neil Kinnock, there was also the shadow of 'unfinished business'. Ashdown and others also felt that the rationale for the French veto, which had effectively prevented a UN resolution from being passed, could be questioned.

Blair and Ashdown considered that if the Iraqi regime were allowed to continue then their government's credibility in fighting human rights abuses would be undermined. Kosovo had shown that interventionism could work , and the judgment was taken that it would also work in Iraq. The decision was made to take military action and within a week the war was under way.[14]

The domestic response to this decision was uproar – marches on the streets, newspaper columns full of condemnation, openly hostile criticism of the decision from within both partners in government. Cook quickly resigned, but with quiet dignity. He made it clear that while he was proud of the achievements of the government, he could not remain a member of a Cabinet which supported military action.

Open criticism of the decision was tempered during the war itself by the unwritten rule that military action was not criticised while troops were in action. Although the war was short and ultimately successful, the political floodgates opened once it was clear that the conflict had ended. Simon Hughes, who had refused to support the action when questioned before the war, resigned from the government once the war it was over. In an interview broadcast on *Sky News,* he also chose to announce that he was leaving the Liberal Democrats to start a new party which would remain loyal to the principles of the liberal tradition – in essence, a party for the vast majority of Lib Dems who did not support the war. Within days, a further forty-one of his Parliamentary colleagues had joined the Social Liberal Party and several high-profile businesspeople pledged money to make sure it would prosper. Those MPs who remained loyal to Ashdown appeared to do so more out of personal allegiance.

The new party quickly captured the public spirit and was soon registering high opinion poll ratings. The split left the policy of 'cooperation' in tatters and Ashdown's personal credibility at something approaching zero. The Labour Party could not continue cooperating with a party that had been decimated in such a way. Blair, already suffering from the euro defeat, the loss of two senior Cabinet members, and now the removal of a prime plank of policy, resigned.

Cook, Brown and Straw all quickly announced their intentions to run for the leadership and after a bloody battle, Brown emerged triumphant. Cook hijacked the press conference to release the result to announce his resignation from the party and his intention to talk to other like-minded 'real Labour Party' members about starting a new party. Cook's position on the war was diametrically opposed to Brown's and the two had never enjoyed a close relationship in government. It would also appear that Cook could not see a senior position for himself in Brown's Labour Party. Cook's announcement took the shine off Brown's win and the new Prime Minister immediately came under pressure to call a fresh general election to give the electorate the chance to give their verdict on the seismic changes going on in politics.

The future

At the time of writing, Prime Minister Brown has indeed called a general election – the first Westminster election to be held under the new electoral system. Many more parties believe that they have an opportunity under the new system, and the electorate will be faced with a choice between seven main parties, excluding the Scottish and Welsh nationalists and Northern Irish parties:

- Democratic Labour – Cook's 'old Labour' party, which has had little time to establish itself as an alternative party of the left. Cook is trying hard to bring the trade union movement with him.
- The Labour Party – the Brown-led 'New Labour' party. Brown is attempting to move the party in a direction appreciated by more traditional Labour voters; his is not a 'new Labour' party in the same way that Blair's was.
- The Conservative Party – the party of the group traditionally seen as one-nation Tories. Hague is, however, struggling to convince the electorate that he can follow this path, and waiting in the wings are a number of potential leadership candidates. Whilst anti-euro, the party remains, in principle, in favour of Europe.
- Conservative Future – a low-profile Conservative backbench MP, Iain Duncan Smith, has led a small band of retired and former Conservative MPs to form a stridently anti-European party.
- British National Party – after some successes in local government, the BNP feels that it has a real opportunity of picking up votes from disillusioned working-class Labour supporters, as well as those from the Conservative Party who feel that they are no longer represented adequately.
- The Green Party – building on its base of support established since the late 1980s, the Greens are looking to use their local council and European experience to prove their worth in the setting of Westminster.
- The Liberal Democrats – Ashdown is struggling badly to hold what remains of his party together but it lacks any real alternative leaders.
- The Social Liberal Party – the anti-war former Lib Dems, led by Hughes, which commands the vast majority of the former Lib Dem supporters and MPs.

The outcome remains far from certain.

Reflecting on the period of 'cooperation', the impression is one of great reform and of a massive shift in British politics. The great irony is that Blair introduced 'cooperation' partly to help distance himself from the left of his own party – yet, in the first term at least, introduced some very left-wing policies. The electoral system the Liberal Democrats fought so long to introduce looks set to condemn them to political obscurity. Ashdown himself took the party into power for the first time in nearly a century, but ultimately split the party with his attitude towards the war in Iraq.

The period will be remembered as a time that reshaped British politics, but its impact has still yet to be fully realised.

Notes

1 With many thanks to Alex Thomson.
2 Jenkins is described as 'a bridge' in Paddy Ashdown, *The Ashdown Diaries: Volume One, 1988–1997* (Penguin Press, 2000), p. 346 – a role he continued to play between the two during their time in government.
3 With service in Singapore, Brunei, Aden and Belfast.
4 Ashdown had been a Labour voter until 1967.
5 Paddy Ashdown, *Citizens' Britain: A Radical Agenda for the 1990s* (Fourth Estate, 1989), pp. 31–32.
6 Tony Blair, speech, 1997 Labour Party Conference.
7 Reproduced in Duncan Brack and Tony Little (eds.), *Great Liberal Speeches* (Politico's, 2001), pp. 423–28.
8 Lib Dem antipathy towards Straw was equally as strongly felt and well-known; see Ashdown, *Diaries,* p. 559.
9 The Labour Party had originally argued that Wales should be offered an Assembly rather than a more powerful Parliament. The Lib Dems argued that it would inequitable if Scotland were to have a Parliament and Wales only an Assembly. Their argument won.
10 See Ashdown, *Diaries,* p. 558.
11 The 1997 Lib Dem manifesto, *Make The Difference,* stated: 'We will replace the Student Loans Scheme with a fair repayment scheme linked to salaries in later life. We oppose top-up fees for tuition.'

What if ...

12 As well as Kosovo, the government committed troops to Afghanistan, Sierra Leone, Liberia and Rwanda. It also unilaterally imposed sanctions on a number of other countries.

13 There had been calls to delay the referendums because of the worsening situation in Iraq, most notably from the former Labour Deputy Leader, Lord Hattersley, but also from newspapers such as the *Independent*.

14 As well as the UK and US governments, there was a small group of countries who supported action without UN approval.

Chapter 21

What if Michael Portillo hadn't lost his seat in 1997?

Iain Dale

'You do know you're in trouble, Michael, don't you?' whispered the particularly conspiratorial voice of Peter Mandelson as they left the BBC election night studios. 'Well, it's certainly not going to be the majority I'm used to,' responded the outgoing Defence Secretary, somewhat despondently.

As he got into his waiting car outside the TV Centre studios the last thing Michael Portillo wanted was to hear the excited babble of his loyal assistants as they argued with each other over the scale of the coming onslaught in the country. After all, it wasn't exactly his fault, was it? For the first time he began to feel a sense of impending doom. Surely he couldn't lose. Could he? After all, Enfield would return a donkey if it sported a blue rosette. His campaign team had berated him for not spending more time in the constituency, but just how could he manage that when he was expected up and down the country twenty-four hours a day? After all, he wasn't superman, no matter what his more zealous supporters might think.

It was already clear that Labour had won – and won big. Just how big was big, though? What kind of rump of a Conservative Parliamentary Party would be left? And would they be leadable? He was sure John Major would immediately step down, so now his moment had come.

The crown had so nearly been his just two years earlier. Everything was in place, yet he, Michael Denzil Xavier Portillo, had hesitated. 'He who wields the sword rarely inherits the crown' was the thought that had guided his decision. If Redwood wanted to risk it so be it, but he wasn't being tainted as Major's assassin. Sure, he'd talked to Redwood, and urged him to stand down in his favour if there was a second round, but Redwood was having none of it. Thank God he hadn't got any further.

But Redwood was history. Portillo is the future. Or that's the thought that was spinning in his mind as he got out of the car at Enfield Town Hall. He was immediately surrounded by the waiting media and a not inconsiderable throng of Labour Party supporters. 'Mr Portillo, are you going to stand for the leadership?' shouted a blonde journalist he didn't recognise from Sky News. 'Fuck off, Portillo!' spat a callow youth. 'Michael, have you considered the possibility of losing your seat?' shouted the man from ITN. Portillo ignored it all and marched calmly into the Town Hall.

He didn't have long to wait before his agent spotted him. 'Not looking good, Michael,' he whispered. 'Twigg's ahead in the bundles, but there's two wards to go – both usually OK for us.' So this is what it had come to. Thirteen years of service yet the voters might be giving him the bum's rush. The bastards.

For the first time he considered what he would do if he lost. Not a pleasant thought. It wasn't exactly as if he was qualified to do anything, having spent most of his working life as a researcher or an MP. He could probably count on being taken on by one of the big City firms, but it wasn't exactly a scintillating prospect for someone who in other circumstances would be anticipating standing for the leadership of the Conservative Party. He thought of the ignominies experienced by his friend Francis Maude when he lost his seat in 1992; he'd even had to take money from some God-awful lobbying company. Still, better to cross that bridge if and when it came to it, he thought, almost shaking his head in shock at the fact that he was finding himself contemplating defeat.

Reality soon dawned. There was a commotion on the floor; angry voices were hurling insults at each other. He thought he saw a punch being thrown but he couldn't make out whose fist it was. But it was clear that the result was imminent. He steeled himself. The Labour candidate, Stephen Twigg, looked as nervous as he was feeling himself. Twigg had fought a good campaign. He looked the part – dashing, tall, well-spoken. Should have been a Tory, thought Portillo, before he was rushed back to reality by the voice of the Returning Officer.

'I, being the Returning Officer for the constituency of Enfield Southgate, do hereby give the result of the parliamentary election. Browne, Jeremy, Liberal Democrat, four thousand nine hundred and sixty-six.' The Liberal vote had halved – an ominous sign, given the likelihood of tactical anti-Tory voting.

The Returning Officer was enjoying the moment, enunciating every syllable at inordinate length. For Christ's sake get on with it, thought Portillo, as the official made a valiant effort to make the next two candidates' results last as long as he possibly could. And then he stiffened.

'Portillo, Michael Denzil Xavier, Conservative, twenty thousand, five hundred and seventy.' Bloody hell, I'm 8,000 down. Just how large can the Labour vote be?

The Returning Officer took a deep breath. He puffed his chest out as far as he could – and it was quite a long way. 'Twigg, Stephen, Labour, nineteen thousand one hundred and thirty seven. I hereby declare that Michael Denzil Xavier Portillo be duly elected.'

The characteristic Portillo smirk was back. The press had still got him to kick around for a bit longer.

The following twenty-four hours disappeared like a blur. Portillo had been truly shocked at the narrowness of his result, but he had clearly been luckier than most. Tory MPs had been losing like ninepins in a bowling alley. One hundred and ninety-one seats. Ye Gods. Even Kinnock had got more seats than that. Rifkind, Olga Maitland, Seb Coe, Marcus Fox, David Mellor – all gone. Who'd want to lead this rump of a party?

Truth was, many would. He knew that. But one thing was for sure, John Major was a goner.

Three weeks later

Funnily enough, the leadership contest hadn't been particularly bruising. Apart from Ann Widdecombe's successful assault on Michael Howard, the whole contest had happened with barely a whimper. The truth was that the press were so obsessed with Tony Blair and his bright, shiny new administration that they paid the Tories little attention.

Portillo had predicted that many would stand for the leadership, if only to put a marker down for the future. Indeed, some acted with what he considered to be unseemly haste. Ken Clarke couldn't wait to throw his fedora into the ring, announcing his candidature only a few hours after the last results were in. Michael Heseltine finally had to rip up his famous envelope when heart problems ruled him out. Serves him right, thought the many people who would never forgive him for the events of November 1990.

Stephen Dorrell raised many a belly laugh when he announced his short-lived candidacy. His lamentable performance in the Major Cabinet certainly did for him in the eyes of his colleagues. William Hague and John Redwood were thought to be big threats. Some expected Peter Lilley to stand but he soon declared for Portillo and ended up running his campaign, fuelling the scurrilous rumours which had been circulating in low-life magazines for years about the truth behind his friendship with Portillo.

But the contest itself was a virtual walkover for Portillo. Howard, Hague and Redwood all withdrew after the first round, leaving

Clarke and Portillo to slug it out. Michael knew he would win. And so did everyone else. The Portillo era had begun.

His first task was to form a shadow cabinet, no easy task with only 190 colleagues to choose from. Ken Clarke had made it clear that if he wasn't leader he didn't want to do anything else. Portillo didn't blame him for that, though his other rivals for the leadership all accepted posts, rather to his surprise. Pundits had expected Peter Lilley to be appointed Shadow Chancellor but instead he became deputy leader and Director of Policy Development.

Portillo made it clear that he wished to emulate the Thatcher opposition in developing radical, exciting new policies which could appeal to a new generation of voters who had never considered voting Tory. Michael Howard agreed to shadow the Foreign Office, while William Hague became Shadow Home Secretary. In a difficult interview with John Redwood, Portillo offered him the Shadow Chancellorship, but Redwood made clear that he would only accept if he, and he alone, had control over economic policy.

'He thinks he's Gordon Brown,' thought Portillo. This was high-stakes gambling for both men. There had been a deep rift between them following the 1995 leadership election, when Redwood had failed to unseat John Major, but both men knew that in these dark days for the party, they needed each other. And so it was that Redwood finally accepted the offer of the Shadow Chancellorship, with no preconditions. Portillo had him by the balls, and he knew it.

The most popular appointment, both in the press and among party workers, was Gillian Shephard as Party Chairman. She made it clear from the start that she was looking to modernise the party structure and change the way parliamentary candidates were selected. Her summer tour of the constituencies did much to heal the wounds of the election defeat. The party workers loved her.

Other eye-catching promotions included the pugnacious Alan Duncan to International Development and former Foreign Office

Minister David Davis as Chief Whip. A few eyebrows were raised at the deeply ironic appointment of the Chingford MP and Maastricht rebel Iain Duncan Smith as a junior whip. Few MPs could mistake the evil glint in Davis's eyes when told of the appointment. He remembered Duncan Smith's histrionics over Maastricht; payback time was approaching.

The first six months of Portillo's leadership were quiet. As Tony Blair's administration found its feet, so did the Opposition. Portillo's performances at Prime Minister's Questions were considered moderately impressive, with him winning more times than he lost. His budget response was described by Peter Riddell in *The Times* as 'masterful in the detailed analysis and impressive in political rhetoric'.

His attacks on the Prime Minister's integrity over the Bernie Ecclestone affair did much to knock the shine off New Labour and dented people's trust in Tony Blair in particular. Portillo's off-the-cuff reaction of 'absolute bollocks' to Blair's 'I'm a pretty straight kinda guy' semi-apology for Ecclestone might not have amused the blue rinses of Tunbridge Wells, but it demonstrated that here was an Opposition leader who knew what Opposition was all about. Taste and decency were side issues. People wanted to know that you were up for the battle, and anyone who wasn't would be disposed of.

A few months later Portillo proved that he meant what he said. In a speech to Yorkshire Conservatives, the new rising star of the party, William Hague, maintained that the Conservatives must be judicious in their opposition, as the 'country no longer wanted to hear from them for a good while'. He said that the party should apologise for what it got wrong during the Major years: 'We should concede and move on'. Portillo conceded that it should indeed be William Hague who should move on and summarily sacked him. The newspapers had a field day, depicting Portillo as Arnold Schwarzenegger in *The Terminator*. His 1995 conference speech had been littered with references to the SAS, so this time, he dared to sack Hague and he won. He replaced him with Francis Maude.

In many ways this set the tone for the following two years. Portillo had demonstrated a toughness that few had realised was there. Any other member of his team who strayed out of line knew they would be for the chop.

The newly strengthened Conservative Research Department, headed by Peter Lilley and Danny Finkelstein, was coming up with radical policies which even a sceptical media was admitting were eye-catching. Selling off housing association properties and introducing proportional representation for local government elections were proving popular on a local level, while plans to give teachers greater powers to discipline pupils put the teaching unions in a huge quandary. Andrew Cooper and Michael Simmonds, the party's directors of campaigns, were having considerable success with targeted direct-mail campaigns in the party's top hundred marginal seats and the Conservatives had even begun to recruit hundreds of new members.

But it was in Central Office's press office that the party was having problems. Portillo decided fairly early on that he needed a high-profile press spokesman who could compete with Alastair Campbell on an equal footing. Breaking with tradition, he employed a firm of head-hunters to identify the right person. After several months of discussion the former editor of the *Sunday Express,* Amanda Platell, was appointed. Portillo liked a bit of glamour and Platell provided that in spades. She made an immediate impact, not just with the press, but with Portillo himself. She gradually began changing his appearance, persuading him to flatten a little the trademark Portillo quiff. 'It makes you look camp', she said with typical Australian bluntness. If she hadn't know better she would swear Portillo's cheeks had reddened.

Platell's main contribution in her first six months was to persuade Lilley and Cooper that a campaign on honesty in politics should be launched. She felt that the perception of Tony Blair's government as honest and straight was a lie which should be exposed. As part of the campaign Conservative MPs were urged to be open about their private lives. Shadow International Development Secretary Alan Duncan shocked many by coming out as a homosexual, something which those in the 'Westminster village' had known for years. His party leader praised him for his 'courage, openness and honesty'; some in his constituency were less forgiving. But an attempt to deselect him, which, due to some neat footwork by Amanda Platell, never made the papers, failed miserably after a 'knocking heads together' visit to Rutland and Melton by the thuggish Chief Whip David Davis.

Gradually Portillo began to make the press take notice of the party's new style, approach and policies. Portillo admitted to himself that Hague had had a point when he said that no one wanted to hear from the party for a while, but rather than be defeatist, Portillo and his advisers decided that they had to take the bull by the horns and make them take notice. Central Office made complaint after complaint about the time allocated to Labour and Lib Dem politicians and any example of media bias was ruthlessly exploited. A charm offensive with political editors and newspaper magnates helped the party make some headway and by the time the 1999 local and European elections came around, even the most sceptical of political journalists was having to admit that maybe, just maybe, the Tories had turned the corner.

In 1997 Portillo had instigated a full-scale review of the party's approach towards Europe. He knew that the splits over Europe that had characterised the Major Government could not be allowed to continue. Major's policy of 'wait and see' on the euro had curiously been adopted by the Labour government, yet for the Conservatives it was no longer an option. Portillo's aim was to develop a policy which was clear-cut on the Euro and yet could not be interpreted as being small-minded, xenophobic or little-Englander. He therefore rang up his old mentor, Lord Parkinson, to ask him to chair a commission on the future of Europe. Their conclusions impressed Portillo and were to form the basis of party policy for the years ahead: the euro was ruled out on principle on constitutional grounds, but the party would press for enlargement of the EU and call a halt to the encroaching powers of the European Union. The main change would be the language used in arguing the party's case over the European issue.

In local government things were beginning to turn around too. An aggressive campaign by the Party on Council Tax rates reaped local dividends and the party's councillors felt a degree of optimism they had not experienced since the late 1970s. The 1999 local election results fully justified that feeling. Portillo was cock-a-hoop; despite a ludicrously low turnout the Conservatives had won a convincing victory. They were on their way back. And he, Michael Denzil Xavier Portillo, was convinced that it was only a matter of time before he and Carolyn would enter No. 10.

Over the next two years everything Portillo did, said or thought was geared towards that aim. He wasn't a showman for nothing and the 2000 party conference was vital in providing the party with a good send-off towards what everyone thought would be an election in the spring of 2001.

The press had been warned to expect something special in the leader's speech. And for once no one leaked. The week had gone well. A raft of new policies had been announced, including on-the-spot fines for the possession of cannabis. Francis Maude had been worried that this might be interpreted as decriminalisation, so the policy was successfully spun by Amanda Platell as 'zero tolerance on drugs'. John Redwood announced the proposed abolition of inheritance tax and a reversal of Gordon Brown's dramatic increases in stamp duty on house purchases. He also promised to overturn Brown's raid on pension funds which, he said, threatened a pensions crisis 'the like of which we have never seen'.

But it was the leader's speech everyone was waiting for. The first twenty minutes were laced with humour and cracks at Blair and his government but somehow no one was listening. They were all waiting for whatever dramatic announcement Portillo had to make. Platell had spun it as being a 'deeply personal moment'. Speculation was rife – indeed, it was threatening to get out of control. Finally the moment came. Portillo paused for what seemed like an age. He continued:

> My friends, for too long the Conservative Party has given the appearance of being split – divided. Over the last three years I have made it my business to lead from the front, but also to listen to all parts of the party on all sorts of issues. I firmly believe the party is now more united than it has been for years. United with a purpose. United in our march towards victory at the next election. I want to lead a party of all the talents. Full of people whose only aim is to do good. Good for our country, good for our people and good for our party. If we are to achieve our aim of despatching this sleazy, miserable Labour government to the dustbin of history I want the most powerful team at my disposal. That's why I am delighted to announce today that Ken Clarke has agreed to rejoin the Shadow Cabinet. Ken Clarke, come on down!

Music blasted out. Balloons fell from the ceiling. Ken Clarke appeared at the back of the cavernous Bournemouth Conference Centre Hall and trotted down the stairs, gurgling with delight and waving to the assembled masses, most of whom were standing and clapping. The symbolic message sent out to the watching voters was clear and hardly needed to be articulated by the professional political pundits. 'Master Stroke' and 'A Conservative Coup' were just two of the headlines in the next day's papers.

Everyone, it seemed, was happy. There was no doubt about it, Portillo was seen as a lucky politician. He had been perceived as a little too smug and pleased with himself, but his leadership of the Conservative Party had changed all that. He looked the part. He looked like a Prime Minister in waiting, which was exactly how he saw himself.

Meanwhile, the Blair Government lurched from crisis to crisis, some self-inflicted, some outside its control. And then came the foot-and-mouth crisis. Even Labour's most ardent supporters felt it was handled badly from beginning to end. At one stage it even threatened to ensure that Tony Blair would have to delay calling an election. But the advice he received from the Ministry of Agriculture was that 'no new cases are now expected'. Unfortunately, an incompetent official had failed to include the returns from both Wales and Cumbria in his prognosis, and two days after the beginning of the campaign dozens of new cases of foot and mouth appeared in the Brecon Beacons and Cumbria. A few days later more cases appeared in Northumberland and Somerset. The crisis was real and the Government was in total chaos.

Michael Portillo came into his own, calling for a state of national emergency to be declared. He proposed sending in troops and announced an imaginative compensation scheme for the affected farmers. Tony Blair continue to fiddle while the sheep continued to burn. His sole contribution was to suggest calling off the election. 'In your dreams, Mr Blair,' proclaimed Portillo, as he continued to make good political capital out of a farming nightmare.

All other issues paled into insignificance, and on polling day the country exacted its revenge.

A majority of more than 140 was not going to be easy to overcome, no matter how bad the government's performance over foot and mouth had been. But seat after seat fell. At 12.03 a.m. Bob Dunn won back Dartford, sixty-fourth on the Tories' target list. Malcolm Rifkind narrowly won back Edinburgh Pentlands, becoming one of five Tory MPs north of the border. But it wasn't until 1.30 a.m. that it became clear that a Tory victory was a distinct possibility. The weathervane seat of Basildon fell and from then on the faces at Millbank became gloomier and gloomier.

At 4.30 a.m. Michael Portillo became Prime Minister. He had a majority of three seats, making serving a full term an almost impossible task. The pundits likened it to Harold Wilson's narrow wins in 1964 and February 1974. A further election within a year looked a dead cert.

How had it happened? The pundits had been confounded but most of them agreed that Labour voters had stayed at home in their droves, while the Conservatives had managed to get their vote out. The turnout was pitiful – the lowest ever – but the Conservatives' once powerful electoral machine had proved it had some life in it yet.

Having kissed hands at Buckingham Palace, Prime Minister Portillo returned to the cheering throngs in Downing Street. They weren't quite the seething crowds who had welcomed the Blairs in 1997, but he enjoyed the moment nonetheless.

As he prepared to make his statement of intent on the doorstep of No. 10 – his 'Francis of Assisi' moment – Amanda Platell peered out of one of the upstairs windows, wondering what the future would hold in store for them all. At that very moment one of her junior staff came rushing into the room, almost breathless. 'Amanda, I think you ought to take this call,' he said. 'Who is it?' asked Platell. 'Mazeer Mahmood from the *News of the World*', came the reply. Platell experienced one of those moments when your stomach seems to hollow itself out. 'What the fuck does he want?' she muttered, almost to herself. 'Amanda, you really don't want to know,' said the flunky. She took the phone.

'Hi Maz, Amanda here,' said Platell in her most sweet and innocent tone.

'Amanda, we've had six researchers who for the last six months have been looking at your leader's private life, going back to his time at Cambridge. And they've come up with some rather interesting conclusions. We're running them on Sunday.'

And the rest, as they say, was history.

Contributors

Matthew Bailey is a PhD student at Newcastle University, researching One-Nation Conservatism. He has written on various aspects of British politics for publications including the *British Journal of Political Science* and the *Journal of Conservative History*.

John Barnes has recently retired from the LSE, where he taught Government. He is the co-author of *Baldwin: A Biography*, co-editor of the *Leo Amery Diaries* and author of various articles on Conservative history and thought. He was a Conservative parliamentary candidate in the 1964, 1966 and 1970 elections.

Duncan Brack is Editor of the *Journal of Liberal History*, and has also edited the *Dictionary of Liberal Biography, Dictionary of Liberal Quotations* and *Great Liberal Speeches*. A former Director of Policy for the Liberal Democrats, he is currently Head of the Sustainable Development Programme at the Royal Institute of International Affairs (Chatham House).

Simon Burns has been MP for Chelmsford 1987–97 and for West Chelmsford since 1997. He was Parliamentary Under-Secretary of State at the Department of Health, 1996–97, and is currently Shadow Health Minister. In 1972 he worked for Senator George McGovern in his presidential election bid against Richard Nixon.

John Charmley is Professor of Modern History and Dean of the School of History at the University of East Anglia, where he has taught since 1979. He has published seven books, the best known of which is *Churchill: The End of Glory* (1993).

Philip Cowley is a lecturer at Nottingham University. His publications include *Revolts and Rebellions: Parliamentary Voting Under Blair* (2002) and *Conscience* *and Parliament* (ed., 1998). He is now researching backbench behaviour in the current Parliament.

Iain Dale is a political commentator and owner of Westminster's famous Politico's Bookstore. He is a former financial journalist and political lobbyist and a Conservative Party parliamentary candidate. He presents a monthly political programme, 'Planet Politics', on Oneword Radio, and he is the author/editor of more than a dozen books and the Director of the Conservative History Group.

Mark Garnett is co-author of *Keith Joseph: A Biography* (Acumen, 2001) and *Splendid! Splendid! The Authorised Biography of Willie Whitelaw* (Jonathan Cape, 2002).

Dr Richard S. Grayson is the author of two books on inter-war British political history and has been Director of Policy of the Liberal Democrats since 1999. He is also the party's prospective parliamentary candidate for Hemel Hempstead.

During the period covered by her chapter, **Dianne Hayter** was the General Secretary of the Fabian Society. Since then, she has been Chief Executive of the European Parliamentary Labour Party, Director of Alcohol Concern and Director of Corporate Affairs at the Wellcome Trust, and, since 1997, a member of Labour's NEC.

Sir Bernard Ingham was Press Secretary to Margaret Thatcher from 1980 to November 1990. Since then he has become a political commentator, contributing to various newspapers and other media outlets. His books include *Wages of Spin* (John Murray, 2003) and his autobiography *Kill the Messenger* (Politico's, 2003).

Michael McManus was special adviser to Rt Hon. David Hunt MBE MP 1992–95, Political Secretary to Rt Hon. Sir Edward Heath KG MBE MP 1995–2000, and Conservative candidate for Watford, 2001. He is the author of *Jo Grimond: Towards the Sound of Gunfire* (Birlinn, 2001) and is currently Political Director of Vote 2004.

David Mills is a political journalist and television producer. Educated at the Universities of York and Edinburgh, he is a former media officer at the Transport and General Workers' Union, is currently the Producer of GMTV's Sunday morning political programme, and also writes a weekly political column for *Tribune*.

James Parry is a historical writer.

Anne Perkins has been a political correspondent for Channel Four News and the BBC, and most recently for the *Guardian*. She has also presented news and current affairs programmes on radio and television. Her life of Barbara Castle, *Red Queen,* was published in June 2003.

Paul Richards is chair of the Fabian Society, and was a Labour parliamentary candidate in the 1997 and 2001 general elections. He is author of several books and pamphlets, including *The Case for Socialism*, and a forthcoming collection of Tony Blair's speeches and articles, to be published by Politico's in 2004.

Greg Rosen edited the *Dictionary of Labour Biography* (Politico's, 2001). His other publications include 'Herbert Morrison' in Kevin Jefferys (ed.), *Labour Forces: From Ernest Bevin to Gordon Brown* and 'John P. Mackintosh: His Achievements and Legacy', in *Political Quarterly*. He is Chair of the Labour History Group.

Neil Stockley was the Liberal Democrats' Director of Policy 1995–97. He was executive assistant to New Zealand Prime Minister, David Lange, and, subsequently, Director of the New Zealand Parliamentary Labour Research Unit. Now a director of a public affairs company, he is a frequent contributor to the *Journal of Liberal History*.

Mark Stuart is a political biographer and researcher, currently working at the University of Nottingham. In 1998, he published *Douglas Hurd: The Public Servant* (Mainstream), and is now working on an authorised biography of John Smith, due to be published in the autumn of 2004.

What if …

Helen Szamuely studied the Russian Revolution and British reactions to it at the universities of Leeds and Oxford, where she produced a doctoral thesis on 'British Attitudes to Russia 1880–1918'. She has written extensively about Russia, the Soviet Union and Communism, and in recent years her main subject has been the European Union.

Robert Taylor is research associate at the Centre for Economic Performance at the London School of Economics, working on the future of the trade unions project. Former labour editor of the *Observer* and the *Financial Times,* he is writing a centennial history of the Parliamentary Labour Party.

Dr Stuart Thomson is a communications and public affairs consultant with DLA Upstream, and an honorary research fellow in the Department of Politics and IR at the University of Aberdeen. His publications include *The Social Democratic Dilemma, Dictionary of Labour Quotations* and *New Activism and the Corporate Response.*

Dr Robert Waller has published seven editions of *The Almanac of British Politics* since it first appeared in 1983, most recently with Byron Criddle (Routledge, 2002). He has been a Fellow of Magdalen College, Oxford, a Lecturer in History at Wadham College, Oxford, and a Lecturer in Politics at Trinity College, Oxford.